MISSIONARY FIRST RESPONDER

Reaching Beyond Broken

KRIS REPP

I0881525

YWAM Publishing
Seattle, Washington

YWAM Publishing is the publishing ministry of Youth With A Mission (YWAM), an international missionary organization of Christians from many denominations dedicated to presenting Jesus Christ to this generation. To this end, YWAM has focused its efforts in three main areas: (1) training and equipping believers for their part in fulfilling the Great Commission (Matthew 28:19), (2) personal evangelism, and (3) mercy ministry (medical and relief work).

Names and identifying characteristics of some individuals have been changed to preserve privacy.

For a free catalog of books and materials, call (425) 771-1153 or (800) 922-2143. Visit us online at www.ywampublishing.com.

Unless otherwise noted, Scripture quotations are taken from the (NASB®) New American Standard Bible®, Copyright © 1960, 1971, 1977, 1995, 2020 by The Lockman Foundation. Used by permission. All rights reserved. www.lockman.org.

Scripture quotations marked NIV are taken from the Holy Bible, New International Version®, NIV®. Copyright © 1973, 1978, 1984, 2011 by Biblica, Inc.™ Used by permission of Zondervan. All rights reserved worldwide. www.zondervan.com. The "NIV" and "New International Version" are trademarks registered in the United States Patent and Trademark Office by Biblica, Inc.™

Verses marked NKJV are taken from the New King James Version®. Copyright © 1982 by Thomas Nelson. Used by permission. All rights reserved.

Missionary First Responder—Reaching Beyond Broken

Copyright © 2024 by Kris Repp

Published by YWAM Publishing
a ministry of Youth With A Mission
P.O. Box 55787, Seattle, WA 98155-0787

Library of Congress Cataloging-in-Publication Data — Pending

ISBN 978-1-64836-151-7 (paperback)

First printing 2025

All rights reserved. No part of this book may be reproduced in any form without permission in writing from the publisher, except in the case of brief quotations embodied in critical articles or reviews.

Printed in the United States of America

International Adventures

A Cry from the Streets

A Way Beyond Death

Against All Odds

Bring Your Eyes and See

Cell 58

Dayuma

Living on the Devil's Doorstep

Love Notes to God

Missionary First Responder

Out of the Ice

River People

Sunrise in the Valley of Death

Taking On Giants

Taking the High Places

The Man with the Bird on His Head

The Narrow Road

Torches of Joy

Walking Miracle

To my precious son, Jacob

Thank you for your sacrifice of love—standing beside me in encouragement and respect as I have followed my heart to reach beyond broken. I love you—Mama

Contents

Acknowledgements

For those who have come and gone, and those still influencing my life—whose names aren't mentioned here—I am full of gratitude. You have prayed for me, supported me, and taught me. You have been the team on the ground enabling me to follow my heart.

Pastor Wayne—your years of teaching provided a solid foundation for my faith.

Robin—your writing workshop was the gift that launched my pen on paper.

Cheryl—your words "The story is in you!" helped me overcome hurdles of doubt.

Jacob, Gary, Renée, and Gail—your ideas, tips, and personal input filled my toolbox as I explored my new world as an author.

Jodie—your long-distance encouragement energized me to finish well as you shared your struggles over writing your thesis at the same time. You were my buddy as we ran the race together.

Warren and Luann—your expertise and grace guided me to the end.

Lord Jesus—Your love compelled me and Your spirit inspired me to fill these pages with the story of a life eternally touched by You.

Crossing the suspension bridge to reach the village clinic in Ecuadorr

INTRODUCTION

Reaching Beyond Broken

When I consider Your heavens, the work of Your fingers,
The moon and the stars, which You have set in place;
What is man that You think of him,
And a son of man that You are concerned about him?

Psalm 8:3

THE MOON, CASTING its dreamy light upon the darkened side of Earth, fills our minds with romantic fantasies. While millions of honeymooners have gazed into their lover's eyes in the moon's reflection, few have walked on it. Moon gazers outnumber moonwalkers.

After four days, six hours, and forty-five minutes of space travel, the first astronauts planted their feet upon the moon's not-so-romantic surface on July 20, 1969. Riddled with craters and covered in a fine grey talcum powder-like dust blended with pebbles and boulders, they came face-to-face with its lifeless terrain.

Describing the lunar surface as "magnificent desolation," Neil Armstrong and Buzz Aldrin—after leaving everything in their familiar world behind—experienced one of the sweetest moments of their lives. Stepping out of the Apollo Lunar Module, they got a taste of honey on the moon.

The time spent getting there, the expenses, and the risks involved, all paled in light of the "one small step for man, one giant leap for mankind" they had taken.

* * *

Me? Jump? You want me to jump?

Placing my hand in His, trusting He knows what He is doing, I jump off the cliff, free-falling with my eyes wide open. My racing heart is surrendered. He tells me to hold on.

Honeymooning with my Creator reminds me of the moonwalker's journey. True to God's economy, the experience is upside down and otherworldly.

Rather than beautiful, dreamy settings, He often takes me to hot and hostile destinations. Like a trip to the moon, some locations require four days of travel to arrive. Landings are rocky and require delicate negotiating. Accommodations are sketchy. Food is testy as opposed to tasty. The risks are high. Sometimes dangerous. The experiences, light years from normal life on Earth, are extraordinary.

Stepping into each moon-like environment, I renew my covenant with my Maker, who reflects His love on me, His bride. Nothing compares to the sweetness of time spent with Him in these places of magnificent desolation, where He teaches me to see from His perspective. Though the experiences may be challenging, even life-threatening, He is there to hold my hand. I am never alone. In the darkest environments His light shines brighter than ever.

Traveling to over half of the countries in the world, I have also seen some of the most beautiful sites on Earth: from the summit of Kilimanjaro to the dunes of the Sahara desert, from the palatial majesty of the Taj Mahal to the simplicity of the thatched Sudanese tukuls, from the calm deep-blue waters of the Caribbean to the turbulent misting cascades of Victoria Falls.

My *favorite* place?

My favorite place is where I am. It is the people surrounding me who make my surroundings beautiful. Their spirit brings beauty to the most barren environments in which I land. Red and yellow, black and white—they are all created in God's image and are precious in His sight. God's Spirit living within me, the sweetness of those surrounding me, and His loving face shining light on all of us, are honey on the moon.

Let me take you there.

Walking and talking with the lions in Zimbabwe

Papa, Nanny, Mom, and I in Canoga Park, California

Chapter 1

Antoine: The Transformation

Therefore if anyone is in Christ, he is a new creature; the old things passed away; behold, new things have come.

2 Corinthians 5:17

"Kristy, what do you want to be when you grow up?"

My childish seven-year-old mind fancifully drifts off to a mysterious continent, full of wild animals and grass huts. A baby in my arms, children tugging on every side, I'm not a teacher or a movie star.

"I want to be a missionary doctor to French-speaking Africa."

French doesn't have a lot of practical use for a young girl growing up in Southern California. With an authentic cross-cultural experience in my backyard, I can cross the border into Mexico or simply stay home and shop at the *carnicerias*. Reality doesn't entice me to get past *gracias* or learn to roll my tongue. My persistent personality is already breaking ground and I am determined to pursue my dream.

All the kids in my neighborhood know that attending summer school is punishment for not having done well during the normal school year, an attempt to catch up with the other kids before fall. It is a sentencing to be avoided at all costs.

At my elementary school, I discover there is a French class being offered during the dreaded summer school session. While my friends are splashing around in their swimming pools, my mind is in another land. Gazing out the window of a sultry classroom, I memorize exotic words like *bonjour* and *papillon*. No swimming pool can lure me away from this intrigue.

Antoine, my pet pollywog, keeps me company. He swims. I study. He is my little French buddy. Days pass as he makes the transformation from a slimy transparent fish into an adorable four-footed frog the size of my fingernail. On a tearful day, I say goodbye to Antoine and watch him hop away to freedom, not realizing I will one day experience a miraculous transformation enabling me to live a life of freedom as well.

The weekends pass quickly, filling time with lots of activities. Church is not one of them. My mom and dad love me deeply. They provide all the material things I desire but fall short of helping to build a spiritual foundation for my life. It's Nanny, my maternal grandmother, that introduces me to Jesus.

* * *

In the early 1900s, Nanny, or Willie Bell MacKenzie, is baptized as a young girl in a stock tank used for watering cattle. With an eighth-grade education behind her, she elopes with Papa, William Franklin Martin. They honeymoon their way from Oklahoma to California, settling in Whittier. Nanny is a woman of rock-solid faith, put to the test when Papa is dying of typhoid fever.

Papa does not share Nanny's Christian beliefs. Lovingly, she pleads with him to get right with his Maker as she watches his diseased body waste away. She fears he may soon find himself face-to-face with the One he has chosen to reject. Riddled with fever, he reaches up and motions for her to turn him over in bed. Heartbroken, she thinks this is his way of saying goodbye. Facedown, on the sweat-drenched pillow, a plea for mercy rises from his parched lips, "I give You my life. Lord, forgive me."

Nanny prayed for years for God to do whatever it took to bring her husband to Him. She later confesses, "If I had known what it would take, I might not have prayed that prayer." Her story teaches me a valuable lesson. Only the Creator, whose love wants to touch our soul, knows what it will take to do so. The stubborn resistance in Papa's heart could only be broken by a near-death experience. My stubborn resistance will take a similar path.

Nanny's prayer is answered. Papa recovers from typhoid. He lives a long devout life and dies a saved man.

* * *

Summer school is over. Friday has arrived. The trip to Nanny and Papa's takes an hour on the freeway. Our family frequently makes the trek to spend the weekend with them in Whittier, passing by Disneyland on the way. I am more excited to see Nanny than the Matterhorn. How can I resist being smothered in affection and spoiled rotten? My thoughts of her are wrapped in love and homemade pie.

It is the late fifties and early sixties, the era when Barbie dolls have just come out. Nanny doesn't drive but that doesn't stop her from getting around town. She takes the bus everywhere. This makes for many exciting adventures together. We head to Richardson's five-and-dime where she lets me pick out any outfit I want for Barbie.

Riding the bus is a fascinating experience. Plopping my quarter in the till and listening to it clink, I grab a seat. When Richardson's is in sight, I reach up and pull on the overhead string. The driver stops right in front of the store at my command.

In my back pocket I carry my little book of dreams: the Barbie catalog. Thanks to Nanny, my Barbie case is filled with every one of the elegant and expensive outfits in the collection. I even have the bridal dress, which she purchased for the extravagant price of five dollars, two dollars more than Barbie herself. She and Papa have spent a lifetime doing custodial work to make ends meet. When it comes to lavish generosity, there is no comparison.

Nanny loves me unselfishly, a love flowing from the spirit of Christ in her heart. She doesn't think twice about putting me first, denying herself to please me. When there is one piece of my favorite pecan pie left, she makes sure my name is written on it. With a smile on her face, she willingly goes without.

Talking about Jesus in her strong Okie accent she'll say, "Ohhhh Kristy, He loves you *so* much!" Then she lives out her Jesus example before me. When Nanny and I are together, it seems Jesus is always with us.

Spending the rest of the summer camped out at her house, I bask in her love. In a small bedroom, I am allocated a special dresser drawer: *Kristy's* drawer. In that drawer is a secret stash of garter belts and nylon stockings. I am fascinated by such big girl things. "I reckon you can wear those to church, honey," Nanny says.

Slipping the silky-smooth stockings on my legs, I fasten the garters to hold them up. Off to church, we go—Nanny, Papa, and me in my nylon stockings, feeling so grown up and important. I love going to church.

Spending less time with Nanny and Papa in the summer and more time with my circle of friends, life is carefree through sixth grade. There is absolutely nobody that tops my popularity list over Nanny, but her influence in my life begins to be overshadowed by the impact of my peers.

In junior high, big troubles begin. Whether or not it is true, I think my parents are too strict. Friends are going to movies and dances while I'm not allowed to join them. Rebellion creeps in and dominates my life. Lying about my activities and whereabouts, I begin experimenting with drugs and alcohol. This pattern continues into high school. The tent stakes that had been grounding me as a child, providing a sense of safety and security, are being pulled up one by one. Only a few positive role models are keeping me anchored.

Mrs. Davis, a high school teacher, is one of them. Gifted at her profession, she makes studying the French language as desirable as reading a steamy romance novel. In three years, I seamlessly glide through her classes and manage to graduate from high school six months early with a few stakes still holding me down.

Like many of my friends, I catch a free ride to university life, using it as a license to party. Performing an academic juggling act, I complete premed classes without skipping a date on my demanding social calendar. Little do I know I am slipping into quicksand.

For the party girl, everything appears fine on the outside. All is not so good on the inside. My soul is empty. Temporary pleasures aren't satisfying the deeper hunger within. No longer am I making a free choice to use substances; I need them to get through the day. Addiction has laid its ugly grip on me. Rational thinking is out the door. Reckless, selfish decisions are guiding my actions. My bad choices are seriously jeopardizing my life and the lives of others. The things I pursued for pleasure now enslave me.

On a beautiful sunny day, I decide to visit my boyfriend, Evan, a ski instructor. One moment I am heading toward the mountain resort in my sports car—the next, I have lost control. Time stops. Everything comes to a standstill. Stepping out, I peer down into the abyss. My drunkenness is rattled. The car has spun out and is facing the opposite direction just inches from the cliff. Something has to change.

Putting my studies on hold for a year, I move to France to work as an *au pair*, not realizing I am running away from myself. I don't get far.

Though I have studied French all my life, I hardly recognize what Maxime, age four, and Benoit, six, are saying when they arrive with their mother to pick me up at the airport. Sitting between two adorable but mischievous bubbles of energy in the back seat, they giggle while talking over me. As they speed-speak in a language I can't understand, *my* bubble bursts. I now understand the meaning of the word *foreigner*.

To enter their modest Parisian flat, we ride a mini-sized elevator cage that awaits us at street level. Its noisy closure bounces off the cold cement walls after the door clanks shut. Watching the internal organs of the cage move past, it slowly lifts us to our floor. Everything seems small. I feel even smaller.

A new day dawns and the foggy city comes alive as I escort the boys to school. Class at Alliance Française fills the morning hours, where I am required to continue my study of the French language. After lunch I shake the tablecloth from our second-floor balcony over the pedestrians below before walking the boys back to school. When their school day ends my time is devoted to their care.

These little ones help me perfect my understanding of the subtle nuances of spoken French. They are the living tools connecting my head knowledge of the language to my lips. They are also the tools God uses to test every ounce of patience within me.

For several months, isolation and loneliness are constant companions. Homesickness fills me with overwhelming sadness. An emotional refugee, my aching heart yearns to escape from this heaviness. Resisting the temptation to buy a return ticket home is a daily battle, despite my contract to stay for a year. Something inside of me tells me to fight the urge to run.

Letters from Nanny arrive each week, my lifeline to a love that continues to embrace me. During these last tumultuous years, she has never withheld her kindness from me. Her Christ-like character and unconditional love have left an indelible impression on my heart, drawing me toward Jesus. Though I have formed opinions about Christianity, I have never read the Bible.

"Nanny," I write, "Would you please send me a Bible?"

Brisk afternoons are spent with the boys at the park. They play while I read my New Testament. Days turn into weeks. A breeze rustles the leaves which are turning vivid colors. Eventually, they let go and die, then float to the ground. Death can be beautiful.

I sense a part of me is wanting to die—my old self. The heavy cloud of depression and loneliness is beginning to lift. A new season is in the air. My thirsty heart is finding springs of refreshment through the words in this Book. Each thin page is bringing nourishment to my hungry soul. Something inside of me is coming alive while, at the same time, storms are brewing on the horizon.

Enjoying a day off, I attend a Sunday service at the American Church in Paris. It is one of those moments in life one never forgets. The choir is singing "Joyful, Joyful, We Adore Thee" as the procession makes its way down the aisle. A presence overcomes me and I begin to weep. He sits beside me, embracing me in my loneliness. Somehow, I know He is with me.

As God reveals new things to me through His Word, I grow stronger. It is the first time in my life I have bravely walked through the door of pain without going around it. No attempts to crawl over. No running. No numbing. He is taking my hand and walking with me. By the time my European contract ends I don't want to go home.

Upon returning to the US, I slip my Bible onto the shelf and dive back into my hedonistic lifestyle. In a physical world, it is easy to push aside things nobler and unseen. Having tasted truth in the words of Christ, my conscience cannot rest. I am more miserable than ever.

Afraid to let go, I hold on tightly to the things that are destroying me. The battle rages within. An internal tug of war is being waged for my soul. I wonder if Nanny is praying, *Dear God, do whatever it takes to bring Kristy to You.*

Perfectly describing the enemy's work in my life, I remember Jesus' words, "The thief comes only to steal and kill and destroy. I came that they may have life and have it abundantly."

God knows what it will take to conquer my stubborn will. Using every circumstance as His tool, He convicts my soul and breaks me.

Turning to Him, I pray: *I give You my life. Lord, forgive me.*

A new creature. Born again. Now, the lifelong process of sanctification, or becoming holy, begins. Certain addictions I am freed of instantaneously: cigarettes and drugs. Others take nearly two decades to conquer: alcohol and food. As a believer, I am not perfect, but a sinner who recognizes my need for a Savior.

Leaving my pre-med pursuits, I enter a nursing program at the age of twenty-one, one week after marrying my fiancé, Rick. Dealing with wounded pride, I tell the Lord I never want to stop learning. Immediately after completing the nursing curriculum, I am thrust into a pilot program for new grads in a combination intensive care/coronary care unit. From there I move into emergency trauma and paramedical nursing, never lacking opportunities to deepen my knowledge of medicine and God's miraculous workings of the human body. Being at the bedside to love and directly care for my patients is in my DNA.

Rick and I are blessed with two beautiful sons, Jacob and Cory. Still young in our Christian faith, we are both dealing with baggage from the past. Struggling with alcohol abuse and an eating disorder while maintaining the appearance of having it all together is a horrible burden to bear. Plagued with shame, disgust, and guilt, I repeatedly turn to God in repentance. Somehow, I know He understands. Though extremely self-disciplined in most areas, I am not able to will my way out of this bondage. My desperation in dealing with my self-destructive behaviors is slowly killing me.

One day, while reading the Scriptures, I notice an equation. Jesus says, "I am the way, the truth, and the life. No one comes to the Father but through Me." He also says, "You will know the truth and the truth will make you free."

I spend the next twenty years getting to *know* Jesus intimately: talking to Him, reading the Word daily, going to Bible studies and church, reading books about every facet of my addictions, and seeking private and group counseling—doing the footwork while leaving the heart work to Him.

Facing daily defeat on the physical battlefield, my behaviors persist. Though unable to see the supernatural transformation taking place within me, I desperately cling to His promises. They are my anchor in the storm. Slowly, an external change begins to take place. Finding fullness in Him, I am not turning to alcohol or food to fill my soul. Seeing my worth through His eyes, I start to respect and accept myself for who I am. Abundant love begins to spill out of my heart.

* * *

Healing and brokenness do coexist. Sadly, after eighteen years, my marriage ends in divorce. Though the scar will always remain, Rick and I maintain a sweet friendship after the breakup. For the boys and us, the balm of forgiveness softens the blow of a broken family and prevents the cancer of bitterness from taking root.

Given the choice, I would opt out of a twenty-year battle with addiction. Yet sweetness lies in the victory gained: patience, perseverance, a greater empathy toward others, and freedom. Would my love for Christ be as deep, as intimate, had I not been given this thorn in the flesh? Would I understand the importance of forgiveness if I hadn't experienced the depth of my Savior's forgiveness toward me?

Life's stage is a battlefield and a classroom. Each day, Christ enters the fight with me. Every step, He teaches me. Weaknesses and shortcomings drive me to Him. When I fall, I brush off my wounded pride and get back up. In my strength, I cannot win. In His strength, I can. Standing on His promises, I no longer seek to fill my deepest needs with the things of this world but in my relationship with Jesus. Like my little French buddy, Antoine, I have been transformed and set free.

Beholding the beauty of the Jordanian desert

Roatán's stilted houses and water taxi

Chapter 2

Roatan, Honduras: Trial by Fire

> Rather, as servants of God we commend ourselves in every way: in great endurance; in troubles, hardships and distresses…in hard work, sleepless nights and hunger.
>
> 2 Corinthians 6:4–5 NIV

It's September 1995. I quit my job, clear out my house, and pack my bags. It doesn't seem much more than a dream. But it is. I am leaving for the foreign mission field. My son, Cory, twelve years old, gets to experience the unique adventure of first-time homeschooling on a tropical island.

This isn't exactly as I had planned. Ben, the head of the sending mission organization, originally invited me to run a medical clinic in Cofradia, Mexico. Having previously worked in Cofradia on a short-term trip, I was familiar with the village and layout of the clinic. Cory and I were both looking forward to spending the year in Mexico, immersed in Spanish and ministry, while his older brother, Jacob, studied abroad in Germany. Just before leaving for the one-year commitment, Ben calls with a change in plans.

"The Mexican government has decided they want a national to run the clinic. Maybe you should consider waiting a while."

"Ben, I am ready to go. Too many things have fallen into place. I believe the Lord wants me on the foreign mission field now. Is there any other option you might have? I will go wherever there is a need."

"Well, I was hoping to send someone to pioneer a medical mission on Roatán. I can't tell you what to expect, but I could use you there."

"Send me," I tell him.

Having never heard of Roatán, I do some homework. The west side of the forty-eight-mile-long island is a scuba diving destination, known worldwide for its extensive barrier reef and exclusive resorts. Helene, a shanty town on the poorer east side of the island, is the proposed location for our mission project. Roatán's widest point is less than five miles across. Caribe islanders speak Caribbean English, a modified Creole unique to the Bay Islands. Garifunas speak Spanish. Cory and I will live among the islanders. Nestled in the blue-green waters of the Caribbean, thirty-five miles off the Honduran coast, the island has a tropical climate: hot, wet, and humid.

A sleepless night just weeks before my final decision to go abroad finds me wrestling with the thought of leaving the job I love and letting go of my financial security. As the Lord would have it, a timely phone conversation with a Christian friend takes place the next day.

"Dan, I feel like God is calling me but I can't get a leave of absence from work. I will have to quit my job. Income from the sale of my house will require my paying capital gains taxes unless I purchase another home. How can I be sure I am making the right decision?"

Dan's counsel speaks to the very core of my faith.

"Kris, over two thousand years ago, Jesus came to tell us we can trust Him when He speaks to us. He is still alive and talking to us today. Are you going to put your faith and security in what man has to promise or are you going to trust in the promises of God?"

Hearing Dan's words, I realize that for me, this means I must be willing to leave my home to follow the God that promises to never leave me. It means putting my trust in Him instead of trusting the things I can see. It means letting go and allowing Him to take me to places I have never been or could ever imagine. It means taking a risk, the risk that my faith is real and that it works.

With a monthly pledge of fifty dollars from one couple and the blessings of my home church as my covering, I cushion a stack of unopened homeschooling books between bottles of sunscreen and bug spray, sit on the suitcase, and zip it shut.

Jim and Fran Olson, an American couple scheduled to travel with us and serve as hosts on the island, have a family emergency, canceling their trip. With two guitars, two suitcases, and a few contact names scribbled on a piece of paper, Cory and I board the plane and begin our mission adventure. After several layovers and connections, we land on Roatán, hoping that someone will be at the airport to pick us up.

Immediately, the hot humid air greets us as we step out on the steaming tarmac. Our ride is slow in arriving. Grateful we have not been forgotten once it does, we take in the tropical scenery framed by vast ocean vistas on both sides of the narrow strip of land.

A small guest room, separate from the Olsons' vacation home, is waiting for us. Their island retreat is located on a hill in the heart of the jungle. I am not sure what we will eat, where or how to buy groceries or exchange money, or much of anything. Unpacking a few items before we are surrounded by darkness, I have plenty of questions and no answers.

On the first night we experience a torrential downpour that lasts for hours. Lightning and thunder shake our room, each peal of thunder lasting up to fifteen seconds. The night is alive with mysterious sounds of all types of creatures as well as the familiar chirping crickets, croaking frogs, and buzzing insects.

Cory tosses and turns throughout the night. Partly due to the excitement of our new post and partly due to all the concerns I have for the days ahead, I get little sleep. Daylight brings relief to my restlessness. In the main house, the housekeeper, Joanna, is making coconut bread, which turns out to be one of my favorite staples during our stay.

Wandering through the main living quarters, I see thick rows of black lines moving on the walls. Ants. There must be thousands of them. They are marching up the wall, across the ceiling, and through the length of the entire room, making their exit on another wall. The contrast of this massive army against the whitewashed room makes their presence even more impressive.

"Joanna, there are thousands of huge black ants in here," I call out, hearing her place the delicious bread in the oven.

"They come with the rain. They will soon leave. Don't worry," she says, unconcerned.

As quickly as they have come, the marching army of visitors leaves, just as Joanna predicts. Learning from experience, I, too, hope to become an expert on the comings and goings of life in the jungle. I journal, "Today I run into a three-foot-long iguana in the house. The kids caught chameleons in jars and I almost stepped on a huge tarantula outside."

* * *

A large group of ex-pats live on the island. Some permanently reside on their yachts. Others have cozy getaways on the Caribbean shores. Cory and I run into them as we stumble our way around town. Word travels fast in this tight community. The ex-pats already know about us before we arrive: the crazy nurse and her son who have come to live in the shanty town of Helene on the east side of the island.

Divers, vacationers, ex-pats—they don't go to the east side. We haven't been yet, but get plenty to fill our ears about it. None is good.

One afternoon, we are invited to visit Elke, an eccentric German woman living in the heart of this zoological paradise. Her open-air dwelling is shaped like an octagon with each of the eight outdoor beams decorated with a bird feeder. Groups of hummingbirds compete for a spot around the feeders to feast on the sugary treat. Just as Cory and I sit down to admire the unusual architecture of the home and the many bookshelves offering hours of leisurely reading, a hummingbird flashes across the room to the feeder hanging on the opposite side of the house. Then another. And another. Tiny, feathered creatures are darting at all angles above our heads. During the next hour, like winged spokes on a buzzing hub, dozens of hummingbirds zip back and forth through the house to opposite feeders. Demonstrating incredible precision, I marvel at their instinctive air traffic control.

Observation and learning are part of my daily routine. Roatán enjoys an event-oriented culture as opposed to our Western culture of time orientation. My initiation to this is a huge source of frustration. In the US, time is a highly valued commodity. Punctuality is expected. Schedules are adhered to and, if broken, an apology is in order. Event-oriented cultures value events more than time. Punctuality is not expected. Schedules are not adhered to, and, if broken, an apology is not necessary.

Example: Communication with my mission headquarters in the US from Roatán is by fax. Relying on a private boat to pick me up and take me to a fax machine somewhere on the other side of the island is my only way to communicate with the outside world.

Today, Dingo is scheduled to pick me up at ten from a designated dock and take me to the fax machine. Just before ten I am on the dock, expecting his boat to arrive on time, taking comfort in knowing the mosquitos will not torment me on the water. The sun is a ball of fire overhead. My umbrella offers instant shade as I pop it open. Island travel without it is a big mistake.

By ten thirty, I am drenched with sweat. Its cooling effect, in combination with the sea breeze, distracts me for a few minutes and I take in the beautiful scenery of the Caribbean coastline: fine white sands, palms swaying gently above. Growing impatient, I slap swarms of mosquitos attacking my body and adding to hundreds of pre-existing bites Skin So Soft lotion brought from home, laced with one-hundred-percent DEET from a gallon can on the Olson's patio, doesn't curb their ravenous appetites. Glancing down at my watch, it is eleven thirty. My stomach growls while the mosquitoes enjoy lunch. At twelve-thirty, a moving speck appears on the horizon. I recognize the boat. Pulling up to the dock, Dingo smiles.

"Jump in! Let's go!"

No apologies. No excuses. Nothing. The event is taking place. That is all that matters.

This may sound like an exaggeration, but it isn't.

* * *

Invited to attend a wedding, I walk with other guests through mud-coated specimens of dead frogs and snakes. A rusty truck splashes through potholes behind us, then stops unexpectedly. The driver, clad in a black tux and starched white shirt glances into the rearview mirror to adjust his tie while waiting for us to climb in back. We don't get far before the truck comes to a halt and the groom steps out to check under the hood. Fortunately, the problem is a minor mechanical issue and the repaired truck takes off with a jolt, mud flying, groom at the wheel, a truckload of guests in the flatbed. Arriving at the wedding an hour and a half after the time it is scheduled to begin, we pile out and enjoy the event.

On Roatán it is not easy to find decent living quarters, something I discover when searching for a place to rent. One rental looks promising. In fair condition, it is located on a nice beach. During our walkthrough, we flush several frightened bats from the bedroom closet. Not crazy about the thought of bats sharing my bedroom, I continue looking. On a cay off the main island is a small bat-free house built over the water. I decide to rent it for the month. During this time, I hope to come up with a plan for the days ahead.

Ben, Jim, and Fran arrive from the US after Cory and I have managed to survive on our own in the jungle wilderness for an entire week. The five of us have a great reunion and a wonderful visit. Joanna goes out of her way to prepare some traditional island meals. Real food is welcome. Discussions regarding the unavailability of property for purchase raises concerns. The decision is made to temporarily put the project in Helene on hold. My year-long pioneer mission adventure has been abruptly aborted after one week.

"Do you want to go back to the States? Maybe the timing isn't right for you?" Ben asks me apologetically. He and the Olsons plan to return to the US in a few days.

Convinced this is merely a test of my commitment and faith, I tell him, "Ben, I'm going to stick it out here on Roatán for a month and seek the Lord's plan." By God's grace, the exact measure of faith I need is given to me in His perfect time. He has filled me with His peace, a sense of His presence, and a rock-solid resolve in my decision.

Several days later, a dory, or long sliver of carved tree trunk fashioned into a water taxi, takes Cory and me to our destination: a cay off of the main island. This is our new home. Our stilted shack sits above rippling water moving in rhythm with the tide. Washing up with the water each day, I begin to notice discarded syringes, needles, and broken vials thrown into the sea by health care workers operating a small clinic at the end of the cay. As one of my projects for the month, I educate the workers, teaching them how to dispose of contaminated articles appropriately. Hopefully, they will develop new habits going forward.

* * *

The familiar odor of cigarette smoke drifts into our hut several nights in a row. I am curious about where it is originating. One evening, a shadow of a figure makes its way to our shed on the narrow dock. Peeking out, I see the window of the shed open and smoke wafting out over the water. Later I notice the shed door ajar, two feet poking out onto the dock. After another sleepless night, I have a sunrise chat with my neighbors.

"Did you know that someone is sleeping in my shed?"

"Oh, it's Kye. He's slow but won't hurt nobody. Children like him plenty and he won't steal a thing."

Returning to our shack, I take some satisfaction in scaring the cockroaches off the walls and countertops of the kitchen before preparing breakfast, resigning myself to the fact that my human houseguest might be here to stay.

* * *

Our home becomes headquarters for the island children who do everything to distract Cory from his studies. They can't wait to pull him away and into the water.

"Hey, Cory, let's go bathin' in the sea!"

Kids here live with their moms. Their fathers are fishermen, working on vessels for months at a time. Many are absent altogether. The island children are unsupervised and don't attend school. The sea is their playground. Once underwater, they escape the unrelenting heat and enter a silent world of mystery and color: sponges, coral, and schools of fluorescent fish. After bathin' in the sea with his buddies, Cory appeases me with bowls full of fresh lobster he has plucked from the underwater sand.

One day he returns from his adventures with the island kids tenderly cuddling an unweaned kitten. Abandoned and without a home, Annie fell into the right hands. Nursing his little orphan by giving her milk through a small syringe, Cory manages to keep Annie alive. We celebrate the day she opens her eyes to behold the world around her. As challenging as this island experience has been for my son, I have seen God's grace poured out upon him. Annie is one of those gifts. His Creator knows how much he adores animals.

Homeschooling is getting harder. The distractions from the children are just one issue. Pouring over confusing curriculum, we both lack concentration in the intense heat. The mosquitos travel in massive clouds, making raids on our patio classroom. We have a running agreement to remind one another, "Don't scratch!"

Our scratching produces open wounds. Sweltering hot humid days blend together as we lose sleep from hundreds of itchy bumps on every extremity. Counting my bites, I reach two hundred on one calf and stop.

My next-door neighbor operates a kennel full of barking dogs. Cory cheerfully tells me, "More dogs than people live on our cay, Mom."

Partying late into the night, revelers on the mainland are heard across the shores. Water taxis travel back and forth until the wee morning hours. Steady tapping from their noisy outboard motors marks each arrival and departure from the parking lot—a dock adjacent to our shack.

* * *

Excited to attend the small Protestant church on the cay, my first Sunday experience bathes my soul with encouragement. After several days, I become aware of the fact there is a service every night: seven days a week. On the cay, all eyes are upon me—the missionary. Pressure to attend church is coupled with the stress of wilderness survival:

homeschooling, hand laundering, buying raw materials and cooking unfamiliar food while fighting off bugs determined to sabotage every effort. It is exhausting.

Struggling before the Lord about this matter of church attendance, I know He is aware of how much I love Him. Attending seven services a week does not validate my love. He has also given me the responsibility of caring for my son. Weekday dinners and homework are priorities. Answering to Him is more important than the opinions of my neighbors, yet living out my conviction is not easy.

On account of the rain and humidity, our clothing never completely dries after washing. Dark clouds prompt me to remove the damp pieces before another downpour. The sun returns and tempts me to put them back on the line. Their musty smell tells me I am losing the battle.

In the afternoons, I try to ignore the constant squawking of the colorful macaws on our neighbor's porch. That brochure I grabbed off the travel agency counter didn't come with a sound bite.

For a little getaway, Cory and I head to the beach. With one hand on the umbrella shielding me from the sun, I use my free hand to slap biting sand flies rather than collecting shells along the beautiful shore. For this rookie missionary, boot camp in Roatán is truly a trial by fire. The pictures look so inviting but life on the island is anything but bliss.

On one of many sleepless nights, I listen to the staccato rhythm of torrential rain on the roof. The noise of the chirping jungle animals rises above thundering clashes in the dark. My face is cooled by a constant trickle of tears. Lighting a candle, the God of the universe reaches down and touches me as I read: *"Rather, as servants of God we commend ourselves in every way: in great endurance; in troubles, hardships and distresses…in hard work, sleepless nights and hunger…"*

This is sufficient. This is what I needed. This is what carries me through the month on Roatán before packing our bags for Guatemala, the next destination filled with a new level of challenges in missionary boot camp.

Cory (right) and his island buddies on Roatán

Stepping off the bus in a Guatemalan village

Chapter 3

Guatemala: Beginnings

For who has despised the day of small things?

Zechariah 4:10

Slumped in a heap on the sidewalk, wearing a heavy gray coat covering all but the hand that holds a sticky plastic container to his nose, a resident of the Guatemala City dump obstructs my path to work. Shoe glue, used by street vendors for their trade, numbs his body and carries him away from the hellish reality of one existence into another. He doesn't know he is in my way.

A strong breeze carries plastic and paper garbage to new destinations. Dust in the air creates an ominous atmosphere, while the familiar odor of burning rubbish invades my nostrils.

Watching my step to avoid sinking my boot into excrement, a mangy dog leads me down the trail to a door, no different from the others. Inside, a stethoscope and two bottles of medication sit on the table in front of Rachel, who is lovingly explaining their administration to a single mother rocking a baby in her arms.

"Kris, let's pray for Maria." Rachel places her hand on Maria's shoulder. I place mine on the baby.

On the periphery of the dump, Rachel, a nurse, and her husband, Troy, have established this ministry to the people who live and work here, searching through mounds of rubbish for recyclable items. By providing a food program, free medical care, and church services, we enter into the private lives of these beautiful people by meeting their basic needs.

At the end of the day, after listening to stories of struggle and heartache, I leave, returning to the comfort of the mission base, where Cory and I are living. *Lord, how can I more deeply understand what these people are going through? I always have a way out.*

On Friday night, after Cory leaves for a weekend retreat with his youth group, I pack a few items and jump on the bus. The driver fiddles with something under his heavily cushioned steering wheel. His seat, the dashboard, and the entire front of the bus are colorfully well-padded with tuck and roll-style vinyl. Pictures of the Virgin Mary hover like guardian angels over his head. Cranking up the volume, mariachi music booms loudly from the blown speakers. The chassis groans and clanks from the all-too-familiar excessive weight it is carrying. While balancing on the edge of the overcrowded seat, I am soon locked into place by riders standing in the aisle. I've seen some sleep in this upright position, supported by those around them. I haven't found an adequate Spanish verb to describe this common situation. I invent one: *sardinar*.

This is the picture of everyday life for most Guatemalans. By using public transportation, the chicken buses, I choose to embrace their culture. Tonight I am going to sleep at the dump, hoping to gain insights by experiencing the world of those I serve.

As I enter the dump, I never cease to be amazed by the huge satellite dishes perched on tin roofs, glaring evidence of unwise credit card purchases made by so many people living here. Large televisions, bought on time, occupy a good portion of space inside cramped living quarters. Sinking deeper into debt, many can't seem to avoid impulsive buying decisions that enslave them. Temptations are the same wherever we go.

Light escapes through the slits of the plywood structure. The soft melody of a hymn rises behind the door I expected to find locked.

Gathered inside our ministry room is a small group of believers holding a church service. A small light bulb, wired to a car battery, casts shadows on their joyful faces. Surprised to see me, they continue praising the One who lifts their spirits out of the despair around them. After they finish, I bid them goodbye and mention I am spending the night.

"Do you have blankets? Food? Water? We will leave the battery so you have light."

Concern for my well-being is overwhelming. Touched by their generosity, I insist they take the battery.

"I have everything I need. Thank you for offering."

Having imagined all types of noise in the form of drunkenness and domestic violence, I am surprised by the hush outside. Settling down on a blanket laid out on a long table, my head begins to throb. Smoldering plastic, a constant presence in the trash heap, does not sleep. Wrestling to find a position to calm the pain between my eyes, the dark quiet hours give way to the first rays of dawn. Silence is followed by the sweet melody of giggling children. Their laughter tickles my ears.

Studying my Bible while pondering the events of my sleepover, I pass the morning marveling at the peacefulness of the environment. The tremendous examples of human resilience I read about in the Bible exist here in the dump. Witnessing an inner strength in those whose faith is tested in these circumstances, I see God's faithfulness prevail. He is with those who turn to Him in the face of hardship.

With nothing to calm the pounding headache now extending to my temples, I decide I cannot stay. Just before noon, while packing my bag, I am reminded: I always have a way out. After an aborted mission in Roatán, I board a plane. After A few hours of inconvenient hunger, I return home to a hot meal. After a night of breathing toxic fumes in the dump, I retreat to fresh air and a cozy room away from a horrible scene. The mystery of destiny puzzles me.

Lord, I am grateful I always have a way out. Please make it my heart's desire to find a way back in.

While Cory attends the Christian Academy of Guatemala, I complete my Spanish homework with the help of Diego, a Mexican missionary living on the Youth With A Mission (YWAM) base. Between Spanish classes and dump clinics, we spend long days ministering to the residents of Tierra Nueva, a squatter's community on the earthquake fault line, thirty minutes by bus from the base.

Carrying a fishing tackle box filled with medications, Diego and I make house calls in the tin and cardboard shacks precariously situated on the steep embankments. Moving from one heartbreaking family situation to another, I feel quite invisible. While Diego talks and ministers to the people, I sit silently, trying to come up with a translation of their conversation in my mind. After consulting me, he provides the desperately needed medication the family cannot afford. Diego then leads us in prayer, followed by my contribution, "Graçias, señor Jesus, amen."

Day after day, this is repeated. Humbling is hardly descriptive of my feelings. One afternoon, heading home to the base, sweat dripping down my face and dust whirling in from the open window of the chicken bus, I crumble. Like a little child, I choke out my frustrations to Diego between sobs,

"I feel worthless. I am doing nothing. I can't understand anything. I can't talk. I am *so* frustrated. I feel like quitting!"

When I finish, he looks at me and says, "Kris, you know those stories you read about the famous missionaries and all their heroic feats? Well, there are many pages of their lives between those stories that go unwritten. Those are the pages you are experiencing today."

Experiencing page after unwritten page, this truth sticks with me while navigating daily life in a new culture.

* * *

Adventure awaits Cory as he surfs the Velcro bus to his carpool—clinging to other riders hanging out of the open door during morning rush hour. He loves it. Hearing stories of people crushed between buses, I don't share his excitement.

Razor wire mixed with broken glass adorn the walls of the YWAM base—security measures in a city filled with crime. Awakened by deafening bullets discharged in the dark morning hours, I tell myself I have failed as a mother, bringing my son to such a dangerous place. Gratefully, the round of gunshots turns out to be part of a birthday tradition: entire packs of firecrackers set off outside a bedroom window.

Pigs and dogs join the forces of bloated roadkill on the steaming asphalt highways. They remain on display for days. Human corpses, covered with sheets after shootings or accidents, are picked up and thrown into the trunks of police cars. Red lights above porches do not represent the nefarious activity I imagine. Relieved to learn their significance, they indicate homemade tamales are for sale inside the home. *Tres tiempos,* posted outside open shops, alert passersby to fresh corn tortillas sold three times a day. Neighborhoods are replete with these homespun businesses where two or three apron-clad women skillfully mold balls of masa for tortillas. Rhythmic slapping echoes in staccatos throughout the streets, while steam rises from the large round stovetop in the middle of the room. Once cooked, piles of tortillas are covered in baskets lined with colorful woven fabric, keeping them hot for hours. I have seen more than a dozen thick tortillas eaten by one person at a single meal.

Putting together a pictorial book entitled "Back To Work Using Our Heads" is an idea that comes to mind while I take note of the ever-present human bearers of burden. With perfect posture, a woman crosses the congested city street balancing two dozen crates of fresh eggs on her head, hands-free. Hot coals sizzle in a primitive welded stove while a man carries it on his head to another destination. Along the road, a "walking tree" travels up the side of the highway. Completely hidden underneath the enormous bundle of branches is a man bearing its load. Strapped to the back of a brightly clad indigenous woman is a baby, completely covered from head to toe by a large shawl fastened around her chest. Signs of life appear only after the mother removes the baby from the cocoon, pulls her breast from her woven *huipil,* and latches him to suckle.

* * *

After dropping the kids off at school, Rachel and I enjoy a cup of coffee in a small café when we hear popping sounds on the street. Jumping up from the table and out the door to see what's going on, we have front-row seats to a real-time cop and robber scene: a getaway car screeching around the corner with armed men hanging out the back door, exchanging rounds with the police who are in hot pursuit. Returning to the shop, we sit and finish our coffee.

While adjusting to the culture, I establish deepening relationships in Tierra Nueva and the dump. Generous funds, provided by supporters, contribute to many substantial projects: housing, clothing, school fees, medication, transportation, hospitalizations, and more. The example of Christ, who addressed spiritual needs after meeting physical needs, is a model I try to follow. To be a channel of love through the support of those in the US who have given their hard-earned income is a tremendous honor I don't take for granted. A rich spiritual harvest follows our work; the Lord is with us.

Having moved from the mission base into a home with other missionaries, including a family, Cory is now speaking Spanish with the Guatemalan neighbors like a native. Struggling with my lack of progress, my pre-dawn thoughts are distracted when I hear little Josiah downstairs in his crib, talking to himself.

"Goo goo, ahhhh, gah…ewe…goo."

"My Spanish sounds like Josiah's. I am not anywhere near where I want to be. Lord, can't You help me become fluent?"

My private pity party is cloaked in the guise of prayer. Questions bombard my mind. Someone is talking to me.

"What's wrong, Kris? Why do you feel you have to master the language before I give you mastery? Could it be pride? One more language on your resumé? Are you self-conscious when you speak? Is that why you don't speak?"

I have to admit my pride is wounded in this battle for control over my tongue.

"Listen to Josiah, Kris. He doesn't care who is listening. He does his due diligence and will be speaking the language within two years. He isn't worried about mistakes in his grammar. Unencumbered by self-consciousness, he just wants to get his point across. He does his work. I do the rest."

One might argue that God isn't talking to me during these moments of internal struggle. I believe He is. Words spoken to my soul by the One who knows the depth of my deprivation, pride, and selfishness hit the bullseye every time. No human on earth sees this hidden part within. It is His alone to scrutinize. In these quiet moments, I am humbled by the wisdom that comes to me, profoundly affecting my life. My mind is calmed.

"OK, I will do my work and let You do the rest."

* * *

Trouble starts to brew at school. Cory becomes more and more defiant. He wants to move back to the States and live with his father; I am concerned he will abuse the freedom he enjoys while living under his dad's roof. Having reaped the positive influence of strong Christian men the past two years, I sense this season is ending.

Seeking His counsel in the early morning, I cry out to the Lord. *"I don't know what to do but my eyes are on You."*

Flipping through the concordance of my Bible, I think of fasting. Prayer, reading the Word, worship, and church attendance have been constants in my life. Unaware of any intentional sin blocking my communication with God, I want to know what else I might do to gain a spiritual advantage. Fasting is something I have overlooked.

Turning to 2 Chronicles 20, I read. *Lord, I don't know what to do but my eyes are on You.*

Didn't I just say that to You, Lord?

Continuing, I read about Jehoshaphat's dilemma. As king of Judah, he is faced with a vast army coming against him and the Israelites. He feels vulnerable. Defeated. God tells him this is not his battle, but God's. Jehoshaphat and the Israelites are to take their stand, worship, pray, and fast. They are to wait for God's deliverance on their behalf.

Reading this over and over, I come to a difficult conclusion. Cory's spiritual life is not in my hands, but God's. This is not my battle. Cory needs to know his father more deeply by living with him. Giving God room to work, I need to take my stand: staying in Guatemala, not trying to control, and placing my trust in Him. Fasting once a week on behalf of my family begins as I close my Bible.

Rachel and I have a habit of meeting at her house and praying together. Her daughter, Lauren, is in Cory's class. This morning, I cancel our prayer time. Writing Rachel a brief note, I explain I am taking Cory to talk with the principal. Nothing more. I leave the note on her door.

As a result of our meeting, plans are made for Cory to finish his remaining month of studies at home, then move back to the States and live with his father. Making more frequent trips back and forth will allow me to visit both Cory and Jacob, who is back from Germany, while continuing to do overseas ministry.

This is one of the longest Fridays of my life. Perhaps the longest day of my life. Heartbroken over our broken family and heartsick to see my son leave, I second guess my decision over and over, questioning if I have truly heard from God. Am I fabricating everything in my mind to justify myself?

Cory leaves for a weekend outing while I drive to Antiqua for a mission conference. Walking across the parking lot, I run into Troy and Rachel. A folded piece of pink paper is in Rachel's hand. She hugs me and hands me the note. On it is written 2 Chronicles 20:12–20.

Opening it I read: "Dear Kris, I don't know what all went on today, only that Lauren thinks it didn't go well. I am praying for you. It's so hard to understand what God is doing in our lives sometimes; to trust that He's working all this out for good when we feel so defeated. You are not alone in this battle, Kris…"

I look up. Against the backdrop of black space, the myriad of constellations is brilliant. From the palette of galaxies, a creamy spray upon the canvas rests as draped raiment, while stars flicker like thousands of fireflies suspended above the planet.

How can it be?

At this very moment, the Creator of this vast celestial universe is reaching down from His seat of majesty to speak to me through ink on pink paper, picking the one star chosen to guide me in the morning: 2 Chronicles 20.

"Yes, Kris, I was speaking to you this morning. I am speaking to you now. You need not fight in this battle; station yourself, stand, and see the salvation of the Lord on your behalf, for the Lord is with you. You are not alone."

* * *

Bumping down another Guatemalan road in another chicken bus, I am talking to an American woman working for an international mission organization. Curious, I ask, "What exactly do you do?"

"I travel all over the world accumulating facts for potential mission trips."

As she explains her fascinating job, I have a sensation, perhaps similar to Elizabeth when John the Baptizer leaped in her womb. My heart skips a beat and my stomach does a somersault.

Maybe it's the road.

Dreaming of how incredible it would be to travel to the far corners of the world while serving God at the same time, I quickly land back on familiar turf.

"Lord, I know You have placed me in Guatemala. Besides, I don't see how this crazy idea would ever work in my situation."

Living in Central America for five years, I am blind to the intricate ways the Lord is weaving the tapestry of my life. The unwritten pages in my book are already written in His. Only He can see my future: one filled with many bumpy, dusty roads throughout the world to compare with these I have come to know in Guatemala.

Kids and I at the Guatemala city dump

Indigenous mountain girls in Guatemala

Chapter 4

Guatemala: The Mountains

I will lift up my eyes to the mountains;
From where shall my help come from?
My help comes from the Lord,
Who made heaven and earth.
He will not allow your foot to slip;
He who keeps you will not slumber.

Psalm 121:1–3

Rolling out of my sleeping bag and off the narrow plank on which I slept, I mentally prepare for the hike ahead. Shorter than the eight-hour trek it took to get here, our medical team hopes to arrive in Santa Rosa after a rigorous two-hour climb in the Guatemalan highlands. Having received a verbal invitation, we look forward to breaking new ground in the remote communist village.

Mike and I have worked together for almost six years now. Living with his family of five in the highland village of Nebaj, he invited me to partner with him in his work. Leading medical teams to areas untouched by the gospel, Mike strategically and prayerfully chooses the villages to visit, hoping to plant churches and reap a harvest of souls in each one. Focusing on this mountain ministry for the last several years, I have been able to provide medical input, dental care, and worship sessions for the frequent teams we host from the US. I call Mike "Mr. Stat Man," deferring statistical, cultural, and "How high? How far? How long?" questions to him.

With a passion for the outdoors, hiking, indigenous people, and bringing the gospel to the unreached, I can't think of a more thrilling place to roll off a plank. Sharing my enthusiasm and a little guilt over my dream job with a friend living in Guatemala City, he assures me, "Kris, you don't have to feel guilty about what you do. It is about as far away from the desires of my heart as I can imagine."

* * *

If it is any indication of how things will go for the rest of the day, the mule drivers decide to strike. Loaded with our medical supplies and waiting patiently on the mountain turf, the mules stand still, like porcelain figurines, while the drivers reach a settlement. After much prayer, we set out for Santa Rosa two hours later, mules and drivers taking the lead.

Heavy backpacks compress the sweaty gear clinging to our skin. Ready to take a break before setting up clinic, we aren't ready for the reaction when we arrive. Watching us through knotholes, the villagers hide in their huts. Those in the open are resisting our visit. We've received word: some think we are there to poison them or steal their land. Some believe we will kill their children for body parts. Hearts hardened and gripped by fear are a breeding ground for lies.

Lynching is not an uncommon way to settle disputes in this area. We shake the dust from our feet and leave, not having planned to spend the rest of the day hiking to the next village, Ixlaj, eight hours away. Ixlaj is another unknown. Will we be welcomed when we arrive, long after dark and bone-tired? Only God knows.

We are met with challenges every step of the way. Torrential rain creates a boggy trail winding through steep mountainous terrain. One of the mules collapses. The load he is carrying must be added to our overstuffed packs.

In the darkness, we tackle the last narrow slalom course through the mud. For experts only: there is a cornfield on the right and a barbed wire fence on the left. Sliding and singing, laughing and sighing, our silliness supplies us with the extra energy we need to cross the finish line. I dodge the barbed wire with my grip, slipping from post to post. After a seemingly endless descent, we pass through a heavy mist settling upon us like a curtain on the final scene of a play. Finally, shadows appear and voices are heard eleven hours after breaking camp this morning. Welcomed with friendly greetings, we have reached Ixlaj.

A rich smoky aroma rises from the crackling bonfire awaiting us. Ignoring my fatigue, I pull out my guitar. Singing songs of worship and joking with the villagers, we are warmed by the fire. Our laughter rises with the smoke, bridging together two cultures in the name of love.

My first patient of the morning, Josephina, is all smiles. Yesterday, she, her husband, their baby, and two other children hiked two hours from their village, Pal, to receive care in Santa Rosa. When the clinic didn't open there, the family joined us for the trek to Ixlaj.

With Josephina's lower wisdom teeth extracted, the five pilgrims begin their long trek home—their load lightened by two less molars. Overjoyed with gratitude, there are no complaints.

Small in stature, strong in might, the Ixil people have no travel alternative. The mountains, considered a curse by some, are home. There are no roads leading to the targeted villages. Everything is carried by mule, a rare luxury, or on their bodies. Without flashlights, they negotiate trails using their *night eyes*, my term for their uncanny ability to see in the dark. Curious as to why we insist on bringing several changes of clothing, multi-packs of snacks, clean wipes, sunscreen, bug spray, and more, they put up with our American ways and love us well.

Decked with cameras and fanny packs, sun hats, and sunglasses, our hikers struggle to the point of exhaustion to reach the villages. In my experience, the buff military types and marathon runners on the team are often the first to drop, overcome by bacterial gastrointestinal competitors.

Fabio, one of the rugged indigenous mountain men, works with our teams. Having survived the bloody civil war, he is a committed Christian with a heart to evangelize his people. Brothers in Christ, he and Mike share a deep bond of friendship. One year, they travel together to the US for a conference in Washington DC, Fabio's first visit to America.

Not long after his return, Fabio, bubbling over with joy, comes up to me after a long hike, while I lay my backpack down in the plywood church. Against the wall are grain bags full of corn, neatly stacked in a large pile, the offering of first fruits. The dormant chapel, with a loudspeaker tied to the top of its tin roof, comes alive during services. Amplified ranchero worship echoes across the mountain corridors and broadcasts Good News. The dirt floor, swept clean with a bush bundle, will be transformed into a bed of fresh pine needles for the worshipers.

"I built a shower for the team." Fabio's smile matches his excitement.

"A shower?"

Pointing at the large cement *pila*, Guatemala's traditional waist-high water basin, I see its base peeking out from under a shroud of blue plastic, supported by tall branches at each corner. The *pila* has been transformed.

Considering our primitive experiences to be unique cross-cultural opportunities, I don't sweat the small stuff like showers. How often does one get a chance to go on hikes and develop friendships with Mayan villagers, while overnighting in their mountain dwellings and eating meals in their homes? Our plan to split up in pairs and stay with individual families this evening thrills me. This is the real thing.

"I put some wood on the ground in the shower. You can stand on it so your feet don't get muddy."

Fabio's smile widens, "I got permission for the team to sleep in the church tonight. You won't have to split up and sleep in separate huts." His creativity and concern for our comfort surprise me. Where did he get all these bright ideas? Later, sipping on horchata while enjoying a black bean and tortilla dinner, Fabio tells me about his experience in the US.

"Now I know why you Americans have trouble on our trails. You don't walk on dirt. I walked from the house to the sidewalk to the car, got out of the car on the pavement, and went inside another building. My feet never touched dirt. You take showers to make you clean every day. I want you to be comfortable here."

Fabio stayed in a very nice home during his stateside visit after he figured out how to use the doorbell. Pizza served for dinner was too rich for his stomach. He is accustomed to a high-carb, low-fat diet. Unable to get comfortable on the feather-light mattress in his guest room, he ended up sleeping on the floor. Projecting the feelings of discomfort and isolation he experienced in our culture, he is determined to keep us united in a cozy, clean, comfortable environment.

Since moving to Nebaj and living among the Ixil, I have experienced a vivid contrast of cultures: community-oriented vs independent, event-oriented vs time-oriented, selfless vs selfish, cooperative vs competitive, and primitive vs developed. While pouring my heart into this work, I receive much more in return. God always works in three hundred sixty degrees: mutual learning and blessing is a two-way street.

* * *

"Can I play it?"

Pulling my guitar out of its case and handing it to the Mayan boy sitting next to me on the narrow bench, I'm happy to share my "baby," a gift for all to enjoy. The view before me is majestic—rolling hills covered in a blanket of grass with endless mountain ranges beyond.

Hiking has jarred my guitar out of tune. The mountain musician is not concerned. Plucking away, boldly fingering broken chords and strumming clumsily, he sings off-key, lost in the pleasure of having an instrument to play. Finished, he takes the guitar in his hands, holding it like a treasure, and looks at it as though capturing its image in his mind. Giving it back after a thirty-minute concert, he thanks me and leaves.

Self-consciousness and self-criticism, two enemies I fight, are nonexistent in such freedom of expression. With growing awareness of the competitive nature of my own culture and the damaging effects it can have, I learn valuable lessons from moments like these.

Having allowed an off-hand criticism of my voice to crush my spirit and silence my song for twenty years, I am still learning the heart of worship. Paled by those more skilled than I and inspiring beginners who are just getting started, any talent the Lord has given me is for His glory, not my own. Competition and comparison damage the realization of what I have been given while placing me in an unloving posture toward others.

"Oh, yeah, I play a little" admits my new friend, Kyle, a young American on the team, brushing his hair away from his face while eyeing my guitar.

"Really, you play?"

"Yeah. I've written a few songs."

"I'd love to hear one," I tell him, handing him my guitar.

Briefly fingerpicking a sweet melody before beginning his song, Kyle stops.

"I haven't played for a while. I don't know if I can remember all the chords. I'll probably make a bunch of mistakes. I don't sing that well."

Pulling the strap over his shoulder to give the guitar back, I insist.

"I want to hear your song! Please!"

Kyle's song is beautiful, so beautiful I have him sing it several times during our week together on the trail. Lyrics penned from the heart of his soul, no composer on earth could write the same. I pray with him, asking the Lord to multiply his talents and help him realize his value as a child of God.

Observing the character of people living in primitive cultures, I believe their lives, uncluttered by material prosperity, afford a depth of development I have missed. They have little to compare with one another: their dwellings look the same, they wear similar clothing, and eat the same food. Reputation is not gained through power, prestige, status, or competition. Stripped of external props, they are known for who they are—their character. Is she mean or kind? Is he stingy or generous? Loving or hateful? Honest or a liar?

Growing in my relationship with Christ, I see His teachings support this truth. Setting my eyes on Him, I yearn to mature in the process he has begun of repairing my brokenness and shaping my character, making me whole in Him from the inside out.

* * *

Housesitting in Nebaj is a great way for me to have a place to stay for brief periods while my missionary friends take breaks and return to the States. Living in this tiny destination village and leaving the house to do simple errands does not go unnoticed. Before I return home, I am approached by more people expressing their needs than those selling their wares. Convinced my green eyes are interpreted as dollar signs, it can be emotionally exhausting to walk across the street. Praying for wisdom, I trust God to help me realize my limitations and wisely discern His will.

During my stay as a housesitter, I look for ways I can bless the owners: repair a screen, mend a torn curtain, wash the windows, stock the refrigerator. "*Mi casa es tu casa*" goes both ways. Privileged to enjoy the comforts of each sweet home, I want to leave it better off than when I arrived.

Some tragedies are out of my control. Waking up to Evan and Jen's dead cat beside her bowl is one of them. I take the limp pet outside and dig its grave. *What did I do wrong?* I feel responsible. Burying the cat in their yard, I dread having to break the news upon their return. They are gracious and suspect an unkind neighbor may have poisoned her.

Leila, an indigenous friend, fills in for a night at Jerry and Jamie's place where I am staying next. After a two-day hike, I return. Dragged to their home by Leila, who only speaks Ixil and has found me on the street, I fear what is ahead. Frantic, she takes me to the rabbit cages in the backyard and points to one that is unlatched and empty. Then she pulls me by my sleeve into the kitchen and opens the refrigerator. Inside lays an enormous, furry dead rabbit. After calming her down, she leaves the house and the rabbit in my care. Another burial.

Sitting on the couch in Jerry and Jamie's cozy abode, I notice the family pictures, personal knickknacks, and books in progress on the shelf across the room. Overcome by a sense of envy, I start feeling sorry for myself, not having a place of my own.

"Kris, this earth is not your home. Your true home is in heaven. Wherever you lay your head is your home for now."

Comforted by my thoughts, I continue to housesit, considering each place my own while making home improvements along the way and trying to keep the pets alive.

"Here. Take this. Whenever you wish, you are welcome. 'My house is your house.'"

I slip the house key onto my empty keyring. Over time, the ring becomes full of house keys, all representing open-door invitations.

"Thank You, Lord, for giving me more homes than I know what to do with until I move into the heavenly palace You have prepared for me."

* * *

Resting to take a water break, our medical team takes in the scenery of a remote trail: switchbacks winding up the steep mountain covered with brush and evergreens. Before we finish our break, we receive word that a man has been injured on the trail ahead. In the middle of nowhere, our medical team descends upon Ivan, a thirty-year-old forensic anthropologist who has been exhuming bodies in the area. Since the war, there continues to be ongoing work to obtain historical information from evidence preserved underground.

At the same time, a Cuban doctor, having received word of the accident in a village hours down the trail, arrives with pain medication. Within minutes, Art and Russ, our team doctors, have the posterior dislocation of Ivan's shoulder reduced and splinted in place.

Ivan and I have several more hours to talk while descending the mountain. Considering the odds, I see this as a total miracle with God's loving handprint all over the case. Ivan sees it as a lucky coincidence. Sharing the gospel with him, I offer an alternative point of view. As we part, he assures me, "I'm thinking about it."

One of my goals is to eliminate the word luck from my vocabulary. I don't believe in luck or coincidence. Every meeting, every event, and every day of my life is orchestrated by an eternal God, who has a plan and purpose for everything.

* * *

The trip to Guatemala City from Nebaj is a long journey. Reaching the base of the mountains, there is a town where temperatures are hot. Traveling with a group of indigenous riders, our chicken bus has a blowout in the middle of the desert lowland heat. The driver orders everyone off the bus while he changes the tire. Surrounded by majestic mountain ranges, I walk with the other passengers toward a crossing where refreshments are sold by open-air vendors. A young man walking beside me strikes up a conversation. Overcome by the picturesque scenery of the valley, I ask him what he thinks about God's creation.

"*¡Soy ateo. Yo no creo en Dios!*" he tells me proudly.

Having established he is an atheist and doesn't believe in God, I ask him how everything around us could have possibly come into being. Rather than offering an answer to my question, he makes sure I understand.

"*¡Soy ateo!*"

"That's interesting," I respond, having listened to him tell me several times that he's an atheist. "I've personally experienced a relationship with the living God, Jesus Christ. He is very real to me, helping me understand the explanation behind the existence of everything around us while also taking care of my everyday needs. He loves you and wants you to know Him."

Leaving me alone in the dust, he walks over to another young man several yards away. Having ended up quite a distance from where we began, it dawns on me I have left my purse behind. My thirst is unbearable.

"Ask the atheist if you can borrow some change until you get back to the bus."

"Are You kidding, Lord? No way! That will give him more reason to mock You after having told him You take care of ALL my needs!"

The atheist is smirking. Humiliated, now standing inches from his face, I blurt out, "Hey, I am really thirsty. Do you have some change I could borrow to buy some water? I'll pay you back when we get to the bus."

He hasn't taken his eyes off me. Certain I've communicated well in Spanish, I am not surprised by his abrupt, "No!"

Turning around, my back facing him and his friend, I slowly walk away, telling the Lord what He already knows: *"They're mocking You, Lord. This isn't about my reputation, but Yours. If You wanted, You could split a rock in front of me and produce water. You did it for Moses. Please do something!"*

I turn around to face the atheist one last time. Two young Ixil girls, colorfully dressed in their indigenous outfits, are now on the path between us, walking toward me. I have never seen them before. One has her arm extended, holding a bottle of cold water.

"You are the doctor who works in our village helping our people. Please take this. It is for you."

Taking the water and thanking her, I hold it in the air, my eyes fixed on the atheist, "*¡DIOS!*"

Singing with the kids in the mountains of Guatemala

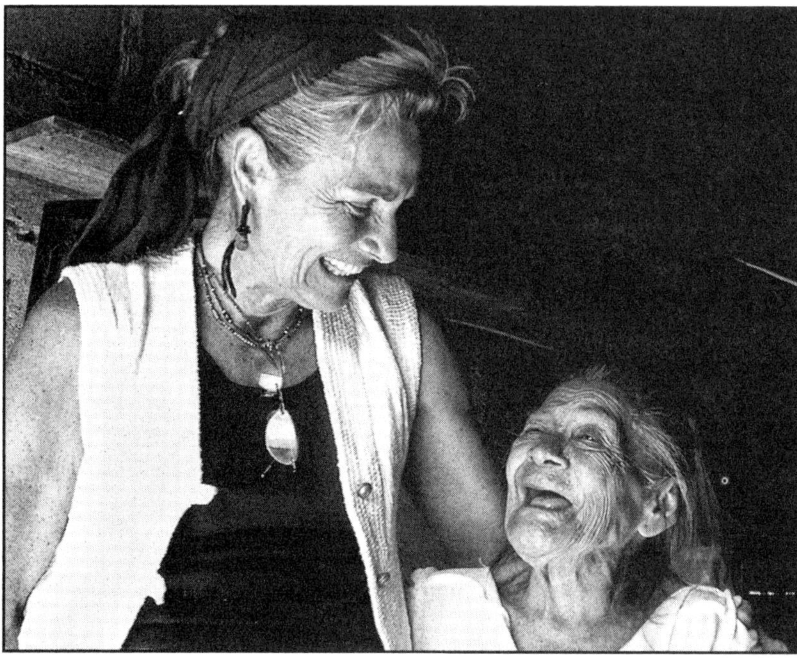

A happy Guillermina— in her home at the Women's Center in Choluteca

Chapter 5

Honduras: Hurricane Mitch

Then they will rebuild the ancient ruins,
They will raise up the former devastations;
And they will repair the ruined cities,
The desolations of many generations.

Isaiah 61:4

"Send me to the hardest hit area."

Jeff, a missionary pilot, is on the line, listening. Static fills my ear while I think back on the week.

Sliding in the mud, pelted by heavy rain, and struggling to pull my boot out of the sludge, I crawl back into the vehicle. This is the third time we will have to turn around. For three days, runoff from the torrential downpours has created landslides, washing out the dirt road and preventing me from leaving the mountains of Guatemala. The rivers of water have now subsided and the road is navigable. Arriving in Guatemala City, I call Jeff, who is a missionary pilot dropping supplies into Honduras, a neighboring country. There, the hurricane has buried thousands of people under debris and sand. I am determined to go and help. Jeff is a perfect contact.

"OK, listen, I'll have Marcelena pick you up at the airport when you arrive in Tegucigalpa. Look for a placard with your name on it. She's with Vida Abundante Church. Let me have your flight information."

Thanking him, I give him my itinerary, hang up, and start packing.

On Oct 29,1998, hurricane Mitch hit the shores of northern Honduras, making its way inland and westward—leaving a path of destruction behind. Relief efforts are in full force when I arrive.

Slinging my guitar over my shoulder, I grab my backpack from the baggage claim, hoping someone in the lobby is holding my name in the air. It won't be easy to make alternative arrangements this late at night.

* * *

My adrenalin is pumping. I can't turn it off. This is my initiation to the emotional roller coaster of disaster relief. Compelled to ride, I buy a ticket and wait in line. Committing myself, I jump into the car clicking its way to the top. There's a pause. Looking straight down, I am hit with doubt, anxiety, and fear. This is scary. What I am getting myself into? Do I have what it takes? Am I equipped to help? Am I supposed to go? Strapped into my seat, I hold on and ride it out. Absorbing the twists and turns to the end, I step out, grateful I waited in line and got on. In the years ahead, I will jump back on the ride many times. Highs and lows will surge; they never go away. Nor will the exhilarating feeling of looking back, knowing the Lord called me to jump in—to go and help those in need. With my arms held up in abandonment, He will never make me ride alone.

* * *

"KRIS REPP," written in bold letters on cardboard, greets me in the lobby. Something about my name being spelled properly is incredibly comforting, like a welcoming hug reassuring me. New to disasters and my first time in Honduras, the Lord knows just what I need.

Marcelena opens the hatch. I throw my baggage into the back. Driving through the capital, our vehicle bumps and twists over broken roadway.

Buckled chain link fences have become solid barriers of mud, trash, and branches. Freight containers lie toppled over sidewalks. Cars tightly embrace telephone poles in mid-air. Tree trunks span three car lengths across the road, blocking entrances to buildings filled with muddy water. The city has been placed in a blender: a mixture of trash, cars, buildings, trees, and mud set on "crush" and poured out on the ground. In the center of town, a huge lake has formed, a body of water dammed by corpses and debris, leaving the stench of death to linger in the air. Authorities believe many of the eleven thousand still missing are at the bottom.

"Jeff tells me you want to go to the hardest hit area. You will spend the night at my house tonight. In the morning, we'll get you on the bus to Choluteca. It's about two hours south, where the Choluteca River empties into the Gulf of Fonseca. During the storm, the raging water gained force as it flowed south through Tegucigalpa and into the gulf, carrying everything in its path."

My mind can't picture much worse than what I see through the windshield. Exhausted by the emotional roller coaster, I crawl into bed in Marcelena's guest room, my head sinking into the soft pillow.

"*Thank You, Lord, for this church and the love extended through it; thank You for Jeff and Marcelena; thank You for the experiences awaiting me. I know they are already written in Your book.*"

* * *

Sweat dribbles down from my visor and into my eye. Confusion over my arrival time keeps me waiting a couple of extra hours at the bus station in sweltering Choluteca. When Pastor Oscar arrives, he takes me straight to his church, a branch of Vida Abundante.

Stretching around the block is a thick line of hungry people. Oscar's wife, Joana, and a dozen volunteers are at work in a small room packing plastic bags with corn flour, rice, beans, lard, coffee, and a gospel tract. Taking my place on the concrete floor, I sit on a tiny wooden chair and begin filling bags with rice. After three and a half hours, with three hundred fifty bags ready for distribution, I sweep flour off the floor while Rosa rescues every stray bean. This is a Thanksgiving I will never forget, counting my blessings while preparing food for those who have none.

An agricultural community, Choluteca sits in the heart of vast melon and sugar cane fields. Trying to imagine what the city looked like before Mitch—now a dune of sand, trash, and destruction—is difficult. Heavy equipment, operated around the clock, moves tons of earth, uncovering buried neighborhoods and bodies. Men shovel ceiling-high mud from houses for the equivalent of three dollars a day. They are grateful for the work. On the wall of one empty house hangs a crucifix, the only item to survive the scourge of death.

Spending hours at the church, I set up a pharmacy, identifying drugs and sorting medication. After emptying twenty boxes, another load arrives on the doorstep. Patients drop in for an exam and share their stories, exposing unseen wounds.

"Our house is still standing but all the furniture and appliances are ruined. We have one bed for all of us and no table. Our family photos were washed away. I still have my children, for which I am grateful. That is more important. Some people have their photos but have lost their children."

Another woman, Glorisel, tells me her husband, an alcoholic, left her two years ago. When Mitch hit, her simple store and adjacent house were threatened. On Friday, Mario, her twenty-four-year-old son, stayed behind to protect the house from looters, convincing his mother to leave.

"I stayed alone in the house," Mario told me. "At ten o'clock Friday night, the water started to fill the room. Everything was floating up to the ceiling. Soon, the telephone cut out and I lost contact with my family. I had to crawl on top of the roof. During flashes of lightning, I could see houses floating by in the river. People, animals, trees, and freight containers surged past me. Cries of terror rose between the rolls of thunder, but I couldn't do anything. Suddenly there was a loud 'thud' and the rest of my house went, dumping me into the water." Mario sighs and continues.

"I was swept downriver in a tempest of crashing tree trunks, houses, and debris. Trying to hold onto something, a wave would come and push me under. I swallowed huge amounts of water. This happened over and over. Thinking it was a branch, I grabbed onto a corpse. My legs cramped and my body ached from the cold. Sharp objects were cutting me. A huge trunk lifted me out of the water and tumbled me as it spun round and round, going down and coming up for breath. By this time, I was forty kilometers downriver. Finally, I was able to grab a tree that was still standing. I tied my T-shirt around it, crawling up and straddling it like riding a horse. My body was cut and bruised. I spent twenty-eight hours there, cupping my hands to drink rainwater."

"What was going through your mind, Mario?"

"I had peace, then I would think, 'You're gonna die.' My pocketknife was with me, so I carved, 'Mario, Jesus still loves you' into a branch. Someday I hope to go back and find that tree. When the sun rose on Sunday, the water had calmed and there was a large tree trunk lying below. I crawled onto it to warm myself in the sun. Helicopters were flying over but they didn't rescue me. Two men in a small boat finally came and took me to shore. My legs doubled over from the weight of my body so they carried me to a hammock where I spent the night. They gave me dry clothes, food, and milk and took me to Choluteca on Tuesday."

Glorisel was certain Mario was dead. Reunited with her son, their Christian faith is stronger than ever. Now living in a different part of town, she is thankful to be out from under the oppression of her old neighborhood.

"My house was surrounded by corruption: drugs, prostitution, robbery. It was a horrible environment. Even though I have lost all my material possessions, I have Mario. I think my life is better."

Human resilience amazes me. Instinctively, we are wired for survival. Hearing their stories and watching the Honduran people rebuild their lives reminds me that whatever I face, God loves me and will be with me in the storm.

* * *

Hot embers feed the crackling fire, shooting sparks in all directions, carried away by the wind. Standing in a circle, the group gathers to pray over property for a new church building. Afterward, I talk with two Americans visiting Vida Abundante. They mention that they have been able to raise over twenty thousand dollars for relief. Impressed, I begin to pray.

"Lord, I believe You can double, even triple that amount. You are Jehovah Jireh, the God who provides. I want to trust You to do something BIG for these people. Please show me what to do."

* * *

Returning to the States, I am hoping to share about Honduras in several churches. Midweek, in the hushed silence of a new dawn, snow begins to fall, covering everything beyond the frosty windows, including my car. While housesitting at my friend's countryside home, I get snowed in, trapped in the beauty of a winter wonderland.

"I've heard about a pastor who is interested in supporting relief efforts for Honduras. His name is Steve. I don't know him but you should try to call him," a friend suggests over the phone.

I make a few phone calls from my snow globe, one to Pastor Steve, whose small congregation is quite a distance from where I'm staying. He seems excited to have me visit. Thankful for the opportunity, I schedule a time to speak, then ride out the storm, trying to believe God knows what He is doing.

"A new church, Lord? A snowstorm? This isn't exactly the BIG I had in mind."

By the time the roads clear and I drive to Steve's rural church, donations have already started to trickle in from other sources. Thirty strangers sparsely occupy seats in a large school auditorium. I can't help but wonder if this trip was worth it. Caught up in worship and blessed by the message, I sense God's presence and set my frustrations aside.

After the service, a young man walks up to me and introduces himself.

"How much money have you been able to raise?"

After telling him, he reaches for his back pocket, "I believe I am supposed to match that amount," he says, then writes a check for five thousand dollars.

Money pours in. The generosity expressed in donations is unbelievable. It is a privilege to be used as a channel of God's blessing.

* * *

Upon my return to Choluteca, I begin to learn the unique nature of disaster relief. Many of the drugs donated to the church have inserts written in English. They require translation, a tedious job. The family with whom I'm staying can't read the labels on the food they've received. "What is this?" they ask. "How do you prepare it?"

A pile of pointed-toe spike-heeled shoes in brilliant shades of blue, orange, and red are stacked in the corner of the supply warehouse—many with no match. With so much work and so little time, the shoes, like a piece of abstract art, remain untouched.

Furniture is scarce. Starting with beds, tables, and chairs, I begin to make large purchases. Pickup trucks with stacks of mattresses piled high above the cab begin to arrive at our warehouse. Later, a truck with one hundred plastic chairs backs into the driveway along with boxes containing a thousand Bibles. Assessing the needs, Joana and I spend hours making deliveries. Dropping me off late one night, she looks at me sweetly, "Our tiredness is another person's rest."

While fasting and praying for direction on how to use the bulk of the money, I keep falling back on James 1:27 (NIV), "Religion that God our Father accepts as pure and faultless is this: to look after orphans and widows in their distress..."

After deciding to invest in property and housing, a parcel with three homes comes up for sale. With Pastor Oscar's help, I sign the paperwork. The receiving families, all single women with dependents, work on the remodeling. Glorisel and Mario, with the others, now have a comfortable home in a beautiful neighborhood.

The months roll on. Doing my homework, I learn housing is abundant for orphans. Children are receiving adequate care, yet elderly women and widows have been overlooked. An idea starts forming: to build a center for elderly women who live on their own.

Though I have raised a good deal of money, I don't want to come up short once I begin. Property is scarce and expensive. Hurricane Mitch didn't leave an abundance of desirable real estate. While attending a city meeting, I am introduced to the mayor of Choluteca. Believing the impossible, I plan to make an appointment to ask him if he has a piece of land he could *give* me—to build a home for elderly women.

Catching up with him is a different story. The demands on his time are great. I'm not able to pin him down.

* * *

I think about last year on this same day when I arrived at the church, sat on a tiny chair for hours, and packed hundreds of bags of food. Tonight we are preparing an American-style Thanksgiving meal at Oscar and Joanna's. Following a trail of fireflies in the darkness, Joanna and I walk to a grocery kiosk in their neighborhood. My apron is wet with gravy smatterings. Pieces of vegetables are wedged in the pockets. "I wanted to speak to the mayor before leaving tomorrow morning but it didn't happen. I couldn't catch him at his office. I guess I'll have to wait until I return."

"You need to speak to the mayor? He lives in that house," Joana points to a courtyard. "Let's walk over there and see if he's home," she says, already heading in that direction.

Nine o'clock at night, in my seasoned apron, I sit down at a backyard picnic table to ask the mayor of Choluteca if he can give me a piece of property big enough for sixteen housing units.

How crazy is this, my BIG God?

Thanksgiving takes on an even deeper meaning. The mayor agrees to give me the property.

* * *

Though I've made huge strides with my Spanish, another language barrier arises. As the construction manager on the building project, I must master a volume of new words: cement, rebar, lumber, nails, financial terminology, and more. It is an exhaustive list. Blessed with a wonderfully patient Christian contractor, Jorge, I put my mini dictionary in my pocket and the building begins.

* * *

Once a week at the church, I arrange twenty-two plastic chairs in a circle with a large box of Kleenex sitting on one of them. People file into the room. I am overwhelmed by the response. They have all come to attend a group session to talk about experiences. To keep it manageable, I have limited the attendance to twenty.

Heartbroken over the stories of suffering I've been hearing, I want to give the survivors an opportunity to share with one another. While waiting for direction, I re-read Dr. Dobson's book, *When God Doesn't Make Sense.*

One morning Joana asks me, "Do you want to attend a seminar? A group from Wheaton College is visiting the church today. They are giving a presentation on psychological trauma."

My pen can't write fast enough. The information I glean is a toolbox packed with everything I need to facilitate a group.

"*Lord, did You send these people from Wheaton to train me?*"

Dr. Dobson's book, available in Spanish, is at the Choluteca bookstore. Providing one for each member of the group, I begin our weekly meetings with a song and prayer, then ask one question, giving each person a chance to respond as we work our way around the circle. Their homework is to read two chapters of the book each week.

"What was the moment you first realized something catastrophic was happening?"

Tears flow while the box of tissue is passed to the next person. Over the six weeks, we forge deep friendships. At the last meeting, I ask, "What is the most significant thing you have gotten out of this group?"

"It is so good to know I am not alone; to realize everyone else is going through the same thing and feeling the things I am feeling."

"We don't [normally] have these kinds of sessions here where we can talk about what we have experienced. This has been such a blessing. Your coming is a gift."

Presenting me with a piece of varnished wood into which they have burned their names, I too, am reaching for the Kleenex as their names are burned on my heart.

* * *

Green shrubs and flower gardens adorn each cinderblock house, a contrast to the barren soil upon which Pastor Steve and a group from his small church broke ground on the women's center six years ago.

Guillermina invites me into her humble home, a mansion by her standards. She has no earthly family but has known her heavenly Father since the tender age of ten. Blowing her wispy gray hair like a soft wind, a fan joins her as she hums the tune I sing. Joy graces each line of her wrinkled brown skin. At ninety-six, Mina is the picture of contentment. She loves her cats, her chickens, and her home. She loves the Lord. For a moment, I catch a glimpse of God in her twinkling eyes.

"Thank You, Lord, for being with me on this ride."

Cristina— in her home at the Women's Center in Choluteca

Enjoying tea in Morocco

Chapter 6

USA: Ground Zero

> Beloved, do not be surprised at the fiery ordeal among you, which comes upon you for your testing, as though some strange thing were happening to you.
>
> 1 Peter 4:12

It is September 11, 2001. "Do you know what is happening in the US?" Hassan sounds anxious.

Ironically, I have run into him on the street in Rabat, Morocco. I am on the way to his house to say goodbye to his family before leaving the country. Motioning me to hurry, we make a running climb up the narrow stairwell leading to his small flat.

Furnished with tapestry-covered cushions, this is home for his family of twelve. Zahra, Hassan's mother, stands in her floor-length *djellaba*, drying a small copper cup with a towel. She greets me in Arabic.

A small black and white television, twelve inches square, is propped on one of the long cushions lining the walls of the room. Tuned into a news program, Arabic figures are scrolling across the bottom of the screen while the reporter announces breaking news.

"Please sit." Hassan motions to a cushion.

A terrible scene unfolds, while a wave of numbness overcomes me. New York City is becoming a disaster zone before my eyes.

Planes crashing into the Twin Towers? How can this be?

Seeing. Not wanting to believe. Fixed on the images, I forget to breathe while I wait for reality to return. I have no words, only a trickle of tears.

Zahra comforts me, gently wiping my eyes with her towel. The other family members express their sadness, consoling me in my grief.

Explaining in broken French what the announcer is saying, Jamila takes my arm in hers and we watch together.

"We are so sorry this has happened. This is terrible." Words pale behind the magnitude of the horrific event before me.

I know my decision to come to their home today instead of yesterday is no coincidence. We are all experiencing this tragedy together by design. Having spent several days with this Muslim family, I feel a deep love for them. Being the recipient of their hospitality has been an honor. Being a recipient of their comfort is a blessing.

* * *

While staying with missionaries Hadi and Naomi on the other side of town, I have spent my days in Morocco finding opportunities to share Christ's love. The couple has lovingly opened their home to me, a stranger, for the week.

"We have a small home church. It has grown to the point we are going to have to split it up again," Naomi explains.

"As it grows and more people come, we must avoid looking suspicious. To keep from drawing attention to the meeting, we break the group up. In doing this, we hope to avoid being reported to the authorities. It is difficult because we come to love one another deeply. Knowing we will eventually have to part ways is hard."

One afternoon I return to their modest apartment, remove my shoes, and set my Bible under the chair.

"Muslims honor the Quran to the degree they place it on top of all other books. In Morocco, we don't set our Bibles on the floor but on a chair or table, to show respect for the sacredness of the Book," Hadi gently teaches me.

Never having forgotten this lesson, I am no longer comfortable placing my Bible on the floor. Though I am not Muslim, I have learned from their example of reverence how to treat God's Word more respectfully.

In the souk, merchants plead with me to buy their wares. Tiny open stalls display rich crafts: hand-tooled leather shoes, brilliant pottery, and tapestry rugs. Cinnamon, cardamom, and other exotic spices fill the air with bouquets of fragrance. Garlands of dried figs and dates hang over bins of colorful fruit, nuts, and raisins. Conversations are just as rich.

Hassan welcomes me into his family's tiny stall. He introduces me to his father, Malik, who is tending his spice shop. We talk for quite a while before Hassan insists on introducing me to the rest of his family. Following him up a narrow stairwell to their flat, I meet his sister, Jamila, also in her twenties, his mother, Zahra, and the other women and children. Unlike the younger generation, his parents don't speak French.

Excusing himself, Hassan returns to his father's shop. I am left to spend the afternoon with the ladies. Mint tea. Flat bred. Laughter. I can hardly believe this is happening. I am in.

In the next several hours, we learn a lot about each other's lives: worlds apart but experiencing similar joys and sorrows in times of celebration and loss. Human emotions are universal.

Invited to return and eat a special meal with the family the next day, I accept. Steam rises from the center of the table, carrying with it a tantalizing aroma of mixed spices. The tagine, a traditional earthenware bowl, is filled to the brim with pieces of lamb, vegetables, and couscous. Sitting on cushions around the large meal, we savor each handful of delicious food. Tea is served. The conversation is lively.

Home videos of the sister's weddings prompt me to ask questions about their celebrations, traditions, and Islamic faith.

"Play us a song," Jamila insists, pointing to my guitar.

"*Lord, what shall I sing?*"

I explain, "This song is about the invisible walls that divide us and how we must let them fall down. At the cross of Christ, the barriers between us are removed."

After the song, Hassan and Jamila ask me to share about my Christian faith. We talk about the gospel and Christ's love late into the afternoon. The loudspeaker echoes the muezzin's call to prayer. Malik andZahra leave for the mosque while the rest of us continue our conversation until we finish the last cup of tea.

* * *

Leaving Rabat, knowing that a personal, loving God has allowed me to share such an intimate time with this family, I marvel at His timing. While physical walls were falling down to drive us apart, spiritual walls were crumbling within to unite us.

Remembering how opinionated I was before reading the Bible, I appreciate the openness of these young adults thirsty for truth. Sharing Jesus' love with them is a joy.

Before returning to the US, I continue my travels through Europe. From the information I gather, medical relief teams are not needed at Ground Zero. Still, the tragedy haunts me. Staying in youth hostels throughout Europe, I find it is haunting the world at large, developing new perspectives on how others view the US.

"If this can happen to America, it can happen anywhere. It can happen to us," Mia, a German backpacker, full of anxiety and fear, pours out her thoughts to me. Amazed at the strength and power my country represents in the eyes of the world, I comfort her.

"There is only one thing that is certain."

Mia listens while I take the opportunity to tell her of Christ's eternal peace.

* * *

Opening my computer when I arrive home to the States, I am flooded with emails. Some are confirming my first trip to Africa, just weeks ahead, but the bulk of them are appeals to minister at Ground Zero, coming alongside people on the streets to share in their suffering.

Having waited for years to get a contact in French-speaking Africa, I don't like the idea of postponing my plans to go. A foolproof sign tells me I must—I can't get Ground Zero out of my mind. I have been a soldier in the Lord's army on foreign ground. The time has come to deploy on home turf.

* * *

Moving the date for my trip to Burkina Faso, I hop on a flight to New York City (NYC) on October 22nd. Greeting me are two friends from Calvary Chapel in Washington state. Brian has already been working here for a while.

"Chad and I are going down to the epicenter. I have security clearance and might be able to get permission for you and him to get through security and tour it with me if you want to go," he adds.

Pushing my fatigue aside, I make the late-night trek with Brian and Chad through lower Manhattan, a city that never sleeps. We catch up on each other's lives and arrive at the scene. Flashing his badge, Brian talks to the police officer stationed at the gate who graciously lets the three of us into the high security zone of the epicenter.

Still ablaze after six weeks, Ground Zero is apocalyptic. Spotlights illuminate the scene, making it appear as though it were a daytime movie set. Like a bustling city in hell, muddy roads service the dump trucks and fire engines while molten pieces of the towers, lifted by cranes, swing to and fro over the fiery pit.

Thick, toxic smoke billows out in grey masses, covering the faces of the backhoe operators and welders. Piles of rubble are stories high, though they have already been shaved down. In every direction I look, skyscrapers have their entire sides blown out, windows blasted, and chunks of metal gouging their exterior.

A lone computer terminal totters on the side of an open skyscraper, its wires naked and exposed. File cabinets and desks on each story are blackened and charred. A light breeze sends a stack of papers to the ground, to their death with others. Tall rotating doors, those leading into designer department stores, usher me into an empty shell of a foyer. Exquisitely beautiful marble floors, covered with debris, now serve as a storage place for gloves, masks, and hard hats.

Walking around the site, I am struck by all the chairs. Pretty, fashionable chairs. All styles, shapes, colors, and sizes. Upright. Overturned. On their side. One here. One there. They are all empty. Those who sat in them were also unique: different styles, shapes, colors, and sizes, all precious people infinitely more valuable than the empty chairs.

Everybody in the city has been affected in some way. Thousands died. Thousands barely escaped. Thousands saw it happen. Thousands lost loved ones. Thousands lost their jobs. Thousands will lose their jobs. Thousands are involved in cleaning up the rubble. Thousands are trying to prevent another attack. Thousands are living in fear.

Our midnight tour ends in a large tent run by the Salvation Army. Inside the tent are work supplies, snacks, hot cocoa, tea, coffee, and exhausted souls. This is where the police, fire, and construction workers hang their helmets and their heads. Faces blackened with soot, bodies weary from twenty-four-hour shifts, they come in for a few minutes of rest while grabbing a new pair of gloves or a cup of coffee, whatever they need to continue working.

Brian taps my shoulder, "It's getting late. We need to go back."

Looking for the person in charge, I know what I want to do.

"Could I spend the rest of the night here? I would love to stay and help," I ask.

"You are welcome to stay tonight. If you want to be a volunteer with us after this shift, you will have to visit headquarters in downtown Manhattan and go through the application process. A security clearance is required."

Exactly the words I wanted to hear. Brian and Chad leave me behind to spend the rest of the night serving and talking to first responders. Their stories reveal not only the physical impact but the emotional and spiritual wreckage it has brought into their lives.

At the end of the shift, with the Salvation Army's address on a post-it in my hand, I walk to the Manhattan headquarters and apply for the volunteer position. During the next few days, I work with the church, talking to people on the streets. Fueled by morning devotions, worship, and prayer, we spread out across greater Manhattan, offering listening ears. In a city where people don't ordinarily say hello on the streets, I have been kissed and hugged by more strangers than ever before.

Checking back at the Salvation Army office, the door swings wide open. I've been accepted for the position and receive my security badge.

On site, while outside the supply and canteen tent, Norm, a crane operator, strikes up a conversation with me. His excavation crane would later be captured in iconic images throughout the world. He invites me to go up into the crane's cabin. Above the smoking wreckage, I listen.

Norm shares the toll this has taken on him and his family. Crumbling under the load of the work, grieving over the friends he lost, and feeling the stress on his marriage, he doesn't know how he can keep going.

"I don't see an end in sight. Something has to change."

After a long pause. I ask, "Can I pray for you?"

"Yes, of course, I would appreciate that!"

In this sacred cabin above the devastation, I appeal to the Lord on Norm's behalf, believing the sovereign God was not off-duty when this happened. Nor are His eyes turned away from Norm today. Trusting in His justice and love, I know He hears my prayer.

* * *

My birthday is normally spent away from home where I find myself among strangers on my special day. The Lord knows, so I don't mention it to anyone, but wait to see what He plans to do. My secret game provides great birthday entertainment. Time and again, I have been amazed: a huge party in my honor in India, my favorite dish served by people I just met in South Africa. Today is my birthday and I wonder what God has up His sleeve.

Taking short puffs off her cigarette, she sits on a bench in front of a small café staring at the crane as it lifts a smoldering red hot beam. Crying. Nervous. Anxious.

"Are you OK?"

"No, I'm not."

Jessica lets me sit next to her on the bench. She witnessed the destruction from her office window. Planes crashing into the Towers.

Buildings falling. People jumping. Now there is an anthrax scare. Taking time off work this afternoon, she decides to face the aftermath. Up close. Raw.

Still grieving the loss of her brother to AIDS, Jessica admits she is hurting. Beyond hurting.

"I want answers. I have so many questions and no answers."

She allows me to explain the gospel to her and listens attentively. Treading softly on her broken heart, I can tell she wants to hear more. As we talk, her spiritual eyes are opened.

She tells me she wants to surrender her life to Jesus, trusting Him for the answers she needs.

"Let's pray."

There is no greater gift than to see a life transformed eternally by a step of childlike faith. Having experienced it myself, I know the peace a relationship with Christ can bring to our lives. Jessica now has that peace.

This is the best birthday gift ever.

* * *

Nino's Restaurant on Canal Street unlocks its doors one mile from the World Trade Center ruins, offering free meals to rescue workers. Open 24/7, I sign up to volunteer for several shifts. Clearing tables and helping serve is another opportunity to demonstrate love to first responders.

Police officers in NYC can be intimidating. Working the same beat, Drew and Mark carry their plates loaded with lasagna and salad to the table. Spotting them in the crowd, I come over and sit across the table from them. They have the appearance of invincible warriors, buff young men clad in uniforms and bulletproof vests.

Softened by the current events, Drew opens up.

"I've been married seven years. My wife left me. We have two kids, four and seven."

I empathize with him, sharing some of the pain I experienced from my failed marriage.

"I couldn't have made it without the Lord," I add.

We talk about everything under the sun while Mark, Drew's partner, stares at me and says nothing. When I begin to share about spiritual matters, I have this crazy notion Mark might arrest me.

Pushing my reservations aside, I know Drew is open to what I am sharing. Giving him a beautiful Bible with special notes to police officers within its pages, he thanks me and gets up to leave.

Mark has moved from the table to stand at a counter. Walking up to him, his dominating presence is now exaggerated by his height.

"Are you working with the Billy Graham group?" he asks.

I saw this coming. I'm in trouble.

With a heart the size of his enormous chest, he says, "Keep praying for Drew, he needs it. We've worked together for a long time. I've been trying to share the Lord with him and have been really frustrated, feeling like it wasn't going anywhere. I know things like this happen to give me a kick in the pants—you being here to talk to him. It's a wake-up call for me. God is in control. Keep on doing what you do."

* * *

Breaking news on the television above the long counter is creating a commotion while I finish my night shift. Noticing several of the police and firemen mobilizing, I learn that an Airbus aircraft has split in two and crashed in a suburb within close proximity of a gas station. The first responders are on their way to Rockaway in Queens.

"Can I ride with your engine company? I'd like to go in." I ask the firemen who are stationed across the street. Explaining to them what I do, they think they can take me. The plan falls through at the last minute. The chief won't let me ride with the company.

Determined to respond to the disaster, I board a subway train and head in that direction, about an hour away. Nobody knows if the crash is another act of terrorism. The entire nation is on high alert. Only residents and first responders can get past security at the scene.

Lord, if You want me there, get me there.

Talking with people on the subway, I meet Zach.

"I was on the eighty-fourth floor of the World Trade Center on 9/11. I lost a bunch of friends. Now I have heart problems."

After talking for a while, Zach wants to know my story. When he learns what I am up to, he says, "I live in Rockaway, two blocks from the crash. My car is parked outside the neighborhood. You can come with me to my car and we'll ride in together. You'll get right in."

Zach is right. With his ID, we drive straight through the security checkpoint.

It's a tough day. Working with people in the neighborhood who are still trying to pull their lives together after 9/11, I spend hours listening to heart-wrenching stories and serving, while responders stack charred corpses into vans: two hundred and sixty-five lives lost in an instant.

On my last day in New York I visit the wooden platform at Ground Zero which overlooks the site. There, at the massive grave are hundreds of dying flowers with new bouquets added to them. Mounds of stuffed animals compete for a spot. Poster boards bear wallet-size pictures of hundreds of men and women. They represent engine companies and squadrons of police who lost their lives. Framed pictures of loved ones never to return home are stacked in piles. The platform's barrier, constructed of wooden two-by-fours, is etched with messages.

"I miss you!"

"Daddy. I love you. Please come home."

"Sweetheart, I'll alway be yours, Emily."

What do I do with all of this?

Quiet and still, I hear a voice. Believing it is His, I am touched: "*This didn't take Me by surprise, Kris. I am a God of love. I am just. Each one who lost their life had a chance for eternal life with Me. Justice will follow. You can trust Me.*"

Tagine dinner with new friends in Morocco

Forging the river on a donkey cart in Burkina Faso

Chapter 7

Burkina Faso: Connecting the Dots

I will also speak of Your testimonies before kings
And shall not be ashamed.

Psalm 119:46

God's ways of directing our lives defy logic. As a child growing up in California, I dreamed of becoming a missionary to Africa, studying French from grade school through college. At forty, I found myself in Central America, struggling to learn beginner's Spanish and far from the drumbeat of Africa. Happily eating beans and tortillas in Guatemala, I wondered if I was mistaken when no contact had been found in five years of searching the African continent. Now, the door seems to be flinging wide open for Burkina Faso, West Africa. Tribal, French-speaking, poor, and predominantly Muslim—it seems like a match made in heaven. Though the picture is not complete, God is connecting the dots.

* * *

I laugh as I think about the unusual conversation I had with my stepmom, Connie, in California, before leaving for Ground Zero. Between sips of coffee, while sharing my frustration over years of searching to find a contact in Africa, she says, "You should email Pascal."

"*Who* is Pascal, Connie? Where is he from? What language does he speak? Is he a Christian?"

Her answer was short.

"Pascal came to San José State University thirty years ago when I was a student there. He's African. His name was on the welcome board so I got in touch with him and showed him around. You should write him." That's all she knew about Pascal.

Always ready to jump on a lead, I write to Connie's faraway friend, telling him about my life and my desire to work in Africa since childhood, excluding only a few minor details—like my friend Antoine. Posing infinite questions and eager to get answers, I click "Send."

When I receive his response inviting me to Burkina, I am amazed. Pascal's newsy email tells me he is "Burkinabé," a native of Burkina Faso, West Africa, and lives in the capital, Ouagadougou. A strong believer, he is a pastor with a heart for evangelism. Fluent in several languages including English, he primarily uses the trade language of Burkina: French.

Pascal's open-arm invitation is accepted. After booking a flight, the countdown begins. My mind is focused on one thing: a scouting trip to West Africa.

My departure takes place after my deployment to New York City. Arriving in Ouagadougou, or "Ouaga," an overwhelming sense of homecoming hits me when I step onto the tarmac. The hot air embraces my face like an old friend as I walk to the terminal, greeting Pascal in the lobby. After an hour of waiting for my luggage with no success, we jump into his old Peugeot truck, which looks like a modern-day covered wagon; a canvas tarp is stretched over an elevated frame covering the flatbed. With a lost luggage claim form in my hand, we head to his house.

I meet Pascal's wife Lisa, a linguist, and their nephew Tim, who works for National Public Radio and will be interviewing chiefs in remote bush villages for a story he is writing. The next morning Lisa looks at me and smiles.

"You want to go, don't you?"

A visitor in their home, I am not about to invite myself to join them. Lisa reads my mind. She loans me some clothes and a few toiletries and we are out the door.

On our tour, we visit Kotoura, eight hours away, in the southwest corner of Burkina. Lisa lived there for ten years while developing a written language for the dialect of the people. It is in Kotoura where she and Pascal met before moving to Ouaga. (In the years to come, Lisa's vacant Kotoura dwelling will be my shelter while holding dental clinics in Kotoura and surrounding villages.)

Listening to the stories shared by the chiefs, being entertained by *balafons*, a traditional gourd xylophone, and watching women with huge mortar and pestle rhythmically beat grain in tandem, I am fascinated.

Returning to Ouaga, masses of people on hand-driven tricycles wait for the traffic light to change. Some drivers, crippled by polio, join motor scooters, bicycles, pedestrians, cars, and trucks in the lineup. The temperature is soaring. One tormented soul wanders naked, digging through trash barrels and settling for a drink of creamy white liquid dripping from a crushed container.

My suitcase, containing more than some Burkinabé will own in a lifetime, never arrives. Living without creature comforts for three weeks is a good initiation into the African lifestyle.

* * *

Three months later, loaded with supplies for the ministry, I leave for my second trip. Plopping onto the noisy belt at baggage claim, I count, "One…two…three…four…five…six containers." Computers, keyboards, monitors, video machine, projector, cassette player, amplifier, speakers, generator, dental supplies, and my suitcase, have arrived. God has accomplished the impossible.

Primers and literacy classes are part of *Vision for Burkina Faso*, Pascal's ministry. His heart is to see his people read and write, enabling them to rise above poverty and become men and women of God. He is also an evangelist desiring that many have an opportunity to hear the gospel in their mother tongue. Along with Pastor Étienne, we combine efforts in fulfilling this vision.

Pulling up to a gas pump, we top off the Peugeot's tank. Influenced by a history of colonization, many dilapidated French vehicles find their way across the ocean to the streets of Burkina. At the pump next to us, the driver hot-wires his truck before departing. Unable to start ours, we do the same. Short of reaching our destination, the Peugeot breaks down miles into the bush, the result of a dying engine. It is not the first time. In the dead of night, deep within the heart of Africa, with baobab and acacia trees as my companions, I sleep on the flatbed with a greater appreciation of its canvas canopy.

"Lord, Your children need a decent vehicle for this ministry. If it is Your will, please provide one."

"We're here!" Pascal announces.

"Yes," I am thinking, *"We're here, but nobody else is!"* Standing in a desolate field, I see one deserted adobe building.

As night falls and brilliant stars populate the sky, villagers appear: walking, carrying babies, and riding bicycles. After the music ends, *The Jesus Film* begins. My heart is smiling as I look out over the crowd. Pastor Étienne is overflowing with gratitude,

"Merci, Kristine! Merci, Kristine! Merci! God has made your dream come true. These villagers will hear the Gospel tonight. Many may never get a chance to leave this village but they are here tonight. Souls will be won for heaven because of this! Merci, Kristine!"

Étienne's joy deeply touches me. Now he and Pascal have equipment for *Vision for Burkina Faso.* They can go to the most remote villages to share God's love through this film in their native tongue as well as several other dialects spoken in the area.

Étienne has a tremendous gift of sharing the gospel by making it culturally pertinent. One day, on our way to a village, we come upon a man, walking alone in the bush. Rolling his window down, Étienne stops and asks the man for directions to our destination. The man points south, telling us he comes from the same village.

Étienne continues, "Tell me, Sir, if you need to get to a village, do you ask someone who comes from that village how to get there or someone who has never been there and doesn't know the way?" The man gives the obvious answer to which Étienne adds, "If you want to go to paradise, there is only One who knows the way, Jesus Christ. If you ask Him how to get there, He will show you the way to Heaven."

In my annual newsletter, I mention the need for a vehicle, then begin praying for the provision. For a year, I wait, receiving one small gift for the project. Thinking it might be my idea and not God's, I am content to leave it up to Him. His timing and answer are always best. At the end of the year, two couples approach me, feeling led to give donations for the vehicle. Between the two, I receive thirty thousand dollars.

Purchasing a used vehicle anywhere is risky, but Africa? Do I drive to a South African auction? Or buy through a dealer? Do I import from Europe? Or seek a private seller? This is how my faith grows. I wait for God to show me what to do.

"Are you sure you want to spend all that money on a vehicle for *Africa*?"

"Won't they just trash it?"

"Who will take care of it? Maybe you should buy something less expensive."

The opinion of others doesn't sway me. As I see it, my African brothers and sisters are children of the King. God's provision is for His children, so they can be about His work. They deserve the best vehicle I can find.

On my next trip to Burkina, prepared to purchase a car, Pascal has good news.

"Kris, a German ambassador has advertised his vehicle. It is an SUV. I think we should check it out."

In mint condition, the car has low mileage and all-terrain capacity. Our offer is accepted. With taxes and other fees required, the total is approximately thirty thousand dollars.

On Sunday, we make one of our first trips in our beautiful vehicle to a little mud-walled church, where the congregation prays and lays hands on it. Fabian, who is blind, places one hand on the hood and slowly walks around the car. He then runs his fingers over the interior and dash, seeing the wonder of God's provision through his fingertips. This beautiful expression of gratitude touches my core.

A heavy-duty rack is welded to the roof for carrying tables, generators, dental, and other equipment. Over the next decade, we take the message of Christ to the unreached in some of Burkina's most remote areas, from the southwest corner to the northeast border.

Early each morning, while touring villages, Étienne meticulously washes and details the vehicle before we set out on another adventure. Maintained in top-notch condition, I can't think of a better investment I could have made. We all know it is a gift from God.

Arriving in Kotoura to stay and work in the dispensary, I am required to meet with a delegation of twenty Muslim men, including the village chief, for permission. Sitting in a circle outdoors, I'm asked why I am here.

"I am a Christian missionary and would like to use my skills to give your people dental care."

"What do you want in return?" the chief asks through an interpreter.

"Nothing," I respond, "My services are free of charge."

There is a stirring among the old men in their flowing robes. One by one, smiles, many void of teeth, grace their beautiful ebony faces.

"Yes, we believe you will be welcomed here by the people. We will allow you to work."

* * *

Amélie, a young Burkinabé, has come with me to translate and assist. She and I settle into our room at Lisa's vacant cottage where there is no running water or electricity. The pit toilet is outdoors. Bernice, a village girl, cooks our meals on a camp stove and brings a supply of water each day. We share our space with the critters: mice which force us to hang our food by a string from the rafters, mosquitos bearing tidings of dengue and malaria, bats in the pit toilet, scorpions on the wall, and snakes on the patio. Knowing my life is in God's hands is a comforting thought.

We see patients in the morning until lunch, walk home and enjoy food prepared by Bernice, then return in the afternoon to work until evening. The fifteen-minute walk each way seems longer in the heat of the day.

"Stop! Don't step on that!" Amélie warns me.

What looks like a natural plant is a gourd bearing a curse. Amélie also keeps me from walking under fetishes hanging from trees. Witchcraft and animism are widely practiced here. Though I don't fear such things, I respect her warnings and steer clear.

Later, as patients arrive, I think about how they have tolerated chronic tooth infections for months. Wounds perforating their cheeks are nature's way of draining abscesses. Some of them have not eaten for days. Their suffering is intense.

A man on a bicycle stops on the trail to show gratitude. "Thank you for pulling my tooth. I was not able to sleep well for months and now I can!"

A pain-free farmer is anxious to return to his field. He will not have to continue paying others to do his job.

Mangos, milk, peanuts, and smiles of relief are the generous gifts I receive for the care I offer. Some travel for hours by foot as word spreads and we treat hundreds of villagers. Unable to see everyone by the end of the day, many sleep on the dispensary patio to have first place in line when I return in the morning.

On Sunday, my day off, I attend the tiny village church. Colorfully clad women, their head wraps matching their outfits, swing back and forth in the aisles. Seashells click against decorative gourd bowls as the women toss them in mid-air to the syncopated rhythm. Naked toddlers boogie down the aisles in perfect timing to the drumbeat. During the sermon, in the heat of the message, a watch-guard gently awakens anyone caught snoozing on the bench with a light tap of his switch.

A group from the church joins our evening outreach. One of them translates the two-hour Jesus movie from the Jula dialect into Senufo. Being able to bring the gospel to this remote village because of the Lord's provision blesses me beyond words. One man, Adama, prays to convert from Islam to Christianity. Later, two more young men accept Christ. *Vision for Burkina Faso* is becoming a reality.

At the end of our stay, Baako, who organizes activities in Kotoura, tells me the leaders of the village are holding a celebration in my honor.

Arriving at seven as instructed, Baako tells me, "You will have to wait. We are going to be a little late in getting started."

Busily making preparations, a handful of men set up the equipment. Powering up the noisy generator, the lights kick on and the PA system is tested. Benches are arranged in a circle. At eight, the balafon players set up their instruments and several women arrive with steaming bowls of food. Potbellied children skate through the dirt. An announcement is made on the PA system for some young girls to bring water. Returning, they sprinkle clouds of dust kicked up by the skaters.

By nine, a crowd has gathered and the benches are overflowing. Most have to stand. Astonished by the numbers, I attempt to count heads and stop counting at seven hundred and fifty. As the formalities begin, the village leaders all take turns expressing their gratitude. The head of the dispensary says, "I know you are a woman sent by God. In all the years you have worked here, not a single patient has returned because of problems."

Asked if I have anything to share, I realize many will hear what I have to say about Christ for the first time. Under the spotlight, with a microphone in hand, and Baako translating, I give God the glory for all He has done to a crowd of more than seven hundred and fifty villagers.

* * *

Occasionally, the nomadic Fulani people pass through and come to my clinic. Fascinated by the men in turbans and the women adorned with silver jewelry, I enjoy our brief encounters. Over the years, they begin to occupy a special place in my heart. A desire to work among them takes root and grows stronger over time.

Working primarily in the southwest corner of Burkina where their numbers are few, I don't have much contact with them. They are concentrated in the northeast corner of the country bordering Niger.

"What do you want your program to be this year?" Lisa writes. I normally correspond with Pascal and am surprised she is asking. I bravely share my heart,

"If you'd like to know, Lisa, I would love to work more with the Fulani."

"I can probably set up an appointment with King Addo after you arrive in Ouaga," she responds.

Set up an appointment with the king?

Lisa tells me she met Addo while attending university in Canada. He lives in Ouaga. King Addo, the Muslim leader of the Fulani people in Burkina, welcomes me into his flat the day after my arrival. Expressing my desire to work with his people in collaboration with the pastors, I am careful to explain our program of evangelism. Miraculously, he is on his cell phone confirming appointments in Fulani villages throughout the northeastern region.

In Psalm 119:46, the psalmist wrote, "I will also speak of Your testimonies before kings and shall not be ashamed." The Lord has given me this opportunity.

Dori, the hub of Fulani life in northeastern Burkina, is a step back in time. Red clay structures are filled with small shops. Wooden donkey carts serve as taxis transporting men, women, and children wearing turbans, flowing robes, and head coverings. While I unload the car, Isai, a pastor, comes to help. As we talk, I can see God is busy at work, connecting the dots.

Isai is from Niger, a country sharing the eastern border of Burkina. Raised in the Islamic faith, he is the son of a Muslim leader. As an adult, Isai converted to Christianity after hearing the gospel at a wedding. Disowning him, his father, and the entire village cast Isai's family out of town. Living under a tree in the desert, he met a French missionary who helped him attend Bible college. Isai speaks French and Fulfulde, the language of the Fulani. His passionate desire is to see the Fulani people come to Christ. I had forgotten I would need a translator from French to Fulfulde. God knew.

* * *

As a child, I loved playing "connect the dots." Using my pencil, I would watch a picture unfold as I traced the sequence of numbers on the page. Connecting the dots, God's picture is taking shape as I walk in obedience to Him. Using both mundane and extraordinary events in my life, He is conforming my plans to His and completing the picture He has always had in mind: a fulfillment of my vision to be a missionary doctor in French-speaking Africa—from Dad to Connie to Pascal to Lisa to King Addo to Isai to the Fulani to Jesus.

Embarking on ministry to the Fulani people, I am realizing my childhood dream, planted in my heart by my Creator.

"*Your thoughts and Your ways are far above mine, Lord. What a beautiful picture You have created.*"

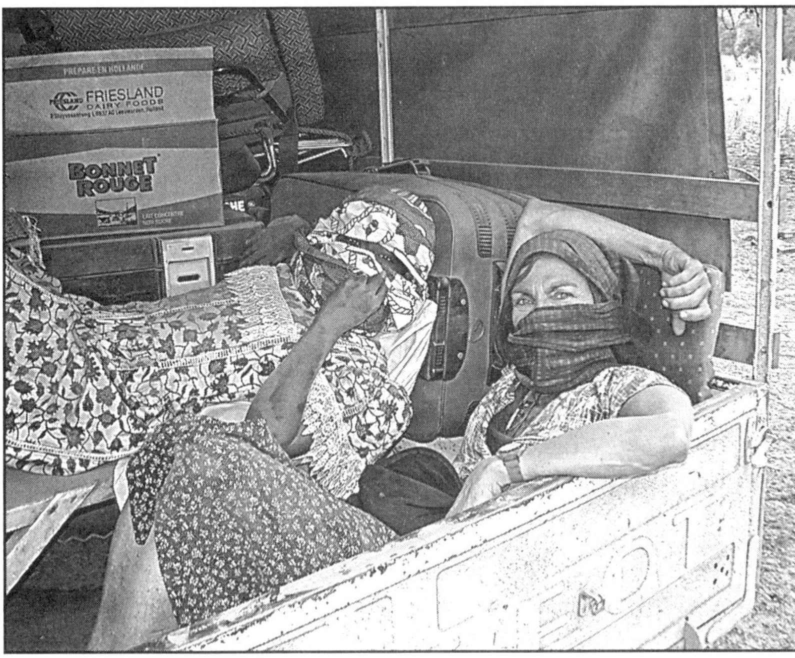

Layered in dirt after the long ride to Kotoura village, Burkina Faso

Arriving on his camel, a Fulani man seeks dental treatment in the desert of Burkina Faso

Chapter 8

Burkina Faso: Le Blanc

For while I was passing through and examining the objects of your worship, I also found an altar with this inscription, "TO AN UNKNOWN GOD." Therefore what you worship in ignorance, this I proclaim to you.

Acts 17:23

After six hours of standing under an acacia tree in the sub-Saharan desert, my clinic day in the Fulani village is finally wrapping up. A thin plastic trash bag hangs empty on the long wooden table. Not a single decayed tooth wrapped in bloody gauze has been placed inside it. Not one dirty instrument is waiting to be cleaned and sterilized. No names have been entered in my logbook followed by the telling numbers #30, #31, and #32 to remind me what teeth I pulled.

Exhaustion from the rigors of a day's work performing dental extractions is real. I have experienced similar physical exhaustion after spending an exhilarating day on the ski slopes or bodysurfing for hours in the ocean. Spending myself on behalf of the Lord brings a joy unmatched by those days. Exhaustion from idle waiting is another story. Physically, emotionally, and spiritually, today's idle exhaustion has drained me on multiple levels.

Knowing there are at least two dozen villagers who could have been relieved of suffering by having an extraction is discouraging; every state-of-the-art tool and medicine needed sit untouched on a table under a tree. With years of practical experience and training, I know I could have blessed them. Instead, I've done nothing.

Mustering up a word of encouragement to myself, I rehearse the reasons for the rough day. Bottom line: They don't trust me. They are suspicious. They are afraid. Why should they trust me? I am the new white girl on the block: *Le blanc*.

Le blanc is the French word used for any foreigner with light skin. I dislike it because I get riddled with it like a target practice decoy as I travel through Burkina Faso. It's worse in the city. The heaviest artillery is fired by bands of small children, empowered by one another's company. They pump magazines at me from all angles, "*Le blanc. Le blanc. Le blanc. Le blanc. Le blanc. Le blanc. Le blanc...*"

Little snipers.

I adore children but these words sting. As much as I realize it isn't meant to be derogatory, I still find the term *Le blanc* hard to swallow. I feel bullied and hurt by those shooting at me. I want to be their friend.

So here I am in another Fulani village for the first time. My clinic consists of an acacia tree, a small table for dental supplies, and a long table for patients. It is strategically located a short distance behind the village huts.

From their vantage point, villagers can feel safe as they peer out from the shadows at *Le Blanc*, who comes with some very gnarly-looking instruments in her possession. There are no bold shouts from the children here. I don't see much sign of civilization at all. My clinic must not look too inviting, even if that observer *does* have a toothache that makes him feel like he has two heads. Daydreaming about another village where my reputation is established, I let my memory comfort me.

* * *

A Fulani man in a royal blue turban and robe rides up on his camel. His calloused feet shod in rubber jellies and a large transistor radio tied around his neck with a shoelace identify him as a herdsman. A Fulani's wealth is determined by his cattle. So important to their culture is their livestock that children are taken out of school to tend the herds. School is not considered important. The cattle are.

The radio provides companionship during the long hours of herding. Fulani women wear beautiful silver medallions and coins as jewelry, a challenge to work around on my extraction table. Balancing huge halved gourds filled with fresh milk on their heads, they trek through the desert in their jelly sandals. Carrying the milk from village to village with their babies strapped to their backs, they sell and trade for other commodities.

Bowing to his knees and lurching forward, the camel enables the nomad to slide forward and down to the ground. Approaching the man-of-the-hut, formalities begin before the nomad explains the reason for his visit. There is no getting to the point until the visitor and host have exchanged the status of near and extended family, predictions of weather forecasts, conditions concerning health, and the world at large. On my first few visits to Burkina, I was charmed by these conversations. Now I suffer from the exhaustion of waiting for the guest to get to the point. In this case: a severe toothache.

Through my translator, my turban-clad patient agonizes, "I have spent many nights in pain. I can't eat or sleep. I have stayed up all night with my herds. I don't have any medicine. It won't stop."

He wants to know how I will remove his tooth. I explain the entire procedure from anesthesia to post-op care. He consents and begins to unwind the yards of fabric wrapped artfully around his head and neck as his camel contentedly grazes in the bush.

Reclining bamboo chairs are traditional outdoor furnishing. Slipping into one is easy; it isn't so easy to slip out. The villagers spend hours in them. Having completed the extraction, my patient rewraps his turban and bites down on a piece of gauze placed in his mouth. He immediately drifts off to sleep in the bamboo recliner and doesn't move the rest of the afternoon.

The next day, he returns with his friend. Both of them park their camels. The friend tells a similar two-headed story of unrelenting toothache and removes his turban. His buddy must have told him what to expect. No questions asked. He is ready. After the procedure, his chair, already warmed by the sun, awaits him. Slipping into it, he dozes off to sleep.

To see these men relieved instantly of their suffering is a great reward. Having gained their trust, more appointments are made by word of mouth. Parking is free. Accepted and appreciated, I start working on the next patient.

* * *

A fly disturbs my daydream. Standing alone, I watch Frederic and Étienne from a distance. The two pastors who brought me to this new village are sipping their mint tea and talking to the Muslim leaders. They are deeply engaged in their discussion. Comfortably reclining in their bamboo chairs while draped in their long robe-like clothing, their casual demeanor adds to the air of détente—their conversation lasts all afternoon.

Throughout the day, I watch Frederic perform his tea-making ritual. It always intrigues me. On our trips, he makes it a point to bring every item needed to perform it: the charcoal stove, the matches, the coals, the teapot, the spoon, the glasses, the mint leaves, and a large box of white sugar.

He begins his ritual by crushing the mint leaves and dropping them into the teapot. Adding sugar and water, he stirs the mixture with his spoon over the red-hot coals. After allowing it to boil for several minutes, the magic begins. Lifting the teapot in one hand and a glass in the other, he pours the steaming liquid into the glass, slowly widening the distance between the glass and the teapot. Next, he pours the contents of the glass back into the teapot, his arms widening vertically in a mesmerizing accordion motion. In its multiple trips through midair, the tea cools. Back and forth, this delicate and calculated juggling act produces delicious results at the perfect temperature.

As the sun perches itself on the horizon, the air grows cooler. Walking across the barren desert toward our vehicle, a young Fulani girl approaches me. Her hair is shaved in a reverse mohawk: from forehead to mid crown, leaving a short curly headband on top of her head. She stops in front of me, her dust-covered arms resting on a distended belly balanced by her thin legs. Her nakedness is adorned by necklaces; one of them is a string of raw groundnuts resembling a popcorn garland. I wonder if "Peanuts" has ever seen the likes of *Le Blanc* in her short three years of life. Locking her dark brown eyes onto my green ones, her expression is tender, not fearful. I extend my hand; her little fingers crawl into my palm.

Peanuts and I walk side by side, hand in hand. After several minutes, I stop.

Dare I try?

I turn toward her, then bend down and gently pick her up. Ever so slowly, I draw her close. She nestles into my arms and, without a word, says, "I trust you."

Soon, Peanuts leaves. A warm sensation settles in my heart. Returning to my dental supplies, I pack them up before pulling out video equipment. As the sun begins to set, Frederic, Étienne, and I enjoy dinner, which rarely varies.

Each of us tears a chunk off the baguette. We share a can of sardines, not sparing a drop of the calorie-rich oil as we take turns dipping the bread into the tin. For dessert: a wedge or two of *La Vache Qui Rit* (Laughing Cow processed cheese) smeared on more bread.

Laughing Cow cheese reminds me of my initial days as an au pair in Paris where I enjoyed it with Benoit and Maxime. Thinking of the intense loneliness I experienced in the beginning, I remember how I persevered and walked through that painful door. Suspecting the isolation and loneliness I felt today could be the painful beginning of something big, I am determined to persist. Like Peanuts, I can take hold of Jesus' hand. He will carry me.

As the sun sets, the video equipment casts a shadow on the clay surface of the mosque. Two small but powerful speakers are strategically placed on the ground to achieve a surround-sound effect. As the projector's beam cuts through the dust particles in the air, music plays and the crowd gathers. Villagers, hidden during the day, begin to appear. The children, usually the first to show up, are eager to grab front-row seats in the dirt to watch *The Jesus Film.*

Two large branches, placed and secured in freshly dug post holes, have a large white sheet suspended between them. As the darkness settles, people fill the entire field, watching the film on both sides of the sheet. Most of the attentive crowd stands during the entire two-hour production, watching scenes that could have easily been shot on location here: long robes, mud houses, donkey carts. I have been told some of these people do not distinguish the difference between reality and the actors in the movie. Quietly commenting among themselves, they are fascinated by the images and the message from the Gospel of Luke.

One man arrives late. He tells us, "I am from another village quite far away but I heard voices in my language. I had to come and see who was speaking."

Before starting the film, Étienne introduces our team. Village after village, I can make out enough of the Fulfulde dialect to understand what he is saying. When he speaks about me, it is always the same thing.

"This American woman who has come to your village has a deep love for the Fulani people. She has used her own money to make a very long trip and offer you free dental care. She has done this because of the love Jesus has put in her heart for you."

Being exalted as a hero every night embarrasses me. I ask Étienne why he keeps telling the people of each village this same story.

"These people need to know what measures you have taken to come here and what a sacrifice you have made for them," he tells me. "They need to know the love God has placed in your heart for them. In their culture, it is the greatest honor for an outsider to come to their village." This isn't about me; it's about them. And God.

As I think about what happened and what didn't happen today, I see I need to be patient with the Fulani people, myself, and God. I can't expect to establish trust with them in one day. By bringing all the ingredients: dental equipment, video supplies, sugar, tea, and a lot of love, God has opened another door to the Fulani people. It may not be fast and easy, but the result will be well worth the wait. Years later, no longer a stranger to these people, my reputation precedes me. The openness to the gospel in this predominantly Muslim area is not something I take for granted, nor is the permission I have been given by King Addo to work here. One evening stands out among the others.

* * *

After holding a clinic in the bush, we return to the village center and prepare for our evangelistic outreach. Advised there is an Islamic religious event scheduled to take place during the film, we begin to pray.

Before we get started, the call to prayer, broadcast from the minarets of several mosques, resounds throughout the village. Men drop to their knees on their prayer mats, paying homage to Allah. I am impressed by the numbers. Far from lacking in devotion, these men are very religious.

Having finished their prayers, I take the microphone to address them. Introducing myself, I cover the formalities. Then, with words prompted by the apostle Paul's address on Mars Hill, I speak from my heart,

"I see you praying. Knowing you are very religious and want to know God, I want to ask: Do you *know* Allah? Can you honestly say you *know* him? *Can* you know him? I have never met a Muslim who has answered 'Yes.' Allah cannot be known. You are worshipping an unknown God. Is Allah pleased with you? Do you know if you will have a place in paradise when you die? I don't believe you have the answers to these questions. I am here to tell you about the One true God who loves you and wants you to know Him. He has paid the price for your sin. You can be forgiven, enter into a relationship with Him, and know with certainty Heaven awaits you. Jesus Christ is the answer to all your questions."

Speaking to the crowd, I am surprised by my boldness. Feeling deep compassion for them, I point them to the truth. After sharing, I sing some songs and turn the mic over to Étienne. I keep waiting for the Islamic event to begin during the two-hour film. The film plays through to the end and the crowd remains, standing through the credits. Not a single interruption occurs over the course of the entire program: our prayers have been answered.

* * *

Reaching villages cut off by water, our SUV successfully forges many rivers. Today we are told we must take a donkey cart to the next village. Our all-terrain vehicle is not going to make the grade. Established in my work among the Fulani, the problem of idleness has been replaced by the sheer exhaustion of trying to meet demands. A donkey cart ride is a great diversion before I get to work.

Telling me he is ready to roll, my escort brays. Another adventure is about to begin. Having loaded the wooden cart with our tables, equipment, generator, and clinic supplies, we secure everything with ropes. Pulled by two strong donkeys, our wagon descends into the river. I take a spot beside the driver, dangling my feet in the cool water. There are several rivers to cross to reach our destination. Our water taxi serves its purpose and we arrive intact; people are waiting, excited for our arrival.

Removing heavy silver earrings and head adornments to enable me to work on their teeth, I have grown accustomed to peering at Fulani patients on my table. Women with thick black lines tattooed around their mouths and one-pound silver bracelets forged around their wrists know what to expect—they are ready for their extraction.

"I can't do any more cases today. We need to leave before it gets dark."

"Please stay. Come and live here with us. We don't want you to go."

They are serious. After years of work, I have won the Fulani's hearts. Miraculously, the Lord has won some of their hearts as well.

Stopping by King Addo's home in Ouaga before I fly out, I share the news about our work among his people and all the Lord is doing. Suffering from terminal cancer, his condition deteriorates with each progressive visit I make over the years. Although he is the Muslim leader of his people, I can't help but wonder if he has secretly accepted Christ as his Savior. Why would he give me access to his people, knowing our team intended to share the gospel? Assuring him of Jesus' love and sacrifice for him, I leave the answers to my questions in God's hands and pray with him one last time.

After Addo's death, the sub-Saharan Sahel where I work becomes off-limits due to the jihad being waged in that region, targeting Christians in particular. Entire villages are being massacred. Many of the perpetrators are Fulani.

I receive an email from Étienne, informing me over eighty villagers have been massacred in cold blood. "The security situation in the country is deplorable. The village of Seytenga, which you visited while you were here, is affected by terrorism. All the men in the village are dead. The only people who were spared were women and children. Please pray for us."

Lord, I pray for Étienne and all the people affected by terrorism. Protect them from ruthless acts of violence. Strengthen their faith amid persecution. Thank you for opening the door for this ministry. Now that it is closed, please continue to draw the Fulani to Yourself. Let them know You, who can be known; the only God who makes Himself known to man.

Making friends with Peanuts

The Mongolian waterman

CHAPTER 9

Mongolia: The Wild East

A voice is calling,
"Clear the way for the LORD in the wilderness;
Make smooth in the desert a highway for our God."

Isaiah 40.3

SOLID BLUE SKIES kiss sand-brown slopes where hairy yaks graze on parched grass. Bumping over a rickety bridge of weathered lumber, another endless wave of rolling hills extends into the distance. Huge rock formations dot the landscape, surrounded by sparse trees and low shrubs.

Our route is as clear as the direction taken by the wandering herds seeking nourishment in this dry land. I have not seen a road for miles. Traveling through the steppes of northwestern Mongolia is like taking an excursion back in time.

Loaded down with road-weary travelers, our old Russian van plugs along while joy bubbles out of the Mongolian girls, our translators, who brighten our ride with their beautiful songs. Four Americans, four

Mongolians, and enough dental supplies to last three weeks are well-packed into this music box on wheels. We are scheduled to hold clinics in village hospitals and private *gers*, the round felt tents of the nomadic herdsmen and their families.

Reaching each destination is a unique adventure. Directions are pointed out by the villagers. A woman with sun-chafed cheeks, clad in pajama-like attire, stands at the entrance to her *ger* and waves us past, while her children ride their imaginary ox cart: a large metal milk can lying on its side. Traffic is an occasional herd of yaks or a family caravan pulling their one-room *ger* on ox carts. Broken apart for transport and strapped down to the cart, they are moving their home to a better grazing spot. The first road sign I notice is simply a –*P*–. Beyond it is a horse hitched to a post.

Tsetserleg Bog is our first destination. While nomadic parents move their herds to pasture, their children winter over in this post-Soviet school building. The kids graciously make space for our team.

After unpacking our two fully loaded vans, we roll our sleeping bags out on the floor of a large room. It has been a long journey. I'm first down and in my bag. Within minutes, I am enjoying a deep dreamy sleep. In my dream, a little creature scurries across my neck. Then another. Consciousness kicks in. *I'm not dreaming.*

Between sleep and wakefulness, I unintentionally let out a scream, arousing everyone in the room. In the corner, the little four-footed racers join their team of miniature Mongolian mice. Busily working overtime in the wee morning hours, they are transferring rice to boots. They haven't touched our bread or cheese. Welcome to another world.

At sunrise, the children stoke the crackling fire. It has kept us warm through the night. A sprinkling of flour falls to the floor as the cook kneads dough for several loaves of bread. Hungry little ones wander in and out of the kitchen through the flour.

Stepping outside to use the latrine, the frigid air smacks my forehead. Between me and the outhouse is a visitor. Pressing tobacco into his pipe, reins in hand, the water man sizes me up. Straddling his ox with a rope passed through its nostrils, his simple wooden cart is carrying a large blue barrel of water. A felt hat, topped with a pom pom and lined with golden trim, sits snuggly on his head. His slanted eyebrows meet the outside corners of his narrow eyes as he puffs on his pipe. Silver ornaments decorate the collar of his heavy wool jacket. Jumping down into the snow, he makes a delivery to the children's dormitory in his knee-high boots with curled toes.

The surrounding landscape reminds me of the cowboy movies I loved as a kid with the waterman adding a unique twist to the plot: The Wild West with an Asian flare.

Two boys finish brushing their teeth, leaning over a long trough with inverted jugs serving as spigots. By tapping a pin in the bottom of the jugs, freezing water is released to rinse their mouths. After greeting the waterman, their boots crunch through the snow, gaining speed as they run back toward the cozy dormitory.

Taking the opportunity to enjoy the kids before breakfast, I pull out my bag of tricks. First, I teach them intricate hand clap games I've embellished through the years. Little girls with big bows on their heads line up to slap my hands and click their fingers. They are quick to learn. With a string, we spin a button and play Cats in the Cradle. The boys find the toys. They sit, tossing a red rubber ball while scooping jacks into their hands. My yo-yo tricks mesmerize them. They all want to try. Like Velcro, they cling to me and delight in these simple forms of entertainment. Technology has not caught up to their corner of the world.

Villagers begin to show up, some traveling from long distances. Hitching their horses to the fence, the line forms quickly. Dr. Bill and I start seeing our first patients of the day.

Communication is my greatest challenge, lost in translation or lost altogether.

"Och, could you please get me a piece of gauze?" I ask my translator.

Smiling, she looks at my patient, "The doctor says to put your hand up if it hurts."

Explaining her interpretation, she answers, "I just tell the patients what they want to hear."

Having to rely on translators to communicate is one of my biggest frustrations. Babel is a reality. There's no question that their English is better than my Mongolian, I can't even get past first names.

"Tseveersagchaa, you will be seen next."

Fortunately, showing the love of God to these people doesn't require me to pronounce their names properly. After receiving dental care and an explanation of the gospel, even Tseveersagchaa accepts Jesus as his Savior.

Dr. Bill and I try to learn terms that are practical for our dental work:

Sain uu. Hello

Timee. Yes

Neekh. Open up

Bitgii nulim. Don't spit

Khazakh. Bite

Bayarlalaa. Thank you

Bayartai. Goodbye

In Mongolian culture, hospitality is assumed. A stranger need not knock on your door, which would be considered rude, but enters after the customary greeting, "Hold back the dog." A welcome reception is expected. Personal space is where you are.

Leaving Bill and his wife Peggy behind without an interpreter one evening, an unannounced visitor arrives in their room. He sits and appears delighted to be there. Locking his eyes on the two of them, he makes himself comfortable and totally at home. Smiling, they stare back, not sure what to do. After several minutes of stare down and uneasy silence, Bill uses his best Mongolian to communicate,

"Sain uu. Timer. Neekh. Bitgii nulim. Khazakh. Bayarlalaa. Bayartai."

The visitor leaves.

On another evening, an elderly herdsman visits the *ger* where we are staying. While we are eating dinner, he walks in and sits on the bed. "I heard there were Americans here and I wanted to see what they were like." Our interpreter translates while I serve our guest fish and rice. He eats dinner, watches us, talks awhile, then gets up and leaves.

Late Saturday night, we pull into a community of *gers* surrounded by a fence forming a crate-like pattern to partition each one. We are hosted by a Buddhist family.

Early Sunday morning, I quietly leave the fenced area around our *ger*, careful to note the number on the gate. After a refreshing hike over the surrounding rocky terrain, I return in time to join our team for church, unlatching gate 7-21. It is the wrong gate.

Like a scout, I retrace my faint tracks in the dirt. Making several circles around the fifty-something *gers*, I peek over each fence while double-checking my bootprints, now leading in every direction. Anxiety mounts, knowing by now that I have kept the group from attending church.

Communication between the few people I pass is nonexistent. I don't know the name of our host. My name is unintelligible to them. My dental vocabulary is useless. At least the people I see know I don't belong here. Perching myself on top of a huge boulder, I sit. Eternity passes.

Lord, please help the team find me. I will sit here until I die. I don't know what else to do.

Imaginary scenarios cross my mind: people talking to each other mentioning the white lady they saw sitting on the rock two days ago, another commenting, "She's still there."

Lost now for four hours and still sitting on the rock, I notice a little girl wandering toward me. She is holding Och's hand. "I felt like we were supposed to come this way."

Thank You, Lord, for being their guide.

* * *

Bringing the gospel to their people comes naturally for Och, the drivers, and our other translator. While patients wait for the anesthesia to take effect, they have time to ask questions and share the message of God's bountiful love. Many give their lives to Christ.

The fragrant scent of sagebrush fills the air as we start morning devotions on a large log, inviting anyone who wants to attend. Many of the villagers come out of curiosity. They are warmly welcomed and get a chance to hear the gospel, often for the first time. Sometimes a comment is made, helping me understand the impact our visits can make: "If you came all this way to give me this care because of Jesus, I want to know Him."

Anticipating an extraction, many villagers are terrified. Traditional workers, known for botched jobs and brutal methods, have proceeded us. Thankfully, this is a new experience for them. The thumbs-up sign is their way of communicating "It didn't hurt."

One of my patients, a young boy, is particularly tense. Grimacing and writhing in his seat, he has his eyes squeezed shut like clam shells. I am finally able to calm and convince him to open his eyes. He laughs at what he sees. I am holding his tooth in my forceps. He didn't even know I'd pulled it.

During our trip, it becomes apparent that people are hungry for spiritual truth. "I want to talk to God. How can I pray? Where do I go?" Baatar asks as he makes the sign of the cross. Saga, the director of the grammar school in Muren Bog, has wrestled with the theory of evolution presented in textbooks. He is trained in physics. Meeting with him and discussing the Bible through our translators, he concludes, "I knew that evolution could not be true. It just doesn't fit with all I understand about the second law of thermodynamics." Baatar and Saga are among the many that surrender to the One who satisfies their soul's hunger for truth.

The work is rewarding. At the end of each clinic, we have a lot of happy customers who return to their *gers* looking forward to a painless night's sleep and eternity with Jesus.

At the end of the day, the time comes to close shop. It's my chance to rehearse the Mongolian math I have learned.

"How many patients are still waiting to be seen?"

"There are two."

"Ok, Dr. Bill will take one and I will take one."

Finishing up with our last two patients, I see more people in the doorway.

"Who are they?" I ask Och.

"They are the last patients."

"How many are there?"

"There are three."

Dr. Bill and I finish the three. Two more appear at the door.

Despite our efforts to explain, another equation is at work. I call it Mongolian math. The patients know, but insist on—no—when it comes to closing time. One afternoon we turn away many who have come long distances and waited several hours.

"You will have to choose one person among you. That will be the last person we see today." Among the group of twelve, an elderly woman with an abscessed tooth is given the spot. The rest leave quietly without a word. In a country where elders are highly honored and respected, I am touched by their willingness to defer to her.

* * *

This evening, in our lone hotel in the middle of nowhere, a group of two dozen soldiers is lodging overnight. Their tall wet boots stand at attention in front of the wood stove while they warm their stocking feet. Uncontrolled fires have broken out in the nearby forest. The men have been working for days to extinguish them.

Obtaining permission from their commander, I share some worship songs and the message of salvation by candlelight, grateful our paths have crossed and hopeful this time together will make an eternal difference.

At daybreak we set out on the endless road, seen only through the eyes of Jargal, our driver. All I can see is miles and miles of countryside. Sheep, cattle, and Cashmere goats graze on the slopes. Wildflowers peek out from under a thin blanket of snow: lavender, yellow, and purple blossoms. A herd of wild horses gallops by. Passing an occasional *ger* decorated with hanging laundry, we make our way to the next village. A woman on a stool, expressing yak milk into a pail, looks up and waves. There's a rare shopping mall—four or five wooden shacks with a common wall selling candy, cigarettes, and large bottles of vodka.

Rivers overflowing with taimen (salmon-like fish) cut through the deep canyons and through the plains. Our invisible road crosses through a dozen of them. Stalling in the middle of one, two feet of water reaches the floorboard and starts to enter the van. Our strong Mongolian drivers push us out. After several heaves, Jargal starts the engine and we enter dry ground.

With a fishing pole in hand, Dr. Bill sets out to try a few passes in the stream. I borrow his other pole rigged with a lure. Enjoying the beautiful outdoors refreshes our strength for the work ahead. It also puts delicious food on our table.

Cradled in the canyon, Bill is knee-deep in rushing water, concentrating on his fly fishing technique. Not having any success with my lure, I hike back to the van where Peggy and the girls are keeping warm. As I pop over the edge of the cliff, I notice a man seated on the expanse of grass, dressed in an elaborate traditional costume and holding a *yatga*, or Mongolian plucked zither, on his lap. We are in the middle of nowhere. I don't have any idea where this man came from or how he got here with his enormous musical instrument.

Bill returns with his catch just in time to hear the Mongolian throat singer begin his concert-at-the-gorge. Afterward, we leave with a full van: our team, the musician, the *yatga*, and some taimen for dinner.

* * *

In Tariat, we work in the village hospital, setting up our clinic in a tiny room. Like the *gers*, there is no electricity. There are no bathrooms. There is no running water. How they care for sick patients under such conditions is unimaginable. Reminded of the blessings I enjoy in the US, I am filled with gratitude. *Lord, forgive me for ever complaining.*

Animals attract flies. Working in areas where there are herds, there are always flies. Though things in this distant country are different in so many ways, I observe that Mongolian flies look and act the same as American flies. Just as annoying, their existence makes no sense to me. In one village, a long white table outside our building is solid black with flies. My goal is to keep them out of my patient's mouth and on the table.

Taking part in some of the people's daily activities is important to me. I feel closer to them when I step into their shoes and share their experiences. A pastime I have learned to enjoy is collecting dung from the ground and flinging it into a basket strapped to my back. Left in the sun to dry, it is later used for fuel for the stove. I learn that dung has additional uses.

* * *

Having spilled scalding oil over half of her body, a mother brings her toddler, Oyunchimeg, to me. Cow dung has been applied to her second-degree burns. The baby is caked in it from head to toe. Using a random jar of Silvadene cream I brought with me in my supplies, I clean the wounds, debride the tissue, and change the dressings twice daily, a treatment I commonly used on burn patients in a major US hospital. We are staying in this village for several days, making it possible to watch the miraculous progress of Oyunchimeg's healing.

Shocked by the application of cow dung, I do some research, learning there are components in the dung that can prohibit the colonization of certain bacteria common in burn infections. These treatments have been used for years in traditional medicine. Hard lesson: the burn trauma nurse from the US doesn't know everything. Still, I am the closest thing to a medical doctor and these patients seek me out.

* * *

Parking his motorcycle with a freshly killed marmot and wooden gun secured on the handlebars, a hunter walks into our *ger* with his finger dressed in burnt goat's hair. Unwrapping the hair, I see the wound, now several days old, healing well. He has come for my advice. Having learned a valuable cow dung lesson, I tell him, "In America, I would clean this, then apply antibiotic ointment and a loose dressing. It looks like it is healing well. There's no sign of infection. I can dress it for you or you can continue your treatment with goat's hair. What would you like to do?"

He is satisfied to leave it as is. I am too.

At the end of the week, I stay behind to rest while the group goes to the clinic. Feeling refreshed in the afternoon, I pay a visit to a depressed, embittered paraplegic man living close by.

Finding Batzorig in his bed, cooped up in a windowless *ger*, I can't help but wonder how difficult his life must be. After dressing his decubitus ulcer, I listen to his story, then he listens while I talk of God's love for him in the midst of suffering. Relaxed and without constraints, we talk for a long time, pouring over scriptures. When I leave, I say goodbye to a transformed man with the peace of God in his heart and bitterness behind him. I would have missed this divine appointment if I had gone to the clinic today.

While the sun is still shining, we take our laundry to the river. Upstream, young girls fill their five-gallon pails with water while watching the four foreigners wash their clothes on the rocks. After a few minutes, with numb fingers, I forgo the sponge bath I'd planned to take and find another excuse to play outside with the children.

As I catch my breath, I realize I've met my match. Exhausted from our rigorous ball game, I offer the kids some snacks, each of them extending cupped hands to receive my gift. It is a beautiful illustration of what I believe the Lord wants us to do: accept His gift of love with open hearts. We don't have to grope or grab. He wants to give freely.

Hanging my freshly washed laundry to dry on the fence, Och walks by and takes it down. "I'm going to wash this for you," she smiles.

At the end of the trip, I spend my last hours enjoying quiet time outdoors on a rock. The familiar odor of sagebrush washes over me as I breathe in the air of the Mongolian steppes, reminding me of where I am and the privilege I've enjoyed being able to work among these people. With my French translation of the Bible in my lap, I read, *"Dégagez un chemin pour l'éternel, nivelez dans la—steppe—une route pour notre Dieu."*

Thank You, Lord, for reminding me why I came to this beautiful land—to "clear the way for the Lord and *make smooth in the desert a highway for our God."*

Mongolian village kids playing on their horse

Harvesting rice with the Thai villagers

Chapter 10

Thailand: Not About Me

The mind of a man plans his way,
But the LORD directs his steps.

Proverbs 16:9

PACKING MY DENTAL suitcase while preparing to leave for Thailand, I receive a phone call. It's Sydney, a nurse with whom I worked in the emergency trauma center in Seattle.

"Since I last saw you, I've experienced a new life in Christ. My faith is growing. I feel called to go on a mission. Is there any chance I could go with you on one of your trips?"

The year is 2004. I haven't seen Sydney for almost a decade but she has been following my mission work through my newsletters. Sipping coffee at an outdoor cafe in Seattle, we catch up on each other's lives.

"I'm getting ready to go to Thailand and spend a week with some tribal people in a rural village doing dental clinics," I tell my friend. "A medical team will join me after the first week."

Seeing her interest, I add a disclaimer: "I don't speak Thai and know very little about the culture. This will be my first time there. I have no idea what to expect, but if you believe God is calling you to go, you can come along."

* * *

Sitting together on the plane, flying into the unknown, Sydney and I begin our adventure to Siam.

"I will never forget the evening you were in the break room at work reading When God Doesn't Make Sense. Do you remember what you said to me?" Sydney asks.

* * *

Sydney's question jolts me, taking me back to that traumatic time in my life when I was bombarded with brokenness and loss. After eighteen years of marriage, my husband and I were heading for divorce.

He'd left me and I'd moved into a rental with the kids after we closed the sale on a beautiful house we'd built together. Before I had time to get settled, a visit to see Nanny brought me face-to-face with her worsening dementia. Days later, her sweet life came to an end. She died of heart failure. My mom, who doubled as my best friend, asked if I would drive her to her doctor's appointment for a diagnostic procedure. In the exam room, she broke the news, "It isn't good, honey. I've got cancer." Six months later she turned sixty and died. Each week I struggled to find childcare to cover my work hours. I applied for a different position at work to obtain health insurance for Jacob, Cory, and me. In light of everything else, insurance and child-care may seem like small things. They were huge. It was all huge and hard and I was overwhelmed. Everything happening in my life became another chapter in the story of one tough year: Chapter 1: Loss, Chapter 2: Loss, Chapter 3: Loss.

My pain was a lonely planet. Grateful for the loving support I received, I still hurt at the end of the day. Life went on, not skipping a beat, while my agonizing world spun out of control. Per diem shifts in the trauma center filled the squares on my calendar.

Lord, I don't know how I can do this. Please help me.

Pushing through the emergency room doors, I carried a thousand pieces of a shattered heart, barely holding them together. Working to save the lives of my patients, I, too, was suffering from an internal hemorrhage that seemed to be draining my very life from me. Taking each day at a time and concentrating on the task at hand, I began to realize something good was happening. In helping others heal, I was healing. Looking beyond my circumstances, my problems didn't seem so overwhelming—tragedies were taking place all around me. Guiding my patients through their pain, whether physical or emotional, lessended my own. God wasn't making sense. My whole life was being pitched and toppled like a boat on a raging sea. Yet, in the midst of it all, I chose to cling to the one thing that would never change—His love.

* * *

Vivid sky-blue fills the small oval window as we pass through the cloud cover, reaching our cruising altitude—"You can now unbuckle your safety belt. Relax and enjoy the flight."

My past relived. Feelings felt. Words forgotten. I turn to Sydney and answer her question,

"No, I don't remember what I said."

Her soft words echo my own—spoken from a broken heart held together by faith—"Syd, I don't know why God is allowing this to happen, but I believe He has a reason and a purpose for it all. I know I can trust Him."

* * *

Sydney and I spend a brief time in Chiang Mai before heading north. We ride the sporty three-wheeled tuk-tuks around town—Thailand's version of a motorized rickshaw. Under the roof protecting us from sun and rain, we take seats on the benches which can accommodate four passengers. Destination confirmed, the driver turns on a dime and weaves forward through thick tuk-tuk traffic, providing cheap entertainment for the afternoon. Buddhist temples offer shelter for the monks in saffron robes walking barefoot in their large courtyards. The aroma of sizzling garlic arouses our appetites at every corner.

Strolling through the side streets of the city, we decide to stop at an open-air soup kitchen for lunch. Packed full, with a chatty lunch crowd of locals, a table clears and we are handed the menu. Everything is in Thai. Looking around the diner, there is not a Caucasian person in sight, except the one sitting across the table from me.

How are we going to order? What are we going to order?

Recognizing this is my first big test in Thailand, I don't want to fail. With pen in hand, I start drawing on a blank page of my journal. The first picture is a bowl of steaming broth. Adding a "+" after the bowl, I draw a chicken and add an " =." The third picture is a bowl of streaming broth with a chicken standing in it. Proudly, I show Sydney my artwork.

The busy young waiter approaches our table and contemplates my masterpiece. Taking his little pad of paper, he scribbles something on it in Thai, looks at me, and smiles, "Ahhh, chicken soup!"

Arriving in Huey Jor, a rural village of Khmu people in the northern area of the country near the Laotian border, the two of us are greeted by Pastor Arthit. Joining his family in his stilted thatched hut, we get settled into our sleeping quarters: simple mats placed on the floor covered by mosquito nets draped from the bamboo rafters. Sydney wonders if the floor will support the weight of our oversized luggage. I love her practical humor: picturing my dental suitcase, like a bomb, crashing through the bamboo floor onto the dirt below.

Anxious to get started on planning a schedule for our clinics in Huey Jor and the surrounding villages, I arrange a meeting with Arthit. Offering dental work to villagers suffering from severely decayed teeth is a valuable service. The satisfaction of seeing their pain instantly relieved will be a tremendous blessing. Sharing my enthusiasm with Arthit, he politely responds, "Ahhh, no. No dental clinic. Khmu busy with harvest. Rice harvest now. No time for dental clinic."

Isn't that why I'm here?

Grappling with my first initiation to a week of humiliating lessons, I tell Syd, "I guess we'll have to trust God and play it by ear."

Over the course of the next few days, we live and eat with Arthit's family, making house visits in the evenings and taking part in traditional dances. Dressing the American ladies in tribal outfits is great village entertainment. Giggling, the Khmu women and girls adjust our vests and headdresses while they instruct us on dance movements. Flowing expressions of the hands and fingers are incredibly challenging for me. The Khmu are people of small stature. My large, not-so-graceful frame must seem bigger than life to them. Their laughter is understandable.

Several times a day, someone brings back an armful of plants from the jungle that ends up in my stomach. I am told, "The Khmu eat what the bugs eat." Every savory dish is seasoned with tiny Thai chilis that are "five-star" hot. Flat, loosely woven circular baskets are filled with the bright red organic staple, sun-drying outside every hut.

Infants barely old enough to chew solid food eat from their mother's hand. Tightly swaddled, the babies enjoy the same five-star dishes the adults eat. Fresh fish from local streams, prepared whole, is eaten by old and young alike. When baby chokes on one of the fish bones, mom gently sticks her finger in his mouth, sweeping it back and away from his throat, dislodging the fine bone. The rescue is chased with a wad of sticky rice. Skinny village dogs finish off the leftover scraps, which are mostly bones. They gobble them down easily without choking.

The food is served in common bowls while we sit cross-legged on woven mats. Small baskets of sticky rice, filled with the steaming staple, are placed next to us and refilled on demand. A bite-sized wad of rice is taken between the fingers and flattened. Food is scooped up from the bowls with the rice, being careful not to touch the rest of the serving with the fingers.

As I savor the spicy delicacies brought in from the streams and jungle, I hear a sniffle and cough from Sydney, who is sitting behind me on the mat. Unlike me, she does not love five-star heat. Wiping tears from her eyes with a tissue she has brought in preparation for the meal, she graciously chokes down the spice that burns every cell of her gastrointestinal tract. Not a word. Winking at me, she smiles, then tackles another challenging bite.

One afternoon, while overnighting as guests with another Khmu family, we take a walk to explore the countryside. Discovering a small village store, we find a little bit of everything on the shelves, and a lot of dust covering the little bit of everything. Most of the items appear as if they have lived there for years. Surprised, I see a package that looks familiar.

Dusting it off, I show Sydney, "Look, Top Ramen!"

I have never been so excited over a package of Top Ramen in my life. Syd shares my excitement. We plan to offer it to our hostess, certain she will agree to add it to our lunch. I enjoy the jungle food, but having something familiar would add a little creature comfort to our adventure. While walking back to the hut, we share mouth-watering ideas about how the ramen might be prepared.

It is amazing how excited one can get over such simple pleasures. Learning to cope with everything different in one's world takes energy. The body and psyche are bombarded on all sides with strangeness and newness. As much as I look forward to cross-cultural experiences, I can't deny that a dusty package of Top Ramen has made my day.

Clutching the noodles in my hand, I find Kat preparing food on the floor of the hut. Squatting over the bamboo mat, she carefully places pieces of chopped bird into a pot of broth. Looking up at me from her position on the floor, she flashes a toothless grin while continuing to chop.

Pointing to the ramen and the pot, I do a little charade in an attempt to communicate with her. I doubt the word ramen is in her vocabulary. Having no trouble understanding me, she shakes her head in an emphatic "No" and cheerfully lays down a piece of tree trunk covered with dry blood.

In a plastic bag is an animal that has a rubbery texture from being singed in a fire. Plopping it onto the chopping block, she begins by slicing the tail and adding it to the pot.

"Sydney?" I call to the other side of the bamboo partition.

"Yes?"

"We aren't going to have ramen for lunch."

"Ok," she replies.

"We are having rat stew."

"Ok," she answers without the slightest hesitation.

A delicacy the family is honored to serve, we eat the bird-rat stew with balls of sticky rice. Because of its fiery seasoning, I can't tell you what rat meat tastes like. Less common than chicken, I know it is a favorite dish among the Khmu.

As we finish our lunch, a little dog watches from the entrance of the hut. "He is so cute. I hope we see him again tomorrow," Sydney whispers.

* * *

On one hot afternoon, Somsack finds us and asks if we can take a look at his hand. The tissue is painful and swollen.

"I was bitten by a scorpion," he tells us through an interpreter.

After giving Somsack some first aid, we pray for him. Filled with gratitude to the point of tears, he thanks us.

Another day, we hike up the mountain to the rice paddies and join the villagers. They teach us how to use their sickles and laugh at our fledgling attempts at harvesting. Their work looks easy until I try. Using a sickle is an art.

In the afternoon, Arthit has me drive his truck to another village. Everything is on the wrong side (for me, anyway). I keep turning on the windshield wiper when I intend to use the blinker. From the passenger seat, Arthit's high-pitched giggle keeps me laughing despite my frustration. Sydney is sitting on the middle console between us. It is a struggle to shift. We get to the end of the road and have to turn around between some fences. Backing up into the fence and denting the rear bumper, I am mortified. Later, I reimburse Arthit for the damage done. He is gracious.

Things aren't going the way I had planned. At all.

My heavy dental suitcase sits in the corner of the hut, a reminder of my grand intentions. It is filled to the brim with anesthetic, gloves, gauze, and all the other supplies I meticulously packed for the trip. It hasn't fallen through the floor. Yet.

Every morning I spend my prayer walk complaining to the Lord. My pride bubble has burst. I feel inept and worthless. I have no clue as to our purpose for being here this week. My prayers sound like a whining child:

Lord, I believe You called me here. Was I wrong? I thought that I was to love these people by giving them dental care. That's not happening. What is the purpose of my being here? I am doing nothing. I am so humiliated. I want to be a godly example to Sydney, but I feel like I have failed her in every way. I don't know the culture. I don't know the language. Every time I turn around, I am making a mistake. As if all this isn't enough, I crash Arthit's truck. Really, Lord? What a bummer! Please, help me trust You and walk in Your will. I want to be obedient. Thank You, Jesus.

* * *

At the end of the week I am spent. Pastor Kham, our Laotian partner, and the team arrive late at night. Lying still but wide awake under the mosquito net thinking about all the mistakes I made during the day, I hear Kham raving as he enters the room.

"Ah, Khmu so sad you leave. Khmu *love* Sydney and Kris. Want you to stay. Be missionaries here. Missionaries to Khmu people."

I listen, not sure I am clearly understanding a word he is saying. He continues. At this point, I am experiencing something between shock and disbelief, not trusting my ears.

"What are you saying, Kham?" I want to be sure I am hearing him correctly from my position on the floor.

"Khmu say, 'Sydney and Kris live with Khmu people, eat Khmu food, eat Khmu chili.' Oh, Khmu *love* you. Want you to stay and be their missionaries."

Kham is passionate and emphatic. His love for his people runs deep. He is speaking on their behalf.

As my mind begins to grasp his words, a floodgate breaks and tears burst from my eyes, quietly drenching my pillow. A moment of reckoning comes when my understanding suddenly readjusts to a different perspective. The spotlight shifts off of me and turns out to the crowd. In this case, the Khmu. There is a saying I love: God created us to be human beings, not human doings. Through experiences like this, I am learning this truth.

Living under heavy persecution and considered the lowliest of tribes in Laos and Northern Thailand, the Khmu suffer from a lack of self-worth and low self-esteem. I have heard them say, "We are like dogs." Little do I realize the impact that our visit has had on the humble people of this tiny village. Living among them this week, eating their food and sleeping in their huts, has validated them as people. Our acceptance of their ways and participation in their daily lives has spoken volumes of love to them. We just needed to show up. God did the rest. He knows what they needed. It didn't make sense at the time. Now it does.

We celebrate our team's arrival with Pastor Khan, sharing a special meal with the Khmu villagers of Huey Jor. At the end of the meal, one after another, they stand to share their hearts.

"When we hear two American women come, we worry. What will we feed them? Where will they stay?"

"You eat Khmu food. You stay in our house, sleep like us. We are so happy."

"A scorpion bit my hand. You came. Took care of me. You prayed for me. You loved me."

"You came to my hut and visited me when I was sick."

The stories continue. I am humbled. Glancing at Sydney, I see her using her tissue: maybe for tears caused by the food, or maybe for tears cried in joy and humility as we bask in God's grace. Maybe both.

God *doesn't* make sense. If I could figure Him out, I wouldn't need Him. Sometimes I learn the answers to "Why?" but more often, I must trust, in faith, that He knows what He is doing. I want to walk the path of obedience even when I don't recognize where it is taking me. As I walk, my words and actions are impacting lives in ways I cannot begin to see.

Like I told Sydney decades ago: "I believe He has a reason and a purpose for it all. I know I can trust Him."

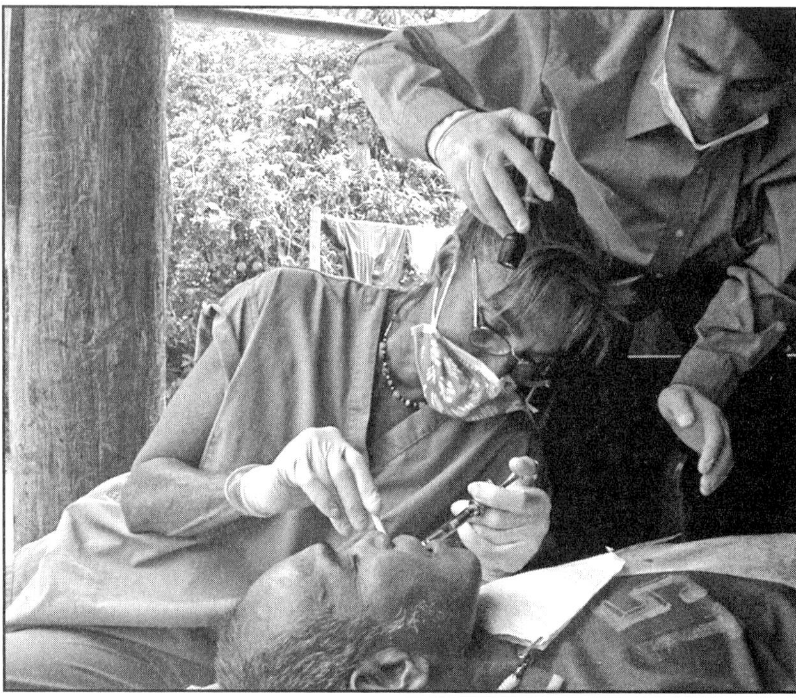

Tooth extraction on a bamboo porch in Thai village

Drawing by Sri Lankan child—a victim of the tsunami

CHAPTER 11

Sri Lanka: Washed Away

So teach us to number our days,
That we may present to You a heart of wisdom.

Psalm 90:12

REFLECTING OFF THE seawater, the sun's rays glisten like tinsel. Along the coastline resorts booked full of tourists share an ocean view with the mosques and temples next to them. Staking out an early morning spot on the beach, sunbathers, laying on colorful beach towels and lounge chairs are engrossed in their novels while children scoop fine white sand into their shovels. Holding hands, a young couple lets the salty water lap between their toes. Two men in sarongs fight the swells to launch their fishing boat, their locks of dark wavy hair blowing sideways in the breeze.

Minutes later, they're gone. All of them. Swept out to sea into the Indian Ocean, never to return, sharing the same fate with two hundred and twenty-five thousand others. The tsunami has claimed their lives.

Responding to disasters, I have been constantly faced with the reality of death: casualties of war; corpses loaded into containers following a plane wreck; victims buried alive in earthquake rubble. Before relief work, I held babies in my arms in the emergency room as they took their last breath and cut clothing off teens who had unknowingly gone out for their last Friday night party.

"Is it safe?"

Whether it is about deploying to a Covid field hospital when little is known about the mysterious virus taking thousands of lives—or traveling to areas of conflict and accepting assignments in war zones—this is one of my most frequently asked questions..

"Is it safe?"

I love the quote from the book *Firestorm* by Jeanette Windle: "Safety is not found in the absence of danger but in the presence of God."

Physical safety is an illusion. The people who drowned during Hurricane Mitch. The victims who perished at Ground Zero. The thousands who washed away in the tsunami. Those crushed in the earthquakes of Haiti, Nepal, and Turkey. When they went to work, when they went to play on the beach, when they lay their heads on their pillows, what would their answer have been when asked, "Is it safe?"

We have bought into an illusion of safety, as though we can somehow control our destiny. Living isn't safe. Underneath this concern for safety is fear: fear of harm and ultimately death. We must experience the presence of the living God in our lives to overcome fear. To fully live we must be ready to die. God's presence in life, and death, is our only true safety.

* * *

The tsunami of 2004 arrives unannounced, unexpected, and unwanted, disrupting life and leaving a trail of death and tragedy behind. At the time it strikes, I am working in Cambodia. Ready to respond to the disaster, I start searching for a contact in Indonesia or Sri Lanka, two of the most severely affected areas.

A church in Colombo invites me to come. Though I have limited information from them, I take a direct flight from Cambodia to Sri

Lanka. Hit with the familiar feeling of doom when I get off the plane, so many thoughts bombard me.

What if there is no ride waiting for me? Will I be able to find a telephone? Can I figure out how to use one if I do? Where will I get currency exchanged? Will I be able to communicate with anyone?

A man looks at me as though to ask, "Are *you* the one?"

I must be the one.

He takes me to the home of a Sri Lankan couple where I spend the night. As I enter their house, I find myself standing in front of a huge fish tank, staring into the eyes of a three-foot-long red-tail catfish swimming in circles with two smaller friends. John, my host, tells me his prized fish recently swallowed two electrical plugs, requiring an operation. Keeping the fish in six inches of water, the vet was able to pull the plugs out of him.

The rest of the contents of the colonial house seem normal, except for the meal served for dinner. The meat looks like blobs of fat. After serving myself a good portion, I am told they are goat udders.

Required to attend a briefing at the church, I grab a cup of coffee and sit down with a group of volunteers. They give us a strict warning. I find their words discouraging.

"The government of Sri Lanka is trying to pass an anti-conversion law against Christianity. We must be very careful in terms of our Christian witness. The predominantly Buddhist majority is hostile toward Christianity. They don't want Christians coming here to give humanitarian aid. They believe we are here solely to proselytize. Your witness must be silent."

Heavy-hearted after leaving the church, I take a walk along the beach.

* * *

Sri Lanka is a tiny country off the southern tip of India where death tolls from the tsunami have reached thirty thousand. Entire tree trunks, driftwood, and wire, strangled by torn clothing and seaweed, clutter the formerly pristine shore. Cracked cement foundations sit naked with piles of rubble, broken brick, and lumber heaped in mounds around them. With folded arms, a young boy stands, looking toward the ocean, the only picture of calm to be found.

Stepping over two halves of a fishing boat, I see a pillow with "Good Luck" embroidered on its case. Broken flip-flops of all colors, sizes, and shapes lay half-buried in the sand without their mate. Women's saris of colorful fabric hang, tangled in the tops of beach palms. Fluttering in the sea breeze, they flag attention to the silenced bed of death below.

A grief-stricken woman wails over her loss as she walks over the heap of debris that was once her home.

How can she possibly bear this burden alone?

Staring blankly, a young man stops before we collide. His glassy eyes reflect the pain in his empty soul.

"I've lost my job, my home, my family. I've lost everything."

He wanders away, through broken furniture and water-logged photo albums, with only his memories to torment him.

Working with a unit of European army medics on the southern coast, we hold our medical clinics in Buddhist temples housing thousands of refugees. Crowds of people stand in the courtyard during the day. At night, warm bodies spread out on hard surfaces, covering every inch of ground and filling stairwells. Coming to us with fish bones embedded in their skin, minor cuts to their arms and legs, and respiratory problems, patients quietly wait to be seen. Most of their physical injuries are minor compared to the gaping invisible wounds left deep in their soul.

"I had my three children with me. Suddenly the wave pulled two of them away. I couldn't hang on any longer. I survived with my one child who has cerebral palsy."

"My wife and my children are gone. I survived with my dog."

Many believe their loss is a result of bad karma, something they did or didn't do, triggering a chain of fateful events in their life, a punishment dealt by some elusive force of energy.

As the days go by, rumors of another tsunami come and go. I always know when they have come. Panic-stricken mothers run frantically down the street clinging to their children whom they have pulled out of school. Fleeing in terror, they flail their arms at approaching vehicles, desperately hoping for a ride to higher ground.

Fear has gripped the entire nation. In this culture of despair, I feel like I am walking around with a set of keys in my pocket—keys to unlock answers to the spiritual and emotional healing of these grieving people. People without peace. People without hope. People who have no understanding of their eternal worth. If only I could tell them of Jesus' love, the love that brings comfort to the brokenhearted, the hope they can have for their future, and the peace in knowing what awaits them in eternity through Christ. My keys remain in my pocket.

One morning, I am reading a familiar scripture as though for the first time:

"Jesus came, the doors having been shut, and stood in their midst and said, 'Peace be with you'" (John 20:26).

The disciples were terrified, fearing the same death as Jesus suffered at the hands of the Jews. Locking themselves in a room after His resurrection, He passes through the physical barriers and appears among them with a message of peace.

The Bible says the Holy Spirit dwells in me. Where I go, He goes. His Spirit defies locked doors. There is no physical barrier He cannot penetrate. The keys to His kingdom come in varied forms: a listening ear, a loving touch, and sacrificial giving. Expressed in many ways beyond words, I *am* sharing the gospel in *all* I do in His name. No barrier can keep Him out. This comforting realization brings His peace.

While working with the army, trying to fit in becomes more challenging with each passing day. Here to help and love the people, I feel a building tension mounting among the medics and realize they have other reasons for being here. They are doing their duty. They are here to get the job done. In the mornings, they complain of hangovers from the night before and bark at each other like bulldogs during the day, showing little empathy for the patients. I decide to put my stethoscope away and grab a shovel. Gutters are blocked everywhere. With another volunteer, I spend hours cleaning them out.

During breaks, my little bag of tricks comes in handy. Playing yo-yo and string games with the children blesses me as I listen to their laughter and see the smiles on their tired faces. At the end of the day, I'm standing in line at a small market when a young Canadian girl in front of me turns and pours her heart out.

"I came here to help. It is terrible. This is *so* hard. I'm exhausted and I can't sleep at night." She hands the clerk a bottle of vodka, pays for it, and leaves.

Humanitarian workers come for many reasons. Often inexperienced, they find themselves unable to handle the magnitude of the situation they face. The stress consumes them. Or, others, veterans at first response, are doing their job, but their heart is not in it. When I see how others are coping, I am grateful to have found healthy ways to deal with my feelings of inadequacy in these overwhelming conditions. Recognizing the fact that a loving God is in ultimate control frees me from relying on my ability to fix things or figure them out and gives me peace amid the suffering and chaos.

A team of Spanish physicians asks me to translate for them. They tell me how their trip got off to a bad start in customs.

"They confiscated all of our medical supplies so they could re-sell them."

Having agreed to meet the team at the orphanage, I take a public bus. The noise is deafening. Traffic and horns. Chants broadcast from the temples. Calls to prayer bellowing from the minarets. Public lottery announcements on public address speakers. Blaring music.

Does this noise pollution protect them from their thoughts?

A woman who smells like a gardenia puts her hand on my shoulder to brace herself. Knowing what we are in for, I will be glad to get off on the other end.

Later, I journal: *"People pay daily to be smashed, crushed, pushed, prodded, shaken, and jerked about while subjecting themselves to a bus driver who cares little for anyone's life: neither his rider's, nor the pedestrian's on the road, nor his own. No wonder people aren't smiling. They live an existence void of hope and joy."*

Leaving the gardenia behind on the bus, a strong odor of urine hits me when I walk through the doors of the old building. Cribs, some occupied by two babies, fill the room. In this orphanage of fifty children, fifteen are under the age of one. The rest are five and younger. Six have special needs. Five employees staff the home. The numbers don't add up. Mothers give birth in the rice fields and abandon their babies. The babies end up here.

We get to work: bathing, holding, feeding, and cleaning the babies. After changing soiled linen, we place them in clean cribs. Most are malnourished. After we finish, a woman holding a switch takes me into a room of rambunctious kids. Jumping on the beds, hitting each other, and tweaking the tuning keys on my guitar, I can't get them to settle down so we can sing. I return to the cribs to serenade the babies.

Riding back to town at the end of the day, I skip the bus ride and take several auto-rickshaws. Negotiating the price when I get on, the drivers up the ante when they drop me off. One intentionally drives me in the opposite direction from where I ask to go.

This experience *is* hard. Yet this is the answer to my prayers: to go to difficult places. When I am least comfortable, I believe I am where God wants me.

Sunila opens a bottle of coconut oil and pours a small well into her palm. Rubbing her hands together, she combs the shiny balm into her long thick hair. Parting off three sections, I weave a French braid, handing her a mirror so she can watch. Her friends giggle, delighted to have a spontaneous beauty salon experience in their group home. This is the second orphanage I visit with the team: one for teenage girls. As I translate for the Spanish counselor, we encourage the girls to talk about their experiences. Sunila, like the other girls, complains of a headache. Tearfully she tells us, "I was on the train with my family. All of them died except for me."

Traveling through the jungle coastline on December 26, the Matara Express, overloaded with holiday passengers, was following its routine schedule when a surge of water halted the train two hours outside Colombo. The force of the wave derailed the carriages. Trapped and unable to exit the eight overcrowded cabins, many passengers drowned when the coaches were overcome by water. Hundreds scrambled to the roof, believing they could find safety, only to be swept away by subsequent swells. As the tsunami forced the carriages against trees and buildings, people seeking cover were crushed. An estimated seventeen hundred people lost their lives, making it the largest single rail disaster in history.

Unable to grasp the extent of psychological and emotional trauma Sunila has suffered, I silently pray: *Lord, comfort her in her sorrow.*

Collect her tears in Your bottle. I pray she would come to know You, the Father who will never leave her.

Sunila sits and sobs, drenched in her pain and sorrow, while the caregiver, passing by, shrugs her shoulders and shakes her head, "She doesn't have a headache. She just cries all the time."

Wiping her tears and turning to leave the room, I hug Sunila before another tearful child shares her story.

* * *

Soggy books, papers, and charts from the school library lay like a patchwork quilt on the grass in the schoolyard, drying in the sun. Thinking about the trauma the younger children have been through and their inability to express their feelings in words, I can't imagine what burdens they are carrying in their young hearts.

A pediatric social worker doing art therapy with the kids lays sheets of blank paper and crayons in front of one group, encouraging them to color. As if asked to show graphic details of the horrors they have experienced, all twenty of them draw pictures depicting their version of the tsunami.

One little girl shyly shows me her drawing. Blue lines, representing water, cover half the page. A stick figure hangs in a crooked palm tree. A second stick figure clings to a tree underwater while other trees lay sideways, colored over with blue. Squares with triangles, stick houses, are covered by blue lines, while another stick figure, immersed underwater, has both arms raised in surrender. What this precious child could never put into words is eloquently expressed in her simple artwork.

* * *

Since the tsunami, the eastern coast of Sri Lanka, one of the hardest hit in the country, has received very little attention. This is the territory occupied by Tamil Tigers, a militant group not supported by the government. The Tamils have a bad reputation with the people. Their cries have been ignored but they desperately need help. Joining a Christian medical team from India, South Africa, the Netherlands, Canada, Cuba, America, and Sri Lanka, we plan a trip to Kalmunai in Tamil territory.

It's still dark when we climb into our van with the medical supplies. Four-thirty is an early start, but we have a long trip ahead. A three-hour ride over rough roads takes us to a military outpost. Breakfast snacks purchased en route are quickly gobbled down before we remove our boots, roll up our pant legs, and begin a two-kilometer trek through wetlands. One of our medical bags is baptized during the trudge through the murky ankle-deep water. Egrets watch us from their perch on cotton-white water lilies as we march single file over the trail to a double dugout canoe. Crossing the deeper water in the canoe, we arrive at another trail. Walking four more kilometers in swampland, with water reaching our mid-thighs, we come to a single canoe crossing. I sit and wait while the canoe makes multiple trips back and forth, ferrying the team and supplies to another landing. Expecting us at the landing is a driver, sitting atop an old tractor hitched to a wagon. The one-hour wagon ride takes half of the group the rest of the way to the school building where we hold our clinic.

Having been without access to healthcare and electricity, the people are happy to see us. Disappearing to pick up the rest of the team, the tractor leaves. We set up as quickly as possible while the crowd continues to grow.

"We need to leave by four-thirty to avoid an elephant stampede. The animals begin their migration to the water sources to drink at that hour," our leader tells us. Getting started so late, it will be difficult to meet the stampede deadline.

Although the examiners finish seeing patients according to schedule, the pharmacy is bottlenecked. For another hour, patients continue to receive prescribed medicine. It is twilight before we leave. Rather than making two trips, the team of twenty-eight packs the tractor wagon like a public bus. We bump along the narrow, elevated passage straddled by two bodies of water. On a rock below is an enormous crocodile who slithers into the water as our listing wagon teeters past him. The first canoe is waiting and makes several crossings without disturbing the elephant's happy hour. Our headlamps guide us back from our landing point: through the wetlands, in the double canoe, and over the trails back to the outpost. We manage to avoid being stampeded, attacked only by a couple of leeches in the water. Singing songs in the van eases the pain of the three-hour road trip back to town. Crawling into bed at midnight, I thank God for a blessed day.

* * *

The foaming surf continues to visit the shore and return to the sea. Watching my step in the rubble, I take one last walk on the beach in Galle before flying out. How beautiful this place must have been before the tsunami turned it into a heap of ruins.

The face of a clock, torn in the center and without hands, looks up from the sand. Only numbers remain. Before the tsunami, it spoke of the passage of time. Then time ran out.

Lord, teach me to number my days, that I may present to You a heart of wisdom.

Sri Lankan boy stands on a beach destroyed by the tsunami

Boat worship in the islands of Lake Victoria, Uganda

Chapter 12

Uganda: The Islands

And He said to them, "Follow Me, and I will make you fishers of men."

Matthew 4:19

KATOSI IS BUSTLING with the activity of fishing boats and their catch. Walking through the tiny port town with my team of Ugandan men, there's no escaping the crowd's curiosity over the *mzungu*, or white-skinned foreigner. I've grown accustomed to the stares of a hundred dark eyes while working on the islands of Lake Victoria.

Lord, keep me mindful that my every move is being watched. I want to reflect You in all I say and do.

Looking for *Yesu Akwagala* painted on the stern, I spot our ministry boat, the only one named *Jesus Loves You*, distinguishing it from all the others. We begin handing our food supplies, tents, foam mattresses, dental equipment, and personal belongings to the porters, identifiable by their thigh-length navy blue overcoats and wet trousers rolled above their knees. For meager wages, they haul cargo and passengers back and forth to wooden boats with plank seats, serving as island taxis, until the vessels have reached capacity. Fishing boats, loaded with mounds of tilapia and Nile perch on ice, compete for parking space as they prepare to leave for distant ports.

The gentle lapping of water on the shore increases in tempo while a fishy breeze picks up. Distracted by this change in climate, I double-check the flotation devices on *Yesu Akwagala*.

* * *

Thinking back on what the men and I call *the day of fear*, I giggle at the memory—my crew, wearing their neon vests all doubling over and bursting out in hysterical laughter.

"Look, they are fleeing. They think we are the authorities coming to check their nets. Nobody else on the lake has money to buy life vests like these, except the authorities!"

In the distance, I see little boats being frantically rowed toward the horizon by fearful fishermen who think the neon authorities will bust them for their use of illegal nets.

* * *

The boat ride from Katosi is not an option. Many island residents are terrified by the water. They don't swim. Drowning is common. With over a thousand miles of coastline, Victoria is the second-largest freshwater lake in the world. Torrential downpours and fierce winds give rise to ocean-sized swells, threatening the most seaworthy vessels caught in the storm.

A porter, his statuesque frame a work of sculptured muscle over bone, is trying to get my attention. Digging his heels into the sand and effortlessly hoisting me up, piggyback style, he trudges through the thigh-deep water to *Yesu Akwagala*, lifting me over the edge, successfully loading the last piece of cargo destined for Lwaje.

Hundreds of islands cover the lake's surface. Traveling between them can take hours.

Among the inhabitants are fugitives, pirates, addicts, and prostitutes; each with a desperate reason for fleeing to one of these remote hideaways.

Island life is anything but exotic. Dilapidated huts constructed of wood scraps, reeds, and metal lamina clutter the rocky banks. Sanitation is nonexistent; everyone has squatter's rights. AIDS, abuse, and addiction have taken up permanent residence.

On the shore: a man scrubs his body, a woman scrubs clothes, a fisherman scales fish, and a child fills a five-gallon jerrycan with water for drinking and cooking.

Toddlers wander barefoot over sharp metal, shards of glass, and fish hooks, playing tag with limping dogs and snorting pigs. Squirming on the ground's rough surface, a naked baby finds relief for her rash-infested body.

Most of the fishing is done at night with illegal nets and small lights used for navigation, the darkness hiding the fishermen from authorities. As dawn breaks, boats pull up to shore with their catch. The scales tip. Prices are negotiated.

Weary fishermen spend the cool morning hours mending their nets. In a dark hut, bootleg spirits are sipped from long rubber tubes dipped in a common pot. Women prepare food to sell; others prepare their bodies. Endless banter takes place at rickety tables where cards are shuffled and bets are waged.

The clandestine activities of the night extend far into the day, blending into the next night of illegal fishing. This is island life.

Lwaje, a three-hour boat ride from Katosi, is my base of operations. Offering free dental care on the islands, I come to lend credibility to the gospel in a practical way. To carry out this ministry, I need a team, including boatmen.

My Christian brothers living on Lwaje are *sittin' on ready* to work with Mama Kris: our two distant worlds brought together by a common purpose, to glorify God. The core group: David, Andrew, Simon, Sylvester, Hallelujah, and Steven is solid. Others join us from time to time.

Pastor David's father died the month he was born, leaving his mother who was lame in one hand, to care for her eleven children. David, the youngest, left school in fifth grade.

"Someone gave me my first pair of shoes when I was sixteen. I moved to Lwaje to fish, hoping to make a living. God met me here. He told me, 'You are no longer a fisherman but a fisher of men's souls.'"

At the time, young David didn't understand. Today he does. He has been able to attend Bible College, pastor and plant several churches, and evangelize throughout the islands. He tells me eight churches have been planted as a result of our ministry. What joy to know the Lord has allowed me to help David fulfill his calling to become a fisher of men.

Gaining insight into what this ministry means to my Ugandan team, I see God's hand in bringing us together. Burning with a desire to share Christ in these dark islands, their poverty hinders them. By providing the resources they need, I help them overcome that obstacle. Living their dream, I come along for the ride. Through the years we have traveled to over seventy different islands. It all started with a trip to Lwaje.

A string of children carry our supplies up the hill to the boarding house, where they live and attend the mission school, a ministry of World Outreach Mission Foundation.

Now fourteen, Elsie's father died when she was ten, leaving her mother with five children. When her mom heard of the school program on Lwaje, she enrolled Elsie. Asking her about the pretty skirt she is wearing, she explains in her Ugandan English,

"Oh, I saved up my mon-ies to buy it by washing cloth-ies. Now I have a skirt to wear to church. I am going to save my mon-ies again, but not to buy another skirt. I don't need another one. I have this one. I will save my mon-ies so that I can give it to my brothers and sisters so they can get an education. I want to be a teacher. Then I can educate people and I will also be able to support my family."

Living out of a small box containing all her personal belongings, Elsie sleeps on one of several bare metal-framed bunk beds in an otherwise empty boarding house. Porridge, rice, and beans are her daily meals. Eating together, she insists on sharing, "Mama Kris, please eat and enjoy."

Such altruism in children is not something I have experienced until spending time on Lwaje.

Lord, teach me through this beautiful child to love others as You do.

* * *

The men endure long hours of hard work. Our boat must be hoisted ashore by a whole posse every time we dock it. On each island, fuel and supplies are carried back and forth from boat to camp. A large canvas army tent, serving as my dental clinic by day and sleeping quarters for the men by night, requires all hands on deck to assemble the frame and stretch the canvas over it. Before we move on, it must be disassembled. Meal preparation is tedious, a full-time job in itself.

Today, the clinic is in full swing. Tackling a difficult molar, I pause and wipe the sweat from my brow. Looking up, I count seventy faces peering curiously into the tent. Removing my mask, I smile and recall a friend's words, "You know that even when we speak the same language, we often aren't able to understand each other. Prayer is the superior form of communication!"

Oh Lord, through this open door, let them watch. May I not show impatience but forbearance and respect towards each person. Let me not sigh or grimace when the task is difficult. Let each word be calm, each touch an expression of gentleness. When tested by the length of time it is taking, or concern about bleeding, let me breathe a prayer of confidence to You. Let my actions speak the language of love.

The tent: my theater. The bedside: my stage. Under the spotlight of hundreds of dark eyes, I embrace these fishbowl moments, trusting He will communicate the deeper spiritual meaning of my actions to my audience.

* * *

Fighting fierce swells, our boat approaches the next island. Hallelujah, our boatman, yanks the rudder to the right and yells something in Luganda.

If Hallelujah is flustered, there's a problem. Sleeping in the supply hut to protect the gasoline from thieves, or guarding our boat when we can't see it from our campsite, he is our watchman and protector.

Hallelujah doesn't speak English but captures my attention by giving me a hearty smile and thumbs up, communicating volumes in a gesture.

* * *

One afternoon, Hallelujah and the kids are circled up on the trail in front of the dorm on Lwaje. Gently pushing my way through the miniature crowd, I see Hallelujah's stick poking at the center of attraction. The snake has met its demise.

It is different from any serpent I have seen: the length of a yardstick and very fat, with a triangular head and a pug nose. Getting the attention of the kids, it isn't about to escape mine. We all let our curiosity get the best of us, keeping a tight circle while Hallelujah uses the stick to rotate the specimen from side to side, displaying different angles of his trophy. A major island attraction, there is no way we are going to let this slip by without proper fanfare.

Later that evening, I can't get the picture of the unusual snake out of my head, nor the fact it was on the path leading to my tent.

Having dinner with Andrew and his family, I know I can count on him for wise counsel, "Pastor Andrew, Hallelujah killed a snake on the trail today. He called it a puff adder. Are they poisonous?"

These common island questions never phase him. Answering unfazed,

"Ah, a puff adder."

In his distinguished African accent, he continues,

"If you do not disturb it, it will not bite you. But, if it bites you, you will die."

* * *

Now in the boat, watching Hallelujah lose his calm, I know we are in trouble. His words sound strong. Responding to his command, the men hoist a scrap metal anchor over the bow to steady us in the wind. The waves are unforgiving. Nobody is agreeing on the right move.

As we are pounded into the rugged coastline, Andrew jumps out, cutting his foot while trying to prevent damage to the vessel.

Like fish drying in the sun, we sit in the tossing boat and wait for permission to hold a clinic on the island. A drunk resident begins harassing me before our answer arrives: permission to work on the island has been denied by the man in charge.

Joining Andrew, the men jump into the water. It takes all their strength to launch us off the rocky landing, pushing through the road-block of disappointed islanders begging us,

"Please don't leave. We want you to stay. Many are suffering. It is only one person who is causing trouble."

Firmly I tell them, "No, I'm sorry. *You* will have to deal with the one who is causing trouble. *We* are leaving."

Amazed by my strength, I know it comes from years of hard lessons on Lake Victoria.

Yes, I am learning how to say, "No."

* * *

On one of my first trips, I am awakened by,

"Your patient is here. He's bleeding. He is *still* drunk."

The messenger and drunk patient are outside my tent at three in the morning. The key word is—still. The patient had been drinking before I pulled his tooth. Lesson: Don't pull teeth on anyone who has alcohol on their breath.

It sounds like an easy call, but it isn't. Suffering from intense pain and without access to dental care, these people are desperate. Most of them drink, some all day. My compassionate heart must be restrained by wisdom.

Early one morning, a young man lies down on my table. A faint but familiar odor on his breath makes its way through my mask. Pastor David is assisting and translating.

"David, please ask him if he has been drinking."

Standing and leaning over him, mirror and probe in hand, I am ready to examine his tooth.

"Mama Kris, he says he is a pastor," David tells me after posing the question and talking with the patient.

"The answer is 'Yes,' right, David?" I insist.

More conversation follows between the two men.

"Yes, he has been drinking," David confirms, adding, "A little."

After explaining the dangers involved, I stick with the verdict,

"No, I'm sorry. My rule applies to pastors as well."

Disappointed, he leaves.

The next morning, while packing up to move on to the next island, David asks, "Do you remember the man you turned away yesterday?"

"Of course, David. How could I forget?"

My resolute "No" is always secretly accompanied by a broken heart. When my patient played the pastor card, my heart bled. Fortunately, I didn't fold.

David continues, "Late last night after you went to your tent, he came back. He told me he *was* a pastor but needed money and moved to the islands to fish. He started drinking and backslid, falling far away from God. He has suffered so much from this toothache and knew you came to bless him, but he could not receive the blessing on account of his sin. God showed him how his sin has brought suffering upon suffering. He turned back to the Lord and asked God for forgiveness."

Today, a year later, this man is attending a Bible study on the island and is continuing to draw close to God.

What a beautiful lesson: My—No—is God's—Go. Not wanting to be perceived as a bad guy, it can be hard to say "No!" I am learning it can be the most loving thing I can do.

* * *

Reaching unmapped territory, I'm told I am the first *mzungu* to step foot on Kome Island. Pastor David, working as my assistant, talks to a beautiful young woman who is waiting for the anesthetic to take effect.

"You just came from a man. When you leave here and go back, they will be waiting for you. Why do you spend your precious life like that? Living like rats and dogs. Don't you know how much God loves you and how valuable you are to Him?"

David "knows" her without her having shared a word about her life of prostitution. As with every patient, we pray together after the extraction. She leaves with a hard heart only to return in the afternoon a changed woman,

"You were right. When I left here, they were waiting for me. I don't want to live like this anymore. I want to give my life to Christ."

As evening approaches, we clear the dental table which becomes our dinner table. Heaping piles of food on their plates, lovingly prepared by Sylvester, the men are all smiles. Listening to their laughter brings me joy. David beams, "I love it when you come, Mama Kris. I eat good food! I gain weight!"

Steven prays, "Lord, please bless those in the States who made this trip possible and provided money to buy this food."

Simon's beautiful smile lifts my spirits as words of gratitude flow from his heart, encouraging me in my weariness after a long day of work.

These men take nothing for granted.

* * *

Lively worship kicks off the evening outreach on a clearing next to thousands of dagaa, silver sardine-like fish, drying on the ground. Music is followed by *The Jesus film* and a message.

Omar is in the crowd. Upon hearing David share, "Jesus is the only way to God," he comes forward, taking the microphone to speak, "I am a highly trained Muslim. I was a marabout and an Imam and received two more years of intensive training to confuse those of the Christian faith. I read in the Quran that I must open my eyes so that I would see paradise. I never saw it. Tonight my eyes have been opened. I have been blind but now I see. This Jesus *is* the Christ. He is the Chosen One of God who has come to show us the way to paradise."

He asks his wife, a believer, to come to the microphone. She is exuberant and filled with joy. Publicly apologizing for his harsh and cruel treatment, he tells her, "I was wrong and tortured you. Please forgive me."

Omar comes to our campsite early in the morning asking David for a Bible.

"You are my pastor. You have shown me the Way. I will keep in touch with you."

* * *

Back at Lwaje, with plans for a picnic, I send my men to the mainland to buy a boatload of food. Emptied of gruel, the cooks tend their stock pots bubbling over with matoke, a plantain-like staple, rice, and beef stew. Armed with plastic utensils and cups of juice, a ribbon of color stretches up the hill, each child waiting patiently to be served. Picnicking on the grass, they become quiet, appearing to savor every bite. When I return a year later, we have another picnic.

Out of curiosity, I ask Beatrice, the headmaster, "Is this special for the children?"

With a puzzled look, she responds, "*Special? Special?* Do you know that these children will be talking about this meal until you come back next year?"

* * *

Music spills out of the small church on Sunday morning. A woven mat is placed on the dirt floor. Lutalo and his wife are on their knees before the congregation to dedicate their lives to Christ. Sharing his testimony, I hear his story for the first time:

"I heard about a white woman coming to give free dental care on the islands. I didn't think it could be true. When I came to ask about it, three different people on separate occasions shared Christ with me, telling me how much God loves me. I was not ready to believe. After I got my tooth pulled and went home, I started thinking about all of this: how it is not possible that someone would come to give this free care to me unless there is a God who truly loves me. I am ready to give my life to Christ, this God of love, who freely gave His life for me."

* * *

Though many obstacles stand in the way: fatigue, illness, near shipwreck, patient complications, bugs, snakes, and storms, to name a few, I love this island ministry. The hardships pale in comparison to the intense joy I experience in relieving such desperate physical suffering, seeing lives changed for eternity, and making fishers of men.

Making fishers of men in the islands of Lake Victoria, Uganda

Sudanese students in their village classroom

Chapter 13

Sudan: Amazing Grace

"My grace is sufficient for you, for my power is made perfect in weakness."

2 Corinthians 12:9 NIV

UNFAZED BY THE storm, the charter plane pilot taxis down the runway. Pelted by liquid bullets released from angry black clouds, our winged cabin bounces violently as it gains altitude. Loaded with a small team of Americans, a Sudanese pastor, and our weight limit of medical supplies, we head north to Bor, Sudan.

Intrigued by the open cockpit, I gaze at the instrument panel and the back of the pilot's head. Outside my steamy window, the landscape provides little variety: dirt, bush, and scattered *tukuls*, or thatched huts. Ninety minutes into the two-hour flight, the co-pilot, now out of his seat and standing before our group announces, "The airstrip where we are supposed to land has been shut down for repairs. What would you like us to do?"

Stuck in mid-air, we look at each other in disbelief. Offering a solution, Elijah, the Sudanese pastor speaks up. "I know of a small runway ninety minutes from Bor."

Heat rises from the provisional airstrip. We unload our luggage and equipment, grateful for our savvy guide who suggested the successful detour. Bidding us goodbye, the pilot adds, "You won't be able to fly out of here. This airstrip is not long enough for a loaded plane to take off."

* * *

After the ninety-minute shuttle to town, we arrive at our destination. Departing from Bor the next day, our Land Cruiser makes slow progress in an attempt to reach Malak village. Pastor Elijah explains the stigma prevalent among the Sudanese government toward lepers, "When they find out they have leprosy, they send them here and forget about them." Less than a year ago, pastors "Papa" Ron and Steve of World Outreach Mission discovered this isolated leper colony where individuals were living without medicine and adequate food.

Caught in the usual Sudanese traffic jam, our four-by-four slides past herds of longhorn cattle. The livestock, driven forward by tall Dinka herdsmen, weave through lorries trapped in mud.

Our vehicle leaves the road and enters the bush. As we begin to think we have lost our way, faint voices in the distance begin to grow louder. Women shouting ululations and young boys rhythmically beating handmade drums appear among the bushes and trees. These are the forgotten ones. They have come from their village to greet us: dancing on feet lacking toes and shaking tambourines with stubbed hands.

Spending the afternoon ministering to *us,* the lepers radiate peace amid severe persecution. What is their secret? On their first visit, Ron and Steve shared the gospel with them. They all placed their faith in Christ and are now filled with unspeakable joy and amazing grace.

Gathered in a circle to sing songs of praise together, I am touched by the miracle of this moment. Of all the villages, peoples, and needs in the entire world, our team has been led to this colony of isolated lepers to provide free medical care, dental treatment, medicine, food, and supplies. *God* has not forgotten them.

* * *

Leaving me behind after a week of fruitful outreach, the rest of the group splits up to fly out, making it possible for the plane to lift off the short runway. My road trip begins. Traveling in a two-ton lorry, Dante, my driver, his friend, and I leave for the World Outreach Mission compound in Morobo. Building a nest in a large metal container behind the front seat, I hope to get a nap during the seven-hour ride. Though the men insist I ride up front with them, Mama Kris gets her way and settles down on top of piles of clothing, a makeshift mattress padding the metal box.

After braving long sweaty hours on the road, enduring harassment at checkpoints, and enjoying rich conversations between naps, we arrive. A young guard armed with an AK-47 opens the gate to the mission property before switching out with the next twelve-hour watchman.

Staying in a small house alone, I am pampered by Benjamin and his wife who live a stone's throw away. Checking in on me, he brings steaming bowls of termite ball soup for breakfast to compliment my fresh roasted ground nuts, a staple during my African trips. Food is scarce. Still hungry and desiring something of substance, I forage through the pantry and find some non-fat, low-calorie Ry-Krisps and a mini-can of Diet Coke left by American guests.

A chaplain in the Sudanese army, Benjamin is my source of intel, providing vital information and security while I work. More than twenty years of war and terrorism have ravaged the infrastructure of Sudan. Hunger, fear, and death are realities of daily life. Facing these difficulties, the Sudanese people press on. Their fortitude amazes me.

Medical and dental care is often out of reach. A young mother who has just given birth tries to ride a bicycle to the nearest clinic and bleeds to death on the way. When emergency transportation is required, the mission's Land Cruiser is used, though not always with success. In the middle of the night, during a heavy storm, another mother is urgently transported to the nearest hospital three hours from Morobo for a C-section. She and the baby die en route.

* * *

When roads become impassable during the rainy season it's impossible to get where we want to go. Pastor Abraham shows up at the mission house and wants to help. He suggests trekking to the villages on his motorcycle.

Strapping my mobile dental clinic on the narrow seat, I take my place: sandwiched between Abraham and the monster suitcase. Navigating areas that defy passage for our mission vehicles, we spend a week holding clinics in the bush. On two occasions we are caught in torrential downpours. The motorcycle, a priceless gift from another ministry, doubles its value.

Two young children sit patiently in the shadows of the *tukul*: my open-air, thatched-roof clinic for the day.

"Hey kids, can you bring your mom or dad here? I can't work on your teeth unless a parent is with you." They leave, returning with their father. Happy to get their painful teeth removed and the balloons I give them, I suddenly remember Inaya.

Bit by a rabid dog, Inaya's father carried her to my clinic. Standing in front of me with his little girl in his arms, he was desperate. I cleaned her wound and explained I didn't have the medication to treat rabies, asking God for a miracle. Now, a year later, I have returned to her village. Reaching into my backpack, I pull out a picture of Inaya and her father. I brought it with me, hoping I might get information about her. Showing the children's father the photo, I ask, "Do you know this child?" He looks at the picture, then at me, and smiles, "That's me!"

I hadn't recognized him as the man in the picture.

"...and...Inaya?" I ask, not expecting a positive answer.

"She is fine. She is at home."

"Is there any chance I could see her?"

Minutes later Inaya rides up on her bicycle, a healthy little girl.

Each year I travel to different villages, giving people in new locations a chance to benefit from my services. Returning to Inaya's village and finding her is a miracle. God's grace is miraculous. Her healing is a miracle.

* * *

I have had the honor of working with some remarkable men and women of God. Abraham is one them: a man of unshakable faith with a riveting testimony. I learn his story one day when he complains of chest pain.

"What's the trouble?"

"I have pain in my chest and back from some old wounds."

"If you don't mind my asking, what kind of wounds?"

Raising his shirt, he shows me two scars from puncture wounds on his chest and two on his back. They are healed.

"Sometimes bands of scar tissue form after injuries heal. That could be what is causing your pain," I tell him.

Having spent the last several days together, I know he formerly worked as a government official. The Islamic leaders were seeking to kill him on account of his faith. One evening, while he was attending a wedding, his brother, staying at his house, was shot. Mistaking him for Abraham, the assassins killed the wrong man. Abraham was eventually captured, imprisoned in a camp, and tortured along with other believers in an attempt to get them to renounce their faith.

"If you want to do something to me, you can just kill me," a Christian policeman among the captives told them. They killed him.

Lowering his shirt, Abraham shares more details. "During my imprisonment, I was chained, brutally beaten, and tortured, all in an attempt to break me. The Lord gave me supernatural strength. When I was captured, I told Him, 'No matter what they do, dear Lord, don't let me deny You.' My stubbornness fueled their hatred. Failing to force me to renounce my faith, they drove meat hooks into my chest and back, then hung me from the rafters. I refused to renounce Christ. At that point, they were finished with me. A guard was ordered to take me and two other prisoners into the bush and kill us. We were blindfolded, marched outside, and forced to walk a long way. I was in terrible pain. Finally we stopped. Then I heard shots in the air coming from the guard's gun. He removed our blindfolds and told us to run, but I could barely walk. I was confused. We didn't know where we were going and ended up walking back into town, where it was not safe. After hiding, we escaped by crossing the border into Ethiopia and then Uganda. I was reunited with my family after three years. They thought I was dead; I thought they were dead. God has used all of this to strengthen my faith. I am not afraid of anything. But, I suffer from pain in these wounds."

Working with Abraham sheds new light on my understanding of God's grace, present in all our trials. Sharing the thoughts he had during his captivity, I realize his mind was made up long before any abuse took place. During the torture, unable to physically endure the pain, the Lord rendered him nearly unconscious, allowing him to endure it. His example of steadfast faith is one I will always treasure; one I hope to follow in times of testing.

Thank You for putting this man of God on my path, Lord.

* * *

While working in a nearby village, Benjamin and Dante swing by with Kazim, a fourteen-year-old boy. They're on their way to the hospital in Yei and ask me to redress his wound: a week-old snakebite on his foot. The witch doctor, claiming Kazim would die if taken to the hospital, kept the villagers and his parents from seeking medical care.

Unwrapping the bandage, I am saddened by what I see. Like an anatomy textbook, the gaping wound exposes bones, tendons, and ligaments. After applying a fresh dressing, I pray for God's intervention. When they arrive in Yei, a doctor is at the hospital, which is not always the case. He believes Kazim will live. He may be able to save his foot.

Witchcraft strongly influences the lives of those who practice it. Prevalent in this area, I am learning how strong those influences can be. Working with another Sudanese chaplain, Peter, at the army barracks in Yei, he explains the powers of evil behind the skills he previously used as a high witch doctor. His training began when he was seven years old. As an adult, he sacrificed two of his children before God turned his life around. Set free from the powers of darkness and death, Peter is now a man of faith.

* * *

Early mornings and late afternoons are the best time to walk on the compound. Next door to the mission house is the school. It has no windows or doors, but more striking is the absence of desks and chairs. The students, adult men in uniforms, sit on large rocks in the dirt, eager to learn. Attending school is considered a privilege. Invited to share a few words of encouragement with them, I tell them they are an encouragement to me.

Many schools are vacant. After months of working without wages, teachers leave. One dedicated villager tells me, "We want our children to go to school but we have no school. We have no supplies. We have no teachers. I am not paid but I am teaching them to read and write so they might have a future."

* * *

Running late on Sunday morning, I arrive at the thatched-roof mud church. Worshipers packing every inch of tight space are clapping, dancing in the red dirt, and rejoicing, their body heat adding to the humid environment. Pastor Simon encourages latecomers to enter, insisting, "Come in, come in. Don't sit down. We are all going to stand and sweat and praise the Lord." His exuberance is contagious.

After church, sitting at a tiny table in a mud hut, Simon and I visit. We are each served an eight-ounce glass of honey. Wondering what I am to do with it, I watch him. I have learned that taking time to observe before making a move can help me avoid a serious cultural faux pas.

Lifting his glass to his lips, he drinks half of the honey in one swallow. Sipping mine slowly, I watch him drink the rest of his in another gulp.

"Do you always drink a full glass of honey?" I ask him.

"If I drink a glass of honey in the morning. I don't have to eat for the rest of the day."

Gratitude, whether arising in exuberant praise or expressed over a glass of honey, abounds in this man of God.

* * *

In Kaya, I work with Saiesha, a Sudanese nurse. Comparing the abundance of Western cultures and our reliance on material resources with their lack of resources, she tells me, "We do what we can do, and, miraculously, God does the rest. His grace covers us."

"Please tell the church in the US of our needs," echoes over the miles as I travel. If only these precious people knew how much we need of what *they* have.

* * *

Finishing a hearty breakfast of two bowls of fried ants, I am ready for the day's work.

Injecting my patient with anesthetic, I peer over my glasses at a petite woman standing beside me, carefully watching my every move. Tihani is a traditional village worker here in Kaya. She has brought her one dental tool with her to my clinic. Observing me intently, I ask, "Would you like to do this one?" She smiles.

Reaching into a small, zippered clutch, she pulls out a thin piece of metal resembling a radio antenna with a tiny flattened spoon-shaped tip. After struggling to put on the unfamiliar gloves, protective glasses, and mask I hand her, she plunges the spoon into the patient's mouth. Within seconds, she pops one root out, and continues to dig frantically for the second, which is now buried under a pool of blood.

Accustomed to working "dry," or without anesthesia, she is naturally in a hurry. In my mind, a dozen terrified faces flash before me, patients who have come to me with painful abscessed roots resulting from failed attempts at a dry run.

"Tihani, I have a tool that can get the root out easily. Let's give it a try." She graciously accepts my offer. Selecting from an assortment of state-of-the-art instruments lying beside boxes of anesthesia and neatly stacked packages of gauze, I choose the best tool for this particular root. Suddenly my simple free clinic takes on an air of sophistication, abounding in advanced technology and supplies.

Lord, I am humbled by servants like Tihani and grateful for Your provision.

* * *

The next day, back in Morobo, truckloads of Ugandan soldiers barrel past my open-patio clinic. Surrounded by a crowd of villagers, eager to have a tooth pulled and seemingly oblivious to the heightened military activity, I sense trouble is brewing.

Another truckload of armed men clad in uniforms passes. Balancing on the frame of the flatbed, soldiers lean into the turn as they round the corner, leaving a trail of dust behind. Later, I am informed the Ugandan army has been deployed to this area of southern Sudan to search for Lord's Resistance Army (LRA) terrorists, led by Joseph Kony. Sighted within a nine-mile radius, they are responsible for raiding several huts and taking two Sudanese hostages.

The next morning, Dante, Benjamin—with his ever-present AK-47 propped against the cab door—and I take the lorry deep into the bush to Wudabi. Checking on a greenhouse crop of new coffee seedlings, I can't help but think this would be a good place for Kony's men to hide out.

Benjamin hangs his head out the window of the truck. "Is it secure?" he asks as Dante turns the lorry around in a clearing. "Secure" means those strange-looking armored trucks scoping the ground for land mines have gone before us and cleared the route for our heavy vehicle.

Heading back on the narrow dirt road, we brush against tall dense bushes. Wedged between the two men, I strike up a conversation with Dante about his faith. He believes the gospel but has never surrendered his life to Christ. Before getting any further, Benjamin orders, "Stop the truck." Taking his gun, he jumps down from the cab and approaches two soldiers standing in the middle of the road. They are wearing red berets.

"Kony's men wear red berets," Dante tells me as we wait.

Questioning them, Benjamin learns they are Sudanese soldiers scanning the road for LRA terrorists. We can continue. My mind starts calculating the odds.

Benjamin and I are saved. If we lose our life today on this road, we will be with the Lord for eternity. What about Dante?

With a greater sense of urgency, I silently pray Dante will seriously consider his need for salvation. I return to our conversation only to be interrupted by Benjamin's command, "Stop the truck."

Though I see nothing, Benjamin, like a game warden sighting a hidden lion in the tall grass, has spotted two suspicious men in the bush beside the road. Calling to the men in hiding, he has Dante slowly inch the truck forward. The men soon appear from within the thick overgrowth. After a brief interrogation, Benjamin feels confident of their innocence and we continue.

"Well, if you believe the gospel, what is keeping you from giving your life to Jesus Christ?" I ask Dante, not waiting for another encounter on the road.

"Nothing!" he says confidently.

Negotiating potholes and splashing through puddles, Dante maneuvers the lorry while praying to accept Jesus as His Lord and Savior. The unknown awaits us on the road ahead, but one thing *is* known: our eternal destinies are sealed in heaven.

Lord, could it be for such a time as this I am here?

* * *

Returning to the US, a culture beckoning me to seek security in circumstances and solutions in a tangible world, I am reminded of the lepers, Pastor Abraham, Pastor Simon, Tihani, Kazim, Saiesha, Dante, and the rest. None have been forgotten. Christ is healing, delivering, providing, and transforming lives today. Though overwhelming needs exist, I can depend on Him.

It is true, Saiesha. We do what we can do, and, miraculously, God does the rest. His grace covers us.

Mobile dental clinic in Sudan

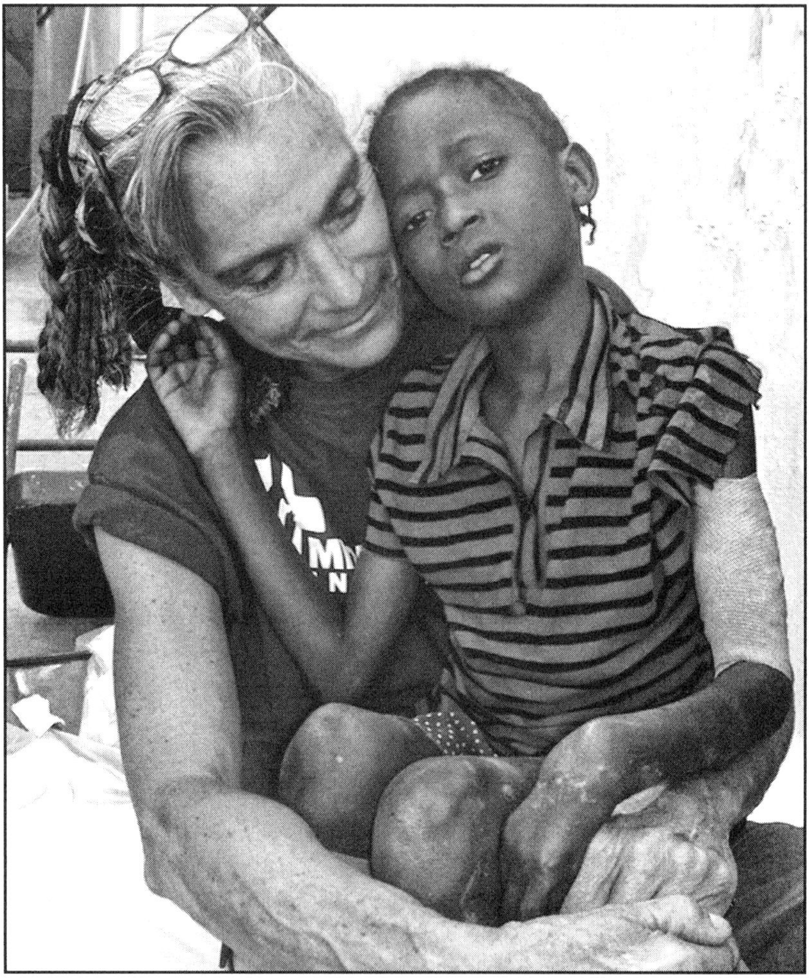

Haitian girl wounded in the earthquake

CHAPTER 14

Haiti: Bringing Baby

> Sing to God, sing praises to His name;
> Lift up a song for Him who rides through the deserts,
> Whose name is the LORD and exult before Him.
>
> Psalm 68:4

ON JANUARY 12, 2010, the headlines bear the grim news: the death toll is estimated to be more than three hundred thousand. Haiti has been devastated by another earthquake. Trying to pray, I can't focus. My thoughts will not leave Haiti. They have already taken me there.

Do You want me to go, Lord?

In a week, I am scheduled to fly to Thailand to join a medical team. Working with the same group each year, I have been looking forward to our time of ministry together. The earthquake has shaken my plans. At times like this, when I can't get persistent thoughts out of my head, I figure they must be important. Honoring commitments is also important. After twenty-four hours of mental turmoil, I give my availability for deployment. If I am called, I will consider it to be a sign I am to go.

"Can you leave this week and stay for a month? A small team of seven will be flying to Portland, Oregon, where the owner of a private jet will meet the group at his hanger. There are no commercial flights into Haiti at this time."

The answer is already clear. "Yes, I can go."

"One caveat, my passport is still at the Pakistan embassy. They are overdue in sending it back after my visa was denied. They know I need it for a trip scheduled for Thailand this week. I expect to receive it in the mail any day."

After a detailed briefing, I call Dr. Helen and explain why I will not be able to go to Thailand with her group. She understands the nature of disaster relief work and the spontaneity it requires. Her gracious response comforts me and helps confirm my decision. Forfeiting my plane tickets, I clear the calendar for Haiti.

Due to arrive a week after the quake, the assignment fits me perfectly: medical disaster relief in a developing Francophone nation. Packing my bags, I check the mailbox daily. No passport. Knowing the fabric of my faith is woven into my body of flesh, I rely on unseen conviction to quiet the squirming uneasiness I am feeling while waiting for a tangible result: an envelope containing my passport.

Departure day arrives. Still no passport. At this point, I am second-guessing my decision.

Did I hear You clearly?

Before the break of dawn, after hours of prayer, I come up with a crazy plan. Arriving at the post office minutes before 8 am, I stand outside, silently rehearsing my plea.

"Click…click," a key unlocks the door to my only hope.

"This is a strange request, but my mail carrier won't arrive at my house until late this afternoon. That will be too late."

Removing some boxes from the counter, shuffling some envelopes around, and unlocking a drawer, the lone clerk prepares to open her station. Peeking over the little window, I continue explaining my desperate situation to her. The adrenalin pumping through my veins is not making this any easier. I would like to give this woman some of it.

"I am supposed to fly to Haiti in a few hours to do disaster relief but I don't have my passport. It is supposed to be en route from the Pakistan embassy. Is there any chance you can check if there is mail to be delivered to my address today?"

She calmly looks up at me. Not knowing if my request is absurd or what she could be thinking, she turns around and disappears into the mailroom. My blood sinks to my toes. Hoping she has gone back to look for my passport and not for more supplies to stock her station, I wait. I pray. My color must be ghost white. I feel like I could pass out.

If You want me in Haiti, Lord...

The door swings on its hinges. Arm waving in the air, she has an envelope in her hand. "This looks like it could be a passport." I stand—and cry.

This is not my idea of how I want my faith to be put to the test, but these memory-making experiences solidify my beliefs. Relief washes over me.

* * *

Strapped to my back like a swaddled infant—Baby—my travel guitar is my companion on every trip.

But Haiti?

Wondering if it would be presumptuous to step off the jet with a guitar on my back, I am reluctant to bring it to this environment of unsurmountable loss and suffering. Only God knows what is best. After seeking His will, I make my decision: Baby is coming with me.

During the flight, so many emotions churn within. Never knowing what I will face, each disaster response does this to me. Anticipating the needs of the victims, the personal challenges I will face, and the adequacy of my knowledge and skills, it is easy to become overwhelmed thinking about the unknown path before me. Reminding myself it is not in *my* strength I go, I turn to the Lord and find peace. He has never failed in providing all I need to accomplish the work to which He calls me.

"Would you like to come up here and take a look?" Our pilot invites me to sit in the cockpit next to him as we cruise at forty-four thousand feet through the sunrise into Port-au-Prince. Below the sublime beauty of the new dawn is a mound of rubble becoming visible as we make our descent. The lack of building codes and a previously damaged infrastructure have exacerbated the devastation.

Touching down, our wheels squeal as they hit the tarmac. Rolling past huge US military cargo planes, helicopters, and trucks, we come to a standstill amidst the deafening engine roar. I am grateful to know our country has already responded and is on the ground.

With no commercial flights, tight restrictions govern all incoming aircraft. Our gracious escort, having donated his time, fuel, and private jet to fly us here, must leave.

"I won't be able to stay with you. They've given me twenty minutes to land, get you unloaded, and take off again," he apologizes and jumps back into the cockpit.

Throngs of people with their fractured limbs propped up on plastic chairs sit behind roped barriers while watching the airport's theatrical buzz of activity. Requiring medical treatment, they are hoping for a way of escape. My pockets fill quickly with paper scraps of scribbled names and phone numbers.

With our luggage and supplies rolling behind us, we find a recessed area behind the small terminal where we wait for our ride. The desperate mass presses in on us. Each request is a pressing need.

The space starts to feel uncomfortably tight. Our ride is nowhere in sight. A young Haitian with dreadlocks, carrying a guitar on his back, appears. Leaving my luggage with the group, I seek him out and ask if he wants to play a few tunes. Leading him a good distance from my team, the attention turns to us, away from the fresh American arrivals. My plan has worked.

We sing a spontaneous song in French. Soon, everyone is clapping.

"You are so beautiful! Yes…You are so beautiful! I want you to take me to America with you!" he smiles and winks.

"You are so kind! Oh yes, so kind! I am old enough to be your grandmother! Your grandmother! I am here to help your people: I can't leave! No, I can't leave!" I reply.

The melody is catchy. The lyrics have the crowd roaring with laughter. We ham it up and enjoy a sweet concert. A healing balm for gaping wounds. Even before leaving the airport in Port-au-Prince, I know bringing Baby was the right decision.

* * *

Mountains of sand and chunks of asphalt bury cars flattened by the weight. Multistoried buildings are sandwiched. Schools missing walls are filled with broken concrete slabs. Stacked on them are mounds of desks precariously balanced at all angles. Broken beams and rebar have prevented them from sliding further. Papers, books, and clothing litter the ground under which children have been unceremoniously laid to rest. Roads percolate with cracks and bumps that must be dodged to reach our remote clinics.

Unsung heroes wait to be treated for their injuries. Many of them were injured while trying to rescue their loved ones as the earth convulsed and their houses collapsed. Thousands are appealing to the US embassy for permission to leave to access medical care. The lines are endless.

Chantal, an eleven-year-old, is one of the fortunate ones. She is due to be evacuated to Florida by the US Air Force. Running out of her house as it began to shake, she was hit by a car and dragged underneath the muffler, sustaining serious facial burns. Still conscious, she realized her mother was trapped in their house. She ran back inside to save her.

The grounds outside the twenty-five-bed hospital are covered with post-op patients. A cement shell, the facility has no windows or doors. Laying in the dirt, traumatized victims with bandaged broken bodies prefer to endure the frequent aftershocks outside. Those inside won't remain. Running or crawling down the stairs and pulling out their IVs as they flee, they make their exit with each jerking planetary hiccough. Large cracks in the new concrete walls are measured daily by a team of engineers from Spain. The findings determine whether we can safely continue surgeries here. Still under construction, the earthquake has moved the date of its grand opening.

Working with an orthopedic surgeon, I provide traction as he reduces femur fractures. The less fortunate are now amputees—four have already been performed this week. Using a special device he has developed, he applies external fixation that does not require X-ray. The patients will be ambulatory within days.

In this bare-bones operating theater, I have a deep respect for both surgeon and anesthesiologist. It takes dedication to work in such a challenging setting. Anesthesia is titrated by keeping a watchful eye on the IV, calculating the drip rate of the medication, and adjusting it manually. No electricity. No suction. No monitors. No modern equipment. All of our observation skills are brought to the table.

The afternoon progresses. Humidity and heat trapped under my surgical scrubs are an effective sauna. Sweat pours from my face into my mask. My entire body is drenched. Finishing up with the day's surgeries, I find some relief in removing layers of protective gear. Sweat is my friend as air hits my skin, cooling my sleeveless arms.

Making rounds, I triage a young man with a large, soiled bandage on his face. Underneath the dressing is a dirty, infected wound. His nose is split in half. As I look at the horrific injury, he says with confidence, "I am a Christian. I know God allowed this to happen to me for His good purposes. He knows I can handle it."

John limps toward me, groaning in pain. He sits and reveals a crush injury to his great toe. Flies swarm around the swollen tissue. The pungent smell of bacterial infection fills the air. Gently cleansing the wound, I watch his facial expression, assuming he is fighting back every urge to scream. He surprises me. Ivory white teeth appear beneath a beaming smile as he begins to sing, "This is the day which the Lord has made. I will rejoice and be glad in it."

* * *

Moving to a guest house on the grounds of a seminary, we pass masses of homeless and injured people. Tarps are everywhere, serving as new homes. Water gushes out of broken pipes. Endless lines of people holding buckets and containers wait to collect the precious commodity and carry it back to their families. Signs read, "S.O.S. We need help here."

* * *

Morning greets me. My journal entry is short: "tremors: 3 am, 4:55 am, 5 am. big boom. try to get out locked door, 7:45 am, cont…stop counting."

Locked in the seminary bedroom to keep intruders from entering, I rethink my strategy. I can't get out during the frequent tremors. Armed forces have protected us at other locations. The 82nd Airborne Division of the US Air Force. Canadian soldiers. At first, it seemed like overkill until I realized safety precautions are necessary to enable us to work. The mobs are desperate.

Outside my room, the hungry, thirsty, irrational, sleepless thousands camp beneath the stars. On these grounds, without a security guard, my best attempt to protect myself is a locked door.

The seminary is in Bolosse, a suburb of Port-Au-Prince. A patchwork quilt of wall-to-wall blankets is draped over the rolling hilltop, each one staking out a squatter's claim to personal space. Two latrines serve the growing numbers. An estimated four thousand people are temporarily residing here. Food has been promised, but not yet delivered.

* * *

In the heat of the day, I start IVs on two severely dehydrated elderly women laying on the grass. Shade is scarce. The sun is scorching. Their blankets serve as bedcovers on the soft green mattress.

Hours pass quickly before the day comes to an end. There is no end to the needs. Laying on my bed, I close my eyes and welcome the night breeze. A soft melody drifts through the screened window. Soon a crescendo carries the tune to a thundering level.

Stepping outside to join in this celebration of life, my heart is filled with His presence. These praise gatherings are the result of an intentional effort made by the directors of the school to help the victims of the disaster keep a spiritual focus amid the chaos and despair. Twice a day, through a PA system, the displaced throng is led in worship. Tonight the stars form a brilliant veil over this multitude as they stand with hands extended to the God who has them covered.

Matters of life and death have always been at the forefront of my mind throughout my career. Intensive care. Emergency trauma. Disaster relief. Miraculous stories in life-threatening situations are beautiful reminders of His infinite grace.

One of the beauties of the healthcare profession is the privilege of entering into a close and private relationship with a perfect stranger in a matter of minutes. Baring body and heart, my patients come to seek a listening ear, someone to whom they can turn for compassion in their time of suffering. To become calloused, cynical, or hardened is not an option. Eye-rolling attitudes must give way to empathetic understanding: this is traumatic for him, even if it seems a small thing to me. Only God knows what he has been through.

Lord, let me feel their pain and cry with them, or get me out.

Caring for the sick and suffering, I am often the first to hear from their heart. In this place of honor, I stand on sacred ground.

* * *

In Baloose, a patient recounts his experience. "I was just relaxing on my couch in front of the TV when something told me in my head to get off the couch, get the family and go outside. I didn't understand where the thought came from, but it was strong. It wouldn't go away. Getting up, I got my wife and kids and took them outside. Then it came. As we stood there, the earth started shaking and the house collapsed into rubble before us. We would have all died if I didn't listen to that voice."

Thousands of others did not hear a voice. This is where I realize I cannot begin to know all the answers why. Trusting in His sovereignty over all creation allows me to leave the answers to Him. He alone has power over life and death. He gives and takes away.

* * *

Laogane is the epicenter of the quake. It is here we spend several days holding clinics on the grounds of a leper hospital. In the early mornings, before the clinic opens, large crowds sit patiently under tarps, hoping to be seen by a doctor. Arriving early is not a guarantee but it does increase the odds.

Seizing a perfect opportunity, I grab a broken cinderblock and sit and sing French worship choruses before a captive audience. Surprisingly, many are familiar with the songs and sing along. As music fills the air and we engage in conversations, I feel the atmosphere begin to change. It is lighter. Frowns are replaced by smiles. Faces don't look as weary. Body language is more relaxed. Sharing God's love, I leave the seeds of the gospel message with them and bid them goodbye. The clinic is opening. I must go, blessed that I brought my Baby to this place.

* * *

Hostility accompanies stress and despair. The environment is tense. A riot breaks out during one of our blanket distributions. The team is forced to pack up and leave. Each experience, embraced by hope, leaves a deposit in my memory bank. Good and bad, God is with me in all of them.

* * *

Exhaustion sets in as we pull into the compound. In the golden hour light, I see the children gathered outside. They're waiting for me. It's time for our daily ritual: the kiddo's after-hours jam session. They are not about to let me slide on my last night. Having barely gotten out of the car, they circle me in anticipation. Pulling out my guitar, we start to sing the worship songs we've rehearsed for a month. French?—I taught them. Creole?—They taught me.

"They be full of life honey!" Nanny's words echo in my mind.

Children always bless me. They bring joy and awaken the child inside. The Bible teaches that Jesus has a special place in His heart for kids. There are so many reasons I can see why.

"Quand l'esprit de Dieu habite en moi, je chante comme David," their little voices sing,

"When the spirit of God lives in me, I sing like David."

As the human magnet train shakes and jumps in dance formation around me, laughter billows out its chimney and stokes my soul with new energy. Revived, I bask in their presence, delight in their innocence, and pray for their future.

Haitian believer's lift their hands in praise in the rubble of their church

Villager making a bamboo dental table

CHAPTER 15

Liberia: Five Answers

"Not by might nor by power, but by My Spirit," says the LORD of hosts.

Zechariah 4:6

WIDE-EYED AND TERRIFIED, Cooper tells his wife, "Let the family know I am in critical condition."

Trying to reassure him, I am getting nowhere. He is frightened and not listening. His wife stands next to him with their baby tightly tucked under her arm. Both are crying. With sweat dripping from my glove, I adjust my headlamp in the afternoon heat and peer into Cooper's mouth to check the surgical site. For hours it has been oozing. A trickle of blood continues to flow despite my attempts to stop it. The socket doesn't want to clot. His strong thirty-three-year-old physique offers no clues as to why his body isn't responding in a normal way. In my work, I depend on the miracle of the clotting mechanism. Today it is not cooperating.

Packing up my dental supplies in the late afternoon, I ask around, "Where is the hospital?"

"You *are* the hospital!"

The answer does not comfort nor surprise me.

* * *

Liberia has been in a civil war for fourteen years. During the peak of a national transition, I make trips here in 2004 and 2005. Soldiers are being paid to lay down arms and participate in debriefing programs. Thousands of United Nations (UN) peacekeeping troops, the largest presence in the world, maintain multiple checkpoints on almost every road. Armed guards, tanks, camouflage draping, sandbags, and bullet-ridden bridges decorate the tropical terrain. Miles and miles of rubber tree plantations dot the landscape. Each trunk bears a small tin strapped to its bark which collects the valuable sap dripping from the wounded tree: reminders of the bloodshed that has taken place in their midst.

Monrovia, the capital, once a thriving tourist destination with a pristine waterfront, has lost its splendor. Mold covers the hollow shells of once-elegant buildings. These serve as makeshift homes for the displaced families struggling to put their lives back together. I try to imagine what the thriving city once looked like before its glory turned to rubble and its long stretch of coastline became a field of human waste. The fresh sea air no longer leaves its fragrance over the sand. Without running water and sanitation, the beach has become an open public latrine, with squatters conversing with one other as they unashamedly pollute the shores.

Dental extractions are a welcome service. I am told there are very few dental workers left in the country. After planning a schedule, I hold several clinics in the capital, then focus on the villages and Internally Displaced Person (IDP) camps in the rural areas. Today's village clinic has gone well until now. Until Cooper.

* * *

Our large guesthouse in the countryside has more rooms than the three of us need. Jerome, my Liberian assistant; Olivia, a Canadian dental technician, and I are very comfortable.

"Cooper, I'd like for you to come to my guesthouse where I can watch you until this bleeding stops." Without hesitation, he agrees. We swing by the village pharmacy to pick up some IV supplies and medications on the way to the provisional hospital.

Knowing I can watch Cooper and keep a vigil throughout the night is reassuring. His sad eyes tug at my heart as I repeatedly explain to him why he must rest, not eat or drink, and keep the IV in his arm. Having done everything possible to stop the post-op bleeding, I wait.

As morning dawns, exhaustion sets in. Neither of us has slept. Perhaps I wouldn't feel so defeated if I hadn't had an equally difficult time with Dennis just days before.

* * *

Happily chomping down on a large piece of gauze wedged in his mouth, Dennis leaves the clinic for home with post-op instructions to bite the dressing for an hour, "If the bleeding starts again, apply pressure and bite!"

I emphasize, "Do *not* spit! Spitting can increase pressure, break the clot, and cause more bleeding, which can be dangerous."

Dennis nods his head.

The next day, leaving the guesthouse in the early morning hours, I set out on the dirt road. My quiet time is interrupted when a rundown taxi, churning up a mound of dust, screeches to a halt next to me. Sticking his head out the back window, a frantic family member insists, "You must come to the house. Dennis has been bleeding all night. He has a bucket of blood at the side of his bed. He is unconscious."

Years of emergency trauma experience combined with respect for the African charm of storytelling help appease any panic trying to assault me. Crowding into the taxi with the extended family, the ambulance flies down the road to the house. Dennis is laying on his bed, interrupting his calm stillness every minute or two to turn and spit into the five-gallon bucket at his bedside.

"He's been doing this all night," his loved ones inform me.

Great! Clearly, he has forgotten what I told him.

He is not hemorrhaging. He is not unconscious. With some minor intervention and education, and a time-out from spitting, Dennis is as good as new.

* * *

Today it is Cooper.

The sleepless night has worn me down and filled me up with frustration and discouragement. Morning light arrives on the wave of hot humid air blowing through the open window. Jerome and Olivia have both left the guesthouse for the day. Cooper has finally drifted off to sleep.

I ask God to speak to me, turning the pages of my Bible to Zechariah 4:6, "Not by might, nor by power, but by My Spirit, says the LORD of hosts."

What are You trying to tell me, Lord? Pouring over these words, I can't understand their significance in my dilemma. I decide to fast and wait for an answer.

Plans for tomorrow are weighing heavy on my heart. The refugees are expecting me. The team is depending on me. In light of today's experience, it is the last place I want to go. Barclay is a camp of roughly 3,000 residents. I predict there will be far too many people expecting treatment. Sending word ahead, I ask the person in charge to make a list of those needing extractions, hoping I will have the courage to not back out.

Right now I don't want to look at another tooth, I whine, directing my words toward El Shama, the God who hears. There is an unusual silence that follows.

I don't hear anything.

The day drags on. Hours alone with Cooper pass slowly. Jerome returns in the late afternoon. It feels like I have been with Cooper for an eternity.

"He is stable," I tell Jerome. "I am going to go on a walk and will stop by the pharmacy to get some more medicine."

Our remote compound is an hour's trek to and from town. Needing a break, I want to clear my thoughts and pray. A walk will do me good.

Well into the journey, negative self-talk persists in dominating the silent conversation: *I'm responsible for Cooper's suffering. I feel like a failure. I want to quit. I don't like it when things don't go well. I don't want to go to the camp tomorrow.*

God hears me. I know He does. I hear nothing.

My arrival is announced by a small bell attached to the door. Christian, the pharmacist, places the supplies I request on the counter. Paying the bill, I try to smile and show him kindness. I am not having a good day.

"By the way, thank you so much for helping my people." He startles me. Like the little bell, he gets my attention. "There are no Liberian dental workers here to help the people. They suffer so much. The people wouldn't have the money to pay if there were. But you don't charge them anything. Thank you for coming."

Offering a valued service free of charge gets noticed. Word gets out. Before I know it, everyone knows my name. Thinking of dental care as a key, it lends credibility to the message of love I want to convey to the people. Here in Liberia, this care is appreciated more than I realize.

The work can be intense and challenging. Liberian teeth are some of the strongest on the planet. Anchored in dense bone, as though super-glued in place, they weren't created to be pulled out. Some cases have taken over an hour from start to finish, leaving both me and the patient exhausted.

* * *

I'm reminded of a lady I saw earlier this week. She comes in at the end of the day to have her tooth pulled. With fifteen minutes left to finish and pack up, I tell her, "I'm sorry. I won't be able to see you. I have to leave in fifteen minutes. There is no way of knowing how long your case will take."

My assistant twists my arm, convincing me she should be my last patient. Reluctantly, I agree.

Gripped with fear, the woman almost leaves before I have a chance to examine her. Praying the Lord would allow the extraction to go smoothly,

I have her lay down, and anesthetize the bombed-out wisdom tooth, a term I use for teeth that have been destroyed, leaving only roots intact.

Fortunately, I extract it easily, thanking God for answering my prayer. After sitting up, she bows her head in silence, shaking it back and forth in disbelief.

"For two years, I had pain every time I ate."

Tears roll down her cheeks and begin to roll down mine.

"If you came all the way from America to do this work here because of the love of Jesus, I, too, want to have a personal relationship with Him."

* * *

Ringing again, the little bell on the door draws my attention back to the pharmacist as another customer enters the store.

"You have no idea what your kind words mean to me, Christian. Thank you."

Crossing the street, I run into Lilly, a Liberian woman who has been assisting me in the clinic all week. She is bubbling over.

"My heart is so full of joy and praise. I have always been shy but now I am bold and want to tell everyone the gospel. I want to teach the children how to brush 'up and down, round and round' so they can have healthy teeth. Oh, thank you so much for coming!"

Marveling at the impact the short time we have been working together has had on Lilly's life, I continue my journey home. My steps feel a little lighter.

Only a few minutes pass before a perfect stranger walking toward me on the road stops to talk. With a huge smile, she introduces herself.

"I am the midwife here in town." Pouring out her heart, as though I were her best friend, she shares, "It is so hard. My work, I mean. Sometimes my patients have bleeding complications and I have to take them to the city. I have nothing. But they get better. Thank you for what you are doing for my people!" The bombardment of gratitude and encouragement continues.

* * *

Parked at the side of the road ahead, I see a familiar name painted across the trunk of the old car. It's our team's taxi. Tossing a bucket of water over his prized vehicle, lovingly named "Fat Boy 2," Dirk, our driver announces with a huge grin, "I'm getting Fat Boy cleaned up for the refugee camp tomorrow!" Though I'm not sharing his enthusiasm, I manage a sheepish smile and continue walking.

My head starts spinning with calculations, an inner voice asking, *"How many thousands of extractions have you done in the past ten years? How many serious complications have you had?"*

But two this week, Lord! I begin to argue.

Do I detect a little pride in your attitude? Don't you realize that you will have complications? It is inevitable. Whose power are you relying on anyway, Kris? Am I not the One who heals? Can you trust Me for Cooper? Can you trust Me for the refugee camp?

My extended walk comes to an end as I reach the steps of the guesthouse. At the same time, a large vehicle pulls into the driveway. Behind the wheel is a lanky man. Graciously, he has given Olivia a ride home. Opening the door, he gets out and greets me.

After introducing himself, the German physician sizes me up, then confides, "Olivia informs me you have had a difficult case. I can tell you are not made of sugar. Nor am I. But these tough cases still get to us. Our work is not easy. We have no backup. The risks are high. Just this week I lost a two-week-old infant. It was very hard. Cooper will be fine!"

This doctor has made a pretty accurate assessment of me. Considering the truth of his tender words, I am hit with the realization of what has just happened during my journey to town and back. I finally make a connection.

Not by might nor by power but by My spirit, says the Lord of hosts.

The German doctor is right: I am not made of sugar. Self-reliance and toughness can get the best of me. God's Word is telling me: it is only by His Spirit that I can do anything at all. Whether the case goes well or not, He is *always* the Healer.

Cooper's bleeding stops. He is thrilled to eat after I remove his IV. Grateful to be relieved of his toothache, he seems to forget the past twenty-four hours on his deathbed in the private hospital. On our way to the refugee camp, we give him a ride to his village in Dirk's sparkling-clean Fat Boy 2. I anticipate another challenging day ahead.

I have no idea what is in store. Please help me trust You.

* * *

Thirty minutes outside the city, we turn off the main road into Barclay, one of the many IDP camps. Thatched huts reinforced with plastic form an endless maze on the sloped clearing. There is no running water. A half dozen pit latrines serve thousands. I have arrived with a small group of Liberian believers.

As we get out of Fat Boy 2, a group of women starts chanting. They are among the huge crowd of people who have been waiting for our arrival. I wonder if this is the beginning of what could be a major riot. After greeting the people, I'm eager to get started.

"Can I see the person in charge? Yesterday, I requested for someone to make a list of patients needing extractions."

A man holding a piece of paper pushes his way through the crowd. Neatly numbered on both sides of the paper titled, "People Who Have Toothaches" are ninety-four names.

Recognizing my responsibility for the obvious breakdown in communication, I realize I failed to mention I would not be able to see more than thirty patients. The list man will have to make adjustments.

"By the way, where will I be working?"

He points to a ten-by-ten-foot bamboo hut.

"Will that work?"

Standing inside on the uneven mounds of dirt, I tell myself, *This will never work!* There are no tables. No chairs. The ground has the topography of an egg crate.

Readjusting my thinking, I tell myself, *This will have to work!*

"What do you need?"

"Well, first I will need a table for my patients."

My interior decorators insist on my telling them the exact height, length, and width of the table I need. I use my arms as yardsticks. Curious as to what they will do with the information, I watch.

Before I can rethink the impossibility of all this, two men appear with shovels. They begin to level the uneven dirt inside the hut. Two other men bring long thick bamboo stalks from the jungle, chopping them lengthwise, while the levelers dig four postholes, perfectly meeting my specifications. I watch their incredible work of art and creativity as a sturdy bamboo bed is woven together with reeds. The inside of this mini clinic is suddenly graced by a custom-built exam table which is securely anchored to the ground. I have to admit, it is one of the best I have ever worked on.

Rich aromas from burning wood and cooking pots fill my mask while I pass the daylight hours working on each grateful patient. Dozens of curious eyes peer between the bamboo slats into my open-air operating room. With their fingers probing their mouths, as if to be searching for a bad tooth, those on the outside are entertained by the action-packed drama in my little hut.

Stepping out of the bamboo clinic to stretch, I am greeted with warm words of welcome and smiles. "Thank you for coming to help us." "Thank you *so* much. We are *so* glad you are here."

The sunset is stealing my time. After completing twenty-five cases I must stop. I look out at a sea of smiling faces: those who weren't fortunate enough to be relieved of years of suffering today. Their toothaches will persist. Yet, they are thankful I came. There is not a word of complaint.

Not by my strength or my power, but by His spirit, do I live. This is the reality He has reinforced through Cooper. Through Dennis. This is the lesson I have experienced at Barclay camp today. This is the truth I am beginning to understand on a deeper level as I leave Liberia. A pharmacist, an assistant, a midwife, a taxi driver, a German doctor: messengers of encouragement delivering a response to my prayer in a timely way. He hears and answers.

Dirk and his taxi—Fat Boy 2—ready for the Liberian refugee camp

Our Tanzanian porters carry our supplies on Kilimanjaro

Chapter 16

Tanzania: The Summit Experience

"Come let us go up to the mountain of the Lord,
To the temple of the God of Jacob.
He will teach us his ways,
so that we may walk in his paths."

Isaiah 2:3 NIV

"There is no such thing as bad weather, only unsuitable clothing." —Alfred Wainwright, *Coast to Coast*

How true. I can find gear for any season. Whether I am facing pounding rain, howling wind, scorching sun, or flurries of snow, my daily prayer walk is a priority. A lifelong habit, this time has become sacred, a time I love and enjoy. Recalibrating my spirit and uplifting my soul, the Lord is ready to meet me, no appointments necessary. Each day, pushing myself past any reluctance to go, I open the door and set out.

If I am in a country or environment where it isn't advisable to venture off too far, I have learned (the hard way) to be creative: pacing guest house corridors or walking in circles around my tent compound. One way or another, I can spend an hour in prayer while benefiting from physical exercise and fresh air. During this time, my thoughts are directed toward Him. We talk. The Creator behind the creation is my guide, teaching me of Himself in these daily classroom lessons, correcting my errors, and growing me up in my relationship with Him.

Rounding the corner and heading up the steep hill toward the World Outreach Mission Foundation (WOMF) guest house in Seguku, Uganda, I return from my walk. Mama Shirley is busy preparing a delicious breakfast in the kitchen. She and Papa Ron are the founders of this thriving mission. Their dedication and love for the Ugandan people stretch across decades. Working in partnership over the years, I have grown to deeply love and respect them.

Mama Shirley looks up from a huge mound of dough, resting her floured hands on top of it, and insists in her sweet convincing manner, "You need to get in touch with Tanya. She is putting together a fundraising team for a group of children's homes we are building here in Soroti. You like to hike. You should talk to her. She doesn't live too far from you in Washington state."

"What are they planning?" I ask her, my curiosity perked. I am flattered she thinks I qualify as a hiker fit for a team.

"Their goal is to summit Mount Kilimanjaro in Tanzania," she says matter-of-factly.

I get a good laugh, then regain my composure, "That sounds like a serious hike, Mama Shirley. I just walk every day!"

She begins to knead the mountain in front of her and replies, "You should get in touch with Tanya."

As impossible as this suggestion seems, I can't put the idea out of my mind. I do love to hike but I have never done anything on this scale. Kilimanjaro? Even the name is mysteriously intriguing. Curiosity gets the best of me. I give Tanya a call.

An avid mountaineer, Tanya is full of enthusiasm. Hiking Kilimanjaro has been a lifelong dream of hers. Trekking is her passion. Christ is her Lord. Meeting the needs of impoverished children in Uganda by doing this fundraiser is a perfect fit for her.

Listening to the excitement in Tanya's voice, I can't help but share her enthusiasm, "Each team member is required to pay their way for the hike, covering the cost of our guides, porters, food, tents, and supplies. I chose a reputable company committed to safety, which bumps up the cost of the trip but is worth it. The excursion will take ten days. We will have meetings at my house over the course of the next year to pray for the trip. We'll get to know each other and fine-tune the plans during that time. I'll schedule a couple of practice hikes in Washington so we can get an idea of how we're doing. I would love for you to come. You should pray about it."

There is a difference between seeking exotic adventure and doing God's will. Sometimes both ambitions join hands. At other times, an " I am going to do this because I want to!" stubbornness prevails. Prayer is my way of discerning the difference.

Am I capable of hiking a mountain of this magnitude? I can try. Challenges attract me. Confident I can raise a sizable amount of support through pledges, I am convinced it is a wonderful cause. But paying for my expenses? In my mind, the cost of the trip is an obstacle. Most every other detail seems to fall in place. Grappling with this hurdle, I ask God to show me clearly if it is His will for me to go and how.

Relying on missionary support for my income, I would never consider appropriating those donations to pay for my expedition expenses. But, what if someone wants to sponsor me for this trip? This is my fleece, my open or closed-door request before God.

"Yes! Of course, we would love to sponsor you! Consider it done!" says the first couple I ask. My answer is loud and clear.

Our team of eight meets and plans for a year: praying for the opportunity to witness Christ's love to everyone He puts on our path. More than a hike and a fundraiser, this is an opportunity to share the gospel with everyone we encounter along the way.

Collecting pledges from friends and family for the number of feet I will travel, I realize I am not alone in this endeavor. Each dollar pledged is given by another member of the team, the non-hiker, who is vitally part of the whole. As I climb, there are those at home who will stand behind me and push me forward through their faithful prayers. The generosity and support I receive are astounding, an incentive to make it to the top. Meeting together to pray and going on practice hikes while raising support, the year passes quickly.

* * *

Arriving outside the guesthouse in Moshi, Tanzania, we are greeted by a group of European tourists sipping mugs of beer while relaxing in the sun at outdoor tables. They've just completed the hike. We're the new crop of hikers, the newbies. One climber nonchalantly describes his conquest, "Everest was a tough one. My first attempt failed and I had to return to base camp. I went back last year and made it to the top."

Nice people, they are admittedly outside of my league. I begin to feel intimidated.

Conversations abound under the shadow of the enormous, snow-covered Kilimanjaro. A hidden gulp slides down the back of my throat as I smile in response to one of the alpinist's questions, "Oh, you're *just doing* Kilimanjaro?"

In the twilight, the eight of us gather on the grass. Replacing the sun's rays, soft moonlight enhances the monstrous mountain looming before us. Leading the team in worship, I am reminded of His strength, which is constantly available to me. Exhausted, exhilarated, nervous, and willing, my mountainous emotions are over the top. Tomorrow we will begin our first of ten days on the trail.

As we finish worship and prayer, Caleb pipes up, "Kris, the Lord is going to give you a song tomorrow. You are going to sing it in Swahili."

Right, Caleb. I suppose I will write a novel before going to bed tonight. Packing up my guitar, I head to my room. My heavy head hits the pillow and I slip into a deep sleep.

Light is beginning to dawn on a new day as I quietly slip outside, taking care not to awaken my roommate. The mountain is the first thing I see; a reminder of the challenge before me. Truly breathtaking and absolutely huge, I pause and reflect on its beauty. This majestic environment ushers me into the presence of the Creator who is behind it.

Praying as I walk, a simple melody enters my mind, playing over and over like a loop. Lacing itself around my prayers, I am unable to shake it.

This has never happened before. Melodies often enter my head while I pray, but leave quickly after a short visit. This morning's melody is different: it sticks.

Checking out at the reception desk, I quickly grab a pen and scrap of paper to jot down the lyrics now pouring into my mind:

I am walking to the mountain of God
It will take the rest of my life
The Father sent His Son
His name is Jesus Christ
To take me to the mountain of God

Allelu…alleluja, Allelu…alleluja
The Father sent His Son
His name is Jesus Christ
To take me to the mountain of God

We are walking to the mountain of God
It will take the rest of our lives
The Father sent His Son
His name is Jesus Christ
To take us to the mountain of God

Allelu…alleluja, Allelu…alleluja
The Father sent His Son
His name is Jesus Christ
To take us to the mountain of God

A gift from God, this song has dropped out of heaven. It came so easily: the words, the tune, the rhythm, and the chords. Simple, with an African beat, it describes the physical mountain I will attempt to climb in His strength and the eternal mountain that is ours as a result of Christ's victory. In the years to come, God uses this song in miraculous ways to minister throughout East Africa to native Swahili speakers.

* * *

Forty-eight porters join our team of eight to carry supplies. We are responsible for our daypacks. Several will hike ahead of the team in the afternoons to set up camp, prepare our meals, and pitch our tents before we drag our weary bodies over the threshold of each day's destination. It is soon apparent the extra money spent with this company was well worth it. We pass other teams eating sandwiches for dinner, sitting in the frigid air on picnic benches set up on the side of the trail. Our team receives the royal treatment: hot beverages and popcorn are served as appetizers while we wait in a large cozy dining tent for a delicious hot evening meal to be served. At the end of each challenging day, I don't mind glamping.

Altitude sickness is not a respecter of persons. Taking time to acclimate to the altitude by ascending slowly can be advantageous. Climbers attempting to reach the top in a hurry put themselves at a disadvantage. Passing hikers having to abort their trek as I ascend makes me grateful for the extra days my body has to adjust. Every day, with the popcorn tent as my goal, I shoot for a mini victory.

* * *

Tori, our leader and senior guide on the mountain, has made three hundred and one ascents before ours. Gentle and soft-spoken, he is a wealth of information. Trained as a high-altitude first responder and an expert on the fauna and flora we pass, he cares for our team as if we were his first.

Volunteering to carry my guitar, Tori willingly translates "Mountain of God" into Swahili, his native tongue. Language has always fascinated me. Swahili is a Bantu language. Compared to others, the basic phrases are simple and pronunciation is easy. Studying my index cards as we climb, I practice all the phrases I have learned, entertaining the porters with my efforts. They call me "Mama Swahili."

Full of energy, these hard-working men bring such joy to our experience. At the end of a day's hike, lining up on the edge of the mountain to greet us, they join in song. Dancing and clapping to a syncopated rhythm, their harmonious voices belt out a chorus as their bright smiles greet us, "Well done! You made it! Well done."

Hours spent on the trail are filled with rich conversation. Forging deep friendships, we openly share our Christian faith with the porters. The Good News *is* Good News to them. Hungry and thirsty for the truth, they pour over copies of *The Four Spiritual Laws* in Swahili, which we have brought. Our personal testimonies captivate them and they begin opening up to us. Listening to their struggles, we spontaneously pray for their needs. One porter asks, "Why is it that over the years so many Christians from Europe, Canada, and America have come to climb the mountain but have never shared the gospel with us? They said they were Christians but they never told us what you are telling us."

I don't have an answer for him. The spiritual soil of the foothills and slopes of Kilimanjaro are ripe for harvest. One by one, the porters express a desire to surrender their lives to Christ. On his three-hundred-and-second ascent, Tori takes his Savior's hand to guide *him* to the mountain of God.

* * *

Brett is at it again. Having finished breakfast, the rest of the team prepares to set out on the trail while he gathers an attentive group of porters around him. Listening as he shares his testimony, the group is visibly touched by his riveting story. His passion for Christ and his physical determination are inspiring. Years ago, critical injuries from a motorcycle accident left him with a significant limp. Through suffering, he has experienced the depth of Christ's love. While pushing past his disabilities, Brett repeats jokingly, "A piece of cake!" as we struggle up the difficult passages on the trail.

On fire for the Lord, Brett's gift is evangelism. He engages almost every person he meets in a conversation about their eternal destiny. This morning is no exception. After hearing Brett's story, the porters express a sincere desire to follow Jesus. Adjusting his backpack, now ready to hit the trail, Brett smiles, "A piece of cake!"

* * *

After several hours of hiking, the sun reaches mid-sky. We stop for a water break.

"I have a headache," Tanya tells me.

I am already unsettled about her respiratory symptoms, having slept in her tent last night to monitor her condition. She was starting to cough and is coughing again.

"You sound like your lungs are congested. I am concerned," I tell her.

Knowing the symptoms of altitude sickness, I realize she may not be thinking clearly if her oxygen level has dropped. Tori checks her vital signs and places an oximeter on her finger.

"Your oxygen level is seriously low. I am afraid you need to be evacuated," he tells her.

Accepting his decision, she graciously allows the porters to cover and lift her into a flat metal basket. Used as a stretcher, it is suspended by a single bicycle wheel with a spring serving as a shock absorber. Porters on each corner of the makeshift ambulance escort her to a lower altitude, holding the basket tightly while running down the mountain over the steep rocky terrain.

When we join her a few days later, Tanya describes her adventure, "The ride was terrifying but once I got to the lower elevation, I immediately felt better."

God allows Tanya to achieve her dream of summiting Kilimanjaro two years later.

* * *

Our last day, an eleven-hour ascent into thin air, arrives. I awaken to two Nalgene bottles forming bumps at the bottom of my sleeping bag. Filled with hot water to warm me through the night, they are now cold. Every move is a tremendous effort. Breathing is labored, even at rest. My knee is sore; it has been bothering me for days. *Will I make it?* Tying my boots, I inhale slowly and wrestle to open the frozen tent zipper.

Through the open flap I see Reagan struggling to walk. Wondering if she realizes how poorly she is doing, I can't imagine her tackling the mountain today. Gratefully, she does not have to be told. She has already made the difficult decision.

"Hey guys, I can't join you for the summit. I have reached my limit. I'm going to stay back."

Like the rest of us, she has pushed herself to the edge. This morning, she hit the wall. Though her heart remains committed, her body is finished. Amazed at her humility, saddened to leave her behind, we all know it could have been one of us. Graciously accepting her limitations, she assures the six of us she will be praying as we say our goodbyes and set out for the peak. Twelve porters stay behind in camp with Reagan.

* * *

At this altitude, the dark slate-like stone and gravel form a stark contrast to the plush vegetation we saw on the lower slopes. Crossing through five climate zones, we have passed through farmland, rainforest, heather, moorland, and alpine regions to reach this arctic desolation. Environmental diversity is not lacking on this mountain.

Brown earth and volcanic rock form an uneven surface for my boots. Our Swahili mantra "pole pole" keeps me moving "slowly" as I fight exhaustion and refuse to stop. Eleven hours since leaving camp this morning, it is now late afternoon. Having required every ounce of mental and physical stamina within, the steep ascent is behind me.

Placing one leg forward on a ledge, I take a big step. Using every ounce of muscle strength I have left, I hoist my body over the top, reaching the summit of Kilimanjaro. What my eyes behold is beyond belief, *Lord, this is like putting one foot in heaven.*

A still small voice whispers, *No, Kris, it is not even close.*

Standing in awe beneath the vast blue heavens, swirls of transparent cloud vapor move over the snow-covered peak toward me. Lightly skimming the glistening snowfield below, they disappear. An amphitheater of aquamarine glaciers sparkles in the sunlight, hues of blues and greens giving depth and dimension to the enormous icicle formations cascading from their surface. Falling to my knees and raising my arms, I worship the Creator of this silent wonderland beyond human description and comprehension. Lingering on top, I try to take it all in, capturing the images in my mind, and storing them in my memories.

Convincing Tori to spend the night in the crater of the volcano is not easy. Rather than making the descent in the morning, he wants us to descend to a lower elevation before dark for our comfort. Our persistence wins over his reasoning and we set up camp in the massive crater. My evening is cut short by exhaustion and a headache. This experience of a lifetime is well worth these minor inconveniences. Saying a prayer for the two that weren't able to be here with us, I close my eyes to this incredible dream.

Days later, we reunite with Reagan, who is excited to tell us about her own summit experience.

"After you left camp, I asked God, 'What is it You have for me here if it wasn't to summit?' The porters had eaten breakfast and were settling in for the morning. One of them came to me with a Bible in his hand, pleading, 'Teach us, Mama.' They placed twelve rocks in a circle. With a captive audience surrounding me, I taught them from the Bible, answering their questions all morning long. Who would have guessed that God had prepared them for this moment? When I finished, I asked if anyone wanted to give his life to Jesus. All twelve of them raised their hands."

Reaching the summit of Kilimanjaro, Tanzania

Ayana and I—jumping on her bedspring trampoline in Kazakhstan

Chapter 17

Kazakhstan: Attacked

> Let us not lose heart in doing good, for in due time we will reap if we do not grow weary.
>
> Galatians 6:9

LIKE A POWERFUL wind with the force of steel, the strength of the blast from behind sends me lurching forward. With umbrella and glasses flying in opposite directions, I hit the ground, landing face down. Struggling to stand, I turn in the dimly lit mist to look into a pair of glaring eyes filled with rage and hatred.

Backed by a large muscular physique, his fist delivers another blow. I am down, my heavy boots and puffy thick vest protecting my body from the rough surface of the sidewalk. Screaming at the top of my lungs, my best attempts to protect myself are futile. My assailant is young, strong, and determined to do me in. In the distance, between strikes, I notice another man heading in our direction. Instinctively, I know he is coming to help my predator devour his prey.

The dimly lit street around me is vacant, surrounded by grey multi-story tenement buildings filled with residents completing their night's sleep. I am hoping someone will be aroused by my screams and come to my rescue. My hopes are not fulfilled. If there *are* people aware of my plight, they are in the shadows, behind the curtains, a safe place to watch and avoid involvement.

Another strike and I am on the ground again, scrambling to my feet only to receive the next blow.

A taxi passes by, its tires splashing through the rain-drenched pavement, leaving no trace of sound as it disappears in the darkness.

As soon as I am up, another blow has me down. The accomplice is approaching.

Lord, I can't fight back. I have nothing left. I think I am on my way to Heaven this morning. Thank You for the peace I feel. I have no fear. I am ready. This man doesn't know You died for him. I must tell him before I go. Maybe he will remember my words.

Teetering, I get up, ready to receive the next hit. Looking into his eyes I scream, "Jesus loves you."

Able to right myself for the last time, I stare at him as his friend approaches. "Jesus loves you," I scream again.

Immediately, his arm is down. His eyes have changed. Rage and hatred have been replaced by fear.

"Money!" he demands frantically, visibly unraveled.

Shaking my head to let him know I have no money for him, he rips my watch from my wrist and turns. Bolting from the scene, he and his friend disappear around the corner of the next block.

Stunned, I stand in the rain; they are gone and I am alive. After composing myself, I find my glasses, pick up my umbrella, and determine to walk back to the hotel. It is still early. I know Dr. Bill and Peggy won't be up for another hour. We plan to go to breakfast before catching our flight to Semipalatinsk to join our host.

Lord, thank You for saving my life. What do I do now? Please give me wisdom.

Pain grips every cell of my body. Miraculously, my face is spared of injury except for a cut below my ear. Most of the trauma is blunt: powerful blows delivered to my core. My cold weather gear cushioned me and protected my frame to some degree. As I slowly walk back, I consider my mistakes.

Though the center of the modern city of Almaty, Kazakhstan is well-illuminated by street lights in the early morning hours, I managed to get caught up in my prayers, not realizing I had entered a poorly lit residential area. Wearing a bright yellow vest and deflecting raindrops with my huge black and white golf umbrella, I was a sitting duck for my assailant, who came without warning from behind. Anti-American sentiments are stacked up against foreigners in this post-Soviet nation. The bottom line—I set myself up as a perfect target for crime.

On the edge of my bed, I start peeling my clothing off to assess my wounds.

Lord, this is our first time in Kazakhstan and the first day of a three-week trip. What good would it do to tell Bill and Peggy about this? Nothing can be done. It is no use to make a police report. I think I can deal with my injuries. I want to stay and carry on as planned. Help me weigh my motives regarding my decision.

I can't come up with any reason to tell my friends. I feel it would ruin our trip. The visible injuries, primarily to my right shoulder, arm, hip, and leg, are covered. My hair can be pulled over the cut on my ear. I decide to keep this to myself unless specifically asked.

Years later, when required to have hip replacement surgery due to injuries suspected to be related to the attack, I feel led to call Bill. My purpose: to ask him and Peggy to forgive me if I wronged them by keeping silent. They graciously accept my apology. Although I felt it was the right thing to do at the time, I now wonder. For years, I have been blessed to care for others in their suffering, yet I rarely allow others to care for me. Not wanting to put a damper on our trip, I thought I was protecting my friends from information that might hurt them, when, in fact, they may have been blessed to care for me in my pain. Did I rob them of that blessing?

* * *

With my fresh wounds throbbing, I sew up some holes in my clothing, wash the raw tissue, then throw on my jacket and go downstairs.

On our way to breakfast, Bill poses his daily question, "How was your walk?"

Prepared with an honest, but short-versioned answer, "It was raining."

Peggy and I sit across from each other at the narrow cafeteria table. Always taking note of details, she glances at my wrist. "You're not wearing your watch."

Without hesitation, I look at hers. "No, but you are wearing yours!"

Silently, I breathe a sigh of relief when she moves on to a different subject. That turns out to be the extent of the questions regarding this morning's walk. Dealing with the pain unnoticed, I am grateful to be carrying on with our original plans.

Filled with thoughts of the attack and sensing the heavy oppression of the environment in Kazakhstan over the first twenty-four hours after our arrival, I admit, *Lord, I don't like this place. The people are unfriendly and indifferent. Besides, I get brutally attacked the first day I am here. I never want to come back.*

The response is convicting, *Didn't you tell me you wanted Me to send you to the hardest places, where others will not go or have not been?*

Nailed. He is right. He has faithfully answered my prayer and I am complaining. Laughing within, I know I'll probably be coming back. *Forgive me, Lord, You are right.*

* * *

The open belly of the khaki-colored Russian plane exposes a set of metal stairs leading into the cabin. Squeezing past the stack of luggage riding with the three of us, I make my way to a metal-framed seat. Never have I seen an airplane like this; I didn't know they even existed. The seat lunges forward as I sit down. A flash of pain shoots through my body.

Vacant ruins, the remnants of buildings ransacked and destroyed during the fall of the Soviet Union, clutter the landscape in the countryside. After the collapse of the communist government in 1991, Kazakhstan was in turmoil. Food became scarce. People were out of jobs. Money lost its value and would not buy the simplest necessities.

Despair and devastation darkened the land. Anything of value, even electrical wiring, was looted from the vacated buildings, leaving ghost towns to echo their traumatic story.

The remains of civilization sleep in overgrown fenced areas: large, above-the-ground tombs filled with silent bones; a generation stripped of opinion and power.

How could I have been so unaware of the plight of these people during that terrible time? Ashamed of my ignorance, I have come to realize the comfort and luxury in which I live often inoculate me from the current events of my times. To pop that protective bubble, I make an effort to keep up to date on what is happening worldwide. If I can't physically respond to the suffering, I can pray for the situation, knowing prayer is a powerful tool: a connection with the One who ultimately rules the world.

Exhausted, I doze off to sleep and am transported in the old flying machine to Semipalatinsk, blissfully unaware of my pain for the two-hour flight.

The airstrip is a stark, colorless field, totally deserted except for the presence of a few Kazakh officers smoking cigarettes on the tarmac. Greeted by a biting wind, we deboard through the belly of the plane with our luggage. The officers will not allow me to take a picture of the nostalgic carrier; I'm forced to capture its image in my mind.

An ornate building with a hollow interior stands alone in the field. Its beautiful marble staircase and chandelier are silent remnants of a more dignified past. They lend no warmth to the frigid atmosphere. Having arrived much earlier than expected, I shiver and pull my cap over my ears as we wait for our ride. Removing my gloves, I grab my guitar, hoping the exercise will warm my fingers as we sing praise songs. The visible vapor lifts from our lips as we are filled with the awareness of His invisible presence.

Seeking a more comfortable spot, we go outside where it is several degrees warmer. Movement on the quiet country road is a welcome sight; a car is traveling in our direction. As it pulls up, a woman gets out, bundled in typical Russian attire, "Are you Dr. Chris?" I ask.

The warmth of her smile is enough to melt the chill that has all but consumed me. Chris, our contact, has arrived to rescue the three of us from our frozen state and escort us to our destination. She is Liberian and attended medical school in Russia. Fluent in Russian, her small ministry team provides preventative health care throughout the countryside while sharing the gospel of Christ with the Kazakh people.

Over the course of the next three weeks, we spend our days in rural villages holding dental clinics in buildings warmed by central heat and fueled by wood stoves. In the evenings, we sit by cozy sizzling fires and enjoy hearty meals made by our Kazakh hosts, peasants with whom Chris is working. In their simple homes, behind frost-covered windows adorned with lace curtains, is a world of relationships uncluttered by time schedules and demands.

* * *

Our village experience lends a drastic contrast to the modernization and booming economic growth of the city. Sliding rows of beads in place as she counts, a village shopkeeper works nimbly with her abacus to calculate our bill. Looking up from under her tall, starched white hat, she thanks us as a horse-driven cart rolls by in the street.

Babushkas layered in scarves, long dresses, sweaters, long johns, and heavy boots sit patiently on wooden benches at our dental clinic. Fashion takes a back seat to practicality for these older women in the bitter cold.

Unfortunately, many residents regularly seek warmth from cheap vodka, a well-stocked item on the shelves of every village market. In a country where a relationship with God has been repressed for over fifty years, drinking serves as a futile attempt to fill the ever-present spiritual void within. In this former Soviet Bloc nation, the majority of the people have not heard the gospel of Jesus Christ. They are unfamiliar with His love.

Lord, never let me forget I was once in that place, trying to fill my spiritual void with substances. Thank You for filling me with You.

As the Good News spreads, the government is cracking down on non-registered Christian churches. Yuri, our driver, tells us of a believer who was jailed for seventy-two hours and fined the equivalent of eight hundred dollars for holding meetings in his home.

"The persecution will get worse," he adds, "but I feel it is inevitable if we are truly dedicated to Christ."

Silent sharing is not easy. The people show little outward response to our witness.

Lord, please help me love when I am not loved in return, and help me not become weary in doing good.

* * *

An elderly babushka tells Dr. Bill, "I just want to die." Her life is empty and meaningless. Hearing her desperation, he takes the opportunity to speak to her about the reality of death and what awaits her on the other side. Seriously weighing his words, she gives her life to Jesus.

What a blessing to reap a harvest of one. God *is* at work. In His time, we pray many more will be convinced of Christ's love, filled with His joy and assured of eternal life with Him.

It is not until we are preparing to leave that it is brought to our attention our faith *did* make a difference. Several of the Kazakh and Russian workers observing us and our treatment of the patients over the last several weeks tell us, "We have never seen such compassion and respect for people as you have shared." God's love has spoken through us. We must not give up, for at the proper time, we will reap a harvest.

* * *

As anticipated, the Lord calls me back to this hostile place. Depending on Him to empower me with His supernatural love, I return to Kazakhstan with Bill and Peggy.

Leaving the warmth of our village cottage to walk and pray, I look forward to my quiet time. The road, framed by wide gravel medians, stretches across the vast flatland, which is occupied by countryside farms. Property lines are marked off with ranch-style open fences set up by the individual landowners.

Crisp air fills my lungs as I fill my mind with gratitude for my life, my health, and the work the Lord has given me. In a split second, a deep pain pierces the back of my thigh. Something has penetrated my jeans.

Before I can turn around, a vicious black dog is growling and barking at me. With the silence and stealth of a lion stalking its prey, he crawled through the wide gap in the horizontal wooden fence and attacked me from behind. Barking after the bite, I had no warning.

I am a few properties down from the cottage of our host and take note of the location before returning. Nastia, a Kazakh nurse on our team, cleans and dresses my puncture wound which is deep and painful. Dr. Chris tells me I will have to start rabies vaccinations at the clinic until we know if the dog is rabid.

Naturally, I want to let the owners know their dog aggressively attacked me without provocation. I don't want the same thing to happen to someone else, particularly a small child. Arriving at the dog's cottage to tell the owners, they refuse to come to the gate. We know they are in the house and continue to knock and wait. Finally, a man comes out and listens to us only to close the gate and walk away in indifference. Later, an irate woman comes to our cottage knocking on the back door. She lashes out in vindictive accusations, "It is her fault the dog bit her!" she yells. Through this experience, I am beginning to understand the imprint fifty-five years of communism has left on the hearts and minds of the people.

Our hosting missionary has one story after another about the breakdown of trust in a culture where there is little respect for truth. Saving face is of utmost importance. Lying to achieve that end is considered a justifiable means. Our Russian driver's words, "Communism devalues human life," are a sad but true reality in a land indoctrinated by it. This is the outcome of a society without God; man has become his own god.

* * *

Returning to our cottage after clinic, I spend an hour with Vincent, a crusty old man willing to sit and talk about religion. Planting seeds in his heart, I enjoy our talks. We've become good buddies.

Stealing me from Vincent, Ayana calls from the backyard. Among the clutter of scrap metal and other rubbish is a rusty bedspring. Smashed down and squeaking loudly with each jump, Ayana on one side of the frame and me on the other, I spend the rest of my day's energy with this sweet little girl on her homespun trampoline. These late afternoon sessions filled with joy and laughter prepare my heart for the hard days ahead.

* * *

Praying for my patients after I finish their extraction is important to me. After asking for permission, I talk to the Lord in English on their behalf. They don't understand my words but God does. Unaware of the impact this demonstration of faith can make, I was surprised when a pastor with whom I was working in Bosnia told me, "Your prayers are powerful. Though the people don't understand what you are saying, they know you are speaking to God on their behalf. They hear you speak to Him as a Person. Many of them have never understood what it means to have a personal relationship with the Father, to be able to talk to Him like we talk to each other. The fact that you relate to God in that way and are asking Him to bless their lives speaks volumes to them."

God knows this feedback is the encouragement that makes everything I have suffered—or will suffer in the future for His name's sake—worth it. He doesn't have to let me know the effect I have had on people, but His faithfulness in doing so keeps me coming back with the assurance it is He who is calling me to these places for His eternal purposes.

* * *

My patient lies on the table. Thick hand-knit woolen socks cover a pair of stained long johns around which her floral dress is tied. Her chest and arms are bundled underneath layered sweaters buttoned from top to bottom. A scarf is neatly tied around her chin. Covering a crown of grey hair, it displays her wrinkled face, etched by the passing of time.

Her extraction goes smoothly. Through my translator, I give her post-op instructions and ask if I may pray for her. She agrees and sits up. Gently placing my hand on her shoulder, I say a simple prayer.

Pulling her rubber boots over her socks, she leaves the bedside and returns to the audience of those warming the benches in the waiting room who have yet to be seen. With a small piece of gauze peaking out of her mouth, her lips begin to quiver and she lowers her head. A flood of tears falls from her eyes, soaking the scarf tied under her chin. My translator, having left the exam room to call on another patient, finds the babushka in her distress and fears something is terribly wrong, "Are you OK? Was it painful?"

She looks up, struggling to speak, "I'm OK. It's just that in all my life nobody has ever prayed for me like that woman just prayed for me."

Bill, Peggy, and I return to Kazakhstan for a third trip the next year, during which I manage to avoid the path of vicious men and dogs. Grateful the Lord gives me the courage not to lose heart, I continue to pray for my assailant and his understanding of my words. I would love to see him again—in heaven.

Clerk uses her abacus in Kazakh village store

Congolese boy turns a somersault in the war zone

Chapter 18

Congo: Checkpoints

> You will hear of wars and rumors of wars but see to it that you are not alarmed...
> Nation will rise against nation, and kingdom against kingdom.
>
> Matthew 24:6, 7 NIV

OUR LAND CRUISER zigzags over the rough surface of the lunar landscape heading north from Goma. Nyiragongo has earned its reputation as a bad neighbor in this town. The volcano's violent eruption in 2002 left a slate of grey, brown, and black stone after the lava cooled, establishing a new floor plan for the remodel that would be built above the buried ruins. One-third of the town melted. Molten lava chased it away. Six years have passed. Dr. Vinnie remembers the disaster like it was yesterday.

"I was in the operating theater. I had to beat it by running on foot. One hundred twenty-five thousand people ran naked for their lives. Hospitals. Schools. Buried. We stood up a large tent to treat the burns.

Due to the heat, we were in constant threat of dangerous gas explosions all around us."

Countless shacks—businesses erected on the volcanic foundation and once operated by roadside vendors—are now vacant and bolted shut. People are still on the run: carrying bundles of clothing, loads of wood, babies, mattresses, and invisible emotional burdens over the lifeless rock, past the windows of our vehicle, and into the unknown. The flow has not stopped. Like one massive living organism, a wave of humanity has replaced the molten lava.

Lined up in front of a small pile of dirt is a group of young boys. Taking turns, they run and jump, lifting off the mound, and executing flips in midair. One rolls on the ground, unable to control his laughter.

One shack is filled to overflowing. Slits between the wooden planks provide peepholes for young teens to gaze at the scenes of the movie projected inside, free of charge. War rages. Life goes on.

A few cars, weaving over the road in front of us, begin to slow as we pass a small house. There seems to be some activity. Men with guns are surrounding it.

Tizo cautions Sebi, our driver, "Be careful!"

Closer, I can see soldiers firing AK-47s and chasing a man in plain clothes. Caught, they forcefully march him down the road at gunpoint.

"He probably tried to defect," Tizo explains.

We make our way past a huge open cattle truck filled with people. A man in uniform wields his gun at the line of vehicles to keep them moving. Watching him ransack a woman's purse, he dumps its contents, takes what he wants, and tosses it to the ground. In the shadow of a ravine, a soldier holds his gun and a young woman next to his side. My stomach turns.

Watching the scenes, I remember being told, "You'd have to be crazy to go to Kanyabayonga. It is the most dangerous place by far."

Words of a well-meaning worker, I appreciate her concern. Running away from volcanoes makes sense to people. Running towards them doesn't. Nor does heading into a red zone during a civil war. Why do I come? There is an inner Voice to whom I will answer in the end. The Voice compels me.

Dr. Mike and I, along with Dr. Dan and Ashley, an American nurse, have been staying in a gated compound on Lake Kivu while working in town. Before we begin, our gracious host carefully briefs our American team, "In the event of an evacuation, you will use the boats docked on the shore. You have a satellite phone. I encourage you to use it once a week to make a personal call to your family."

We enjoy a relaxed breakfast at the compound before leaving for the clinic. The smell of freshly brewed java teases my senses. I savor the first sip, matched only by its inviting fragrance. Dominique serves the food as she reads my mind, "These people, they see you come here during our war to help. It is like the aroma of good coffee."

Tucking a couple of leftover bread rolls into my backpack, I jump into the rig. On the way to work, our driver stops in the middle of the road. I notice all the other vehicles have stopped. All the people on the street have stopped. Everything is still.

"The raising of the flag. It is the law. Everything must stop. See." He points. I look out my window. A government official is harassing a taxi driver. "He didn't stop soon enough."

I watch the official write the license plate number on his palm while another pokes his head inside the taxi. "They will demand money so they can buy food," our driver says.

Desperate. Hungry. Angry.

Watching law enforcement break down amid lawlessness, yesterday's fiasco flashes through my mind. A surreal moment. I rewind the scenario in this theater of war scenes:

Someone in our car pulls out a camera. A passerby notices. Immediately, we are surrounded by a mob, hitting and kicking our car, closing in on us. In the thick of the commotion, an impressively large, uniform-clad man appears out of nowhere. His commanding appearance demands respect. *Is this an angel?* Whatever he says calms the storm of hostility brewing around us. We are able to drive away.

* * *

While unpacking my stethoscope, thermometer, and a couple of pens at the clinic, I ask the nursing assistant, "How was your night? Did you get a good rest?"

"Yes, despite the hunger."

I give her one of the bread rolls from my pack.

By noon, I am beginning to feel my body weaken. My stomach growls.

A mother with two young children sits down in my exam room and starts to cry. "I am a tailor but my sewing machine is broken. I don't have any money."

"Do you have other children?" I ask.

"I have six more children. They are at home. We don't have food. None of us have eaten today."

Putting my arms around her, I hug her while my heart breaks. After praying for her and placing a bread roll and bottle of water in her hand, she leaves.

Getting through the day is a struggle. My energy level is drained. Hunger and thirst demand my attention, distracting me from my work. My backpack is empty.

Returning to the clinic the next day, I slip into a tiny storage room at noon and close the door behind me. Pulling a bread roll out of my pack, I quickly gobble it down and rinse my mouth with a few gulps of water. Ridden with guilt, I derive no pleasure in eating it. It doesn't help knowing I need to take care of myself. I try to wash down the guilt with another sip of water.

This is so hard, Lord. Help me hold on.

The next day we visit the prison. A grateful prisoner thanks us, "You don't know how much it means that you have come. We just get sick in here and they let us die. Or they let us get sick so we have to go out to a hospital where we die."

Leaving the prison, a Congolese woman rides back to town with us. Unwrapping a moldy sandwich, she eats it.

Tizo talks about our road trip. "We will leave early tomorrow morning. Dr. Dan and Ashley will stay in Goma. They'll continue working at the clinic. Dr. Mike, Kris, and I will head north with Sebi."

Stopping at a small market, Tizo adds, "We can buy some bread. We will be working, so we will eat once a day."

* * *

Dr. Mike is a brilliant man. A geologist. An emergency room physician. An intellectual. An atheist. I share my testimony with him. He makes it clear, "I'm not interested. I don't believe in God."

"One of us is wrong, Mike. At least consider what I have shared. Christ loves you more than you can imagine!"

I have a similar conversation with Dr. Dan, "Do you ever doubt your faith?"

"Oh yes, I come in and go out."

Honored to work with these men, I know there is a reason we are together.

Lord, help me demonstrate Your love without words.

Ashley is a woman of faith. Our room is a refuge where we pray together, taking our burdens to the Lord. She is an angel sent from God.

* * *

Leaving Dan and Ashley at the Goma clinic, we set out. Our team of four heads in the direction of Kanyabayonga, through the red zone. We plan to assess thirteen rural clinics and hospitals over the next four days. Dr. Mike is in the back of the rig, sorting through our duffle of medical supplies.

Our white Land Cruiser, with a red cross painted on the door, doubles as an ambulance. Driven by Sebi, a local, it bears a no-arms sign in the window. Tizo sits in the middle.

Tizo, a nurse, has an impartial relationship with the leaders of Mai Mai (militia), CNDP (rebels), RPF (Rwandan Hutu rebels), and FADRC (Congolese army). These are a few of the groups currently waging war in the Congo. I don't know how he gained his reputation. I do know he is a believer and a peacekeeper. After two hours at the negotiating table, he was able to obtain permission for our trip. Days later, running into a United Nations (UN) worker at our furthermost destination, I come to respect Tizo's charisma and clout even more.

"How did you get here?" the UN peacekeeper seems puzzled.

"We took the main road from Goma."

"The UN won't let us travel that road. We have to drive around."

Reminded of the saying in *Firestorm* by Jeanette Windle, "Safety is not found in the absence of danger, but in the presence of God," I am grateful for the eternal Peacekeeper's presence in my life.

* * *

This chaotic civil war has ravaged the Democratic Republic of Congo (DRC) for decades. Killing, looting, and gender-based violence are carried out with impunity. Soldiers take over civilian homes. Child soldiers are recruited, then desensitized. Rape is a weapon of war used to undermine the society.

I have never seen so many pregnant women in my life. Arriving in village after village, bright sarongs, each wrapped around a tiny life within, are everywhere. Walking miles through the bush, women come to spend their final weeks of pregnancy in town as they wait to give birth—victims of war who had to choose between one of two options: to be raped or killed.

The hilly grass knolls in front of the rural medical clinics have become temporary camping grounds. Avoiding the potential dangers at checkpoints along the roads, the women arrive by foot. Banana leaves serve as umbrellas shielding from torrential downpours. The more fortunate ones find rest in mud wards with dirt floors. Protected by a tin roof, they sleep on bamboo cots covered by grass, while the less fortunate spend the night outdoors, waiting for the clouds to clear and their restlessness to turn to slumber.

Every clinic worker has a tragic story to tell. Dr. Mike asks the questions while I translate and take notes.

"Rebels have taken all of our stock. We have no medical supplies."

"Soldiers drank the formula intended for malnourished babies. The babies died."

"Mothers do not respect the calendar. They are birthing their babies in the bush."

"The military demand special treatment. They force us to care for their friends and families. Nothing is left for others."

"We saw two hundred and fifty rapes this month."

Solar panels and generators are gone. Water sources are depleted. Unpaid workers glean from their crops to feed their families. Many towns are empty. In one field, a huge tent camp hovers around a UN installation, with people nesting under the wings of an icon of security.

The emotional and economic trauma of war has touched every person we meet. We lodge in the ransacked home of Jean-Luc, head physician of Kayna Hospital. The forest has been home for him and his kids for the past two weeks. Further north, his wife remains in Butembo. Returning home to find his windows shattered, doors torn down, furniture destroyed and belongings taken, Jean-Luc goes straight back to work at the hospital. All of the other physicians have fled.

Jean-Luc's grown children graciously host us, putting beds together in our rooms and cooking in a new pan they purchase at the open market, a replacement for those stolen. Frying tilapia and cabbage over an open fire, eighteen-year-old Julien tells us, "This is the fourth time in the last two years we have had to flee to the jungle."

Amazed at the hospitality and resilience of Jean-Luc and his family, I'm grateful for their sacrificial provisions on our behalf—offering us a red-carpet treatment in the red zone. As bedtime approaches, I make myself comfortable in my room and bolt the door. Tizo has gone to town to advise the military of our presence. *Thank You, Lord, for Yours."*

In the morning, we thank our gracious host and set out for the next village. Rounding a sharp turn on the mountain road, we meet our competition: a couple of young boys speeding by on their *chukudu*. Throwing all caution to the wind, the brave thrill-seekers get a few minutes of freedom on their traditional wooden scooter loaded with bulging grain sacks. With the hot air peeling across their foreheads, they fly downhill, forgetting what lies behind and closing their eyes to what lies ahead.

Around the bend lies another checkpoint. Mike pulls a quarter loaf of bread out of the duffle and hands it to me in the front seat. Flicking a marijuana butt into an empty tin, a boy soldier approaches the ambulance, kitchen knife in one hand and gun in the other. His bloodshot eyes scan the interior of the ambulance. When interrogated about our medical supplies, I offer the bread instead. Taking the bait, the boy waves us through, returns to his post, and begins to eat. The tactic has worked again.

It's day four and evening is upon us. To finish, it takes longer than we expect. After completing our assessments we still have a long drive through a large national park before arriving back in Goma. Not the best situation. The darkness makes us a vulnerable target in this remote area.

Checkpoints are more frequent. We give one rebel the equivalent of one dollar in change and pass through another post by tossing a liter of fruit juice to the guard. Having made progress towards Goma, we arrive at a checkpoint where we are stopped by a group of three soldiers. They're not satisfied with the half loaf of bread we offer.

"Give us some medicine!"

"Give me a cigarette."

"Why are you afraid?" One soldier questions me, obviously trying to intimidate me. His hostility is palpable.

Dr. Mike is dealing with the patient we are transporting to Goma: a pregnant mother. Her two young boys sit quietly on the bench seat beside her. She has been vomiting since we picked her up. Her nausea has not been helped by the winding mountain road. She continues to vomit while we are being interrogated.

"Sir, I am not afraid. We have a *very* sick patient. We need to get her to the city quickly," I respond, grateful I can speak French.

Surely he could see how fast we were barreling down the road before we stopped. I don't mind him thinking it was due to the urgency of the case. We were actually trying to get out of the national park to a more secure spot before dark to avoid encounters such as this. The tension escalates as he turns his attention to the medical supplies.

"What's in those bags? Open them up." Their blinding flashlights pierce through the darkness and penetrate the windows of our ambulance. Everything inside is scrutinized. We are in a fish bowl.

Lord, thank You for Your peace that surpasses understanding.

As I pray silently for the situation, the soldier addresses me again.

"Madame, pray for us." Looking at me with a serious face, he is no longer hostile.

"I *do* pray for you," I answer, shocked by the sudden vulnerability he displays.

"We need your prayers, Madame," he pleads, then pauses, "Go!"

Tizo flicks the switch and bolts out of the checkpoint. Our ambulance picks up speed, the red emergency light cutting through the night air. As he dodges potholes, a sudden downpour pounds against the windshield. Our patient continues to vomit.

Tightly clutching a can of sardines that have taken on the value of a box of gold, I pray we have gotten through the last of the checkpoints. Our cache of gifts has been exhausted except for this last item on my lap. I have nothing left but a tin of fish. *Could these sardines actually save my life?*

It seems illogical, but so does the futility of this entire war.

We cannot afford to slow down for the young mother's comfort. Darkness is upon us. Tizo's favor and our humanitarian profile have helped us get this far without incident, carried on the wings of angels.

My heart breaks for our patient. My heart breaks for the people whose empty huts we pass. My heart breaks for the young soldiers bearing mounds of psychological wounds below the surface of their uniforms. My heart breaks for a future generation of unwanted children. My heart breaks for the hungry and the homeless. My heart breaks for the multitudes. My heart breaks for the Congo. This is the reality of war. It is heartbreaking.

This is too heavy for me, Lord. I give it all to You.

* * *

Life is so full of contrasts. Late into the night, we reach our beautiful refuge in Goma. As we drive through the gate, the guard locks it behind us. A cheerful face greets our team of weary travelers. Françoise, who calls me "Mama Musique" is jumping and dancing as she joyfully welcomes us back inside the compound, reminding me of the sweet moments I shared with her before our journey began.

Having completed our work, we pack our bags the next morning. As we prepare to leave, Dr. Mike tells me how much he respects me and enjoyed working with me.

Grabbing a private moment with Dr. Dan, I have a chance to talk heart-to-heart with him. Curious to know, I ask, "What impacted you most on this trip?"

Hesitating, his eyes tear up, "Probably getting to know you. You are a remarkable woman. I have never met anyone like you. Ever."

Taken back by his words, I realize my prayers have been answered. During this painful experience, we have all been in the presence of Someone far greater, who is always at work, whether we know it or not.

"If you see any good in me, Dan, it is Christ."

Congolese boys and their chukudu

My ride to the airport as I leave Laos

CHAPTER 19

Laos: The Tragedy

Call on Me in the day of trouble;
I shall rescue you, and you will honor Me.

Psalm 50:15

"PLEASE COME. YOU are welcome. However, you are not to tell anyone you are Christian. You are strictly forbidden to pray with your patients. You must only work in the one village we designate and may not transport patients from other villages to your clinic. You will be accompanied by police escorts at all times. You are welcome."

After explaining the severe restrictions placed upon our group, an official of the Communist party, the Patriotic Front (PF) adds, "There you can suffer for Jesus."

For five years our Christian medical team has been repeatedly denied permission to work in Laos, a communist country. Anti-American sentiments and persecution of Christians run strong, fueled by the propaganda of the PF. Trusting God's timing, the mission organization continues to bless Laotian villages with generous financial donations for water pipelines and other projects. With persistence and prayer, the door opens.

Our team is set to go, but our police escorts tell us they aren't ready to leave Luang Prabang (LPB). While we wait, an exception is made for us to attend a service at an indigenous house church. Without special permission, this would be illegal. Forbidden to speak but allowed to sing, I carefully choose songs expressing Christ's love and joy. The room is filled with the voices of passionate worshipers. Tapping their feet to the beat, the police guards, required to attend, seem to be enjoying the music. The Laotian pastor preaches on the parable of the sower. One of the officers is touched and asks for a Bible, "I want to read this Book."

Kip, another Laotian pastor who has partnered with our team in Thailand for years, introduces me to the police officers, "This is Dr. Torture. She pulls teeth." His endearing nickname has never warmed my heart; I'm not sure it's going to make my "welcome" any warmer in Laos.

* * *

A candle illuminates a blank page in my journal as black ink records the events of my day: *It started raining this afternoon and then rained for the rest of the day. It hasn't rained for months here and it isn't the rainy season. The people see it as a good omen. They believe our group brought it.*

Closing my weary eyes, my mind takes me back to the road leading to Pak Xeng. After a two-day delay, we begin our three-hour journey to cover sixty kilometers. Rugged mountains surround our van on both sides, separated by a steep gorge. Stilted bamboo huts peek through the dense jungle vegetation on their vertical slopes while locals fish from tiny boats dotting the waterways below. After hours of twisting dirt roads, we arrive at the end of the world: Pak Xeng.

A large bridge leads into the obscure town. We join the exodus of peasants completing their pilgrimage alongside our van, seemingly undaunted by the driving rain. Walking for hours, they have come to be treated by the foreigners. According to their animist beliefs, we have brought the rain with us to bless their crops which have been suffering from drought.

Stepping out of the van, there is no one to greet our team and no accommodations prepared for our stay. We check in to a nearby guest-house where a small shared space is furnished with rustic, slatted beds and a single squatty potty.

After arranging our luggage on the floor, hunger drives us back to the street. Chilled and wet, there aren't many options. An open-air café with dog kabobs sizzling on the grill is our best bet. Sitting on the bench, the group orders water buffalo, fish, and rice, which come back to bite three team members later in the day.

Finished napping by two, the district governor eventually finds our group. His heavy-eyed greeting is all too familiar, "You are welcome." A half-day of clinic begins.

* * *

During our visit, hundreds more make the long pilgrimage to reach us. They come for minor surgeries, dental extractions, and medicine. With an annual income equivalent to twenty dollars, free medical care is a tremendous blessing.

If we have been strategically hidden in Pak Xeng to be prevented from making an impact, it is apparent God has different plans. We treat two thousand patients from twenty-two villages. During three and a half days of outreach, God sends rainstorms to grace our presence.

Lord, thank You for Your favor.

* * *

A year has passed and we are hoping to return to Pak Xeng. After meeting with the PF, our request is denied. At the same time, we are assured, "You are welcome. You can work in a different village."

Hoping to extend my trip, I write our host. "Do you mind if I stay in Laos an extra week after the team leaves?"

"Of course, Dr. Torture, that would be fine. There is always work for you to do."

My heart is lured by this open door to a Communist country and I am grateful for the open arms of our hosting ministry. Excited to see what lies ahead, I book my ticket for a three-week stay, knowing the Lord will direct my steps.

Sentiment hasn't changed in a year. Determined to control our movement and activity, the PF sends us to Phonxay, twenty-five kilometers from LPB on a dusty road. We will work under police guard.

A cool breeze makes me thankful for the open space where my dental table is set up. Across the courtyard sits another table used for minor surgeries. As I get started, I notice a thin, petite woman sitting on a chair outside my room. Trying not to stare, I keep glancing back at her. Protruding from her neck and dangling like a grotesque ornament over her chest is an enormous goiter the size of her head. My heart breaks for her. She probably comes believing we can heal her.

I've seen it time and again: a father hoping we can untangle the twisted body of his teenage son who is crippled from birth; a husband seeking a cure for the wife in his arms, her body riddled by bulbous tumors of terminal cancer. Arriving with grand expectations, they are uneducated about disease and ignorant of our limitations. To them, foreign doctors have god-like powers.

As a medical professional, I work to promote health and healing. It is humbling to realize how little I can do in many situations. When I first entered the profession, I told God I never wanted to become hardened to the suffering of my patients. Grateful He has honored my request, I believe I am more sensitive to their suffering today than when I was younger. My faith enables me to cope, knowing I can trust Him to take over when I can do no more.

After the woman is examined and given an explanation of her condition, financial means are provided for her to seek treatment for her goiter in LPB.

Lord Jesus, be with this woman. Please touch her with physical healing, spiritual healing, and eternal salvation. Have Your will for her life.

Dr. Helen, one of the two surgeons on our team, is asked to examine a seven-year-old boy. Pulling his T-shirt over his head, his mother reveals a disfiguring tumor on the back of his neck. Palpating it while listening to the translation of the woman's inconsolable pleas to remove it, Helen tells the mother what she doesn't want to hear: "I am very sorry but I cannot operate on this. If you like, we can cover your expenses to go to LPB and have an x-ray taken. That way I'll have a better idea of what I am working with. Otherwise, I won't be able to do the surgery."

The mother is full of reasons she cannot go to LPB and insists her husband, who is working in the fields, would not allow her to go. Begging and pleading, she does not want to take no for an answer. Helen stands firm and the mother reluctantly leaves.

Returning the next day, this same woman, in her desperation, brings her son back to be seen by another surgeon. Dr. Ben is fluent in Thai, having worked in a mission hospital in Thailand for over a decade. Because of the similarity of the two languages, Ben can communicate with the woman. He listens to her story. After examining the boy, he consults with Helen. He feels comfortable performing the surgery. The preparations are made, with Helen agreeing to assist Ben.

From my vantage point, I can watch some of the activity going on around the boy who is on the minor surgery table across the courtyard. While working on my dental patient, I glance over occasionally, curious about how things are going.

As I finish my case, I notice there are more people gathered around the boy's table.

"Bite down," I tell my patient while putting the gauze in his mouth. I look up again, this time into concerned eyes. Dr. Bob, who has been observing the boy's surgery, is suddenly at my bedside. His request is urgent. "Do you have epinephrine?

"Yes, I always carry it with me."

"We need it. The boy has coded."

My stomach tenses as I break the vial and draw up the medication used to kick-start a heart that has stopped beating. Rushing to the boy's bedside, the rhythmic compressions against his small chest continue while I manage to squeeze between those doing CPR to give the injection. The code has been in progress for several minutes. Pausing to check his status, there are no pulses. The epinephrine does nothing. He is gone.

We have lost a child. A sick feeling grips my whole being. His lifeless body lies on the table, a dozen helpless hands surrounding him. I'm haunted by the stillness. Numb, I continue to go through the motions of appearing useful, while knowing it is useless. What do I do? Someone, please tell me.

Dear Lord, be with his mother. Be with us all.

I've had many conversations with myself over the years about the risk of death with surgery. Isn't that why we have to sign all that paperwork as patients in the States? Surgery is *always* a risk, but more so in mission settings, where it is done with limited resources and sketchy information concerning a patient's history. Having relieved thousands of their suffering through surgery, I have made the difficult decision: the benefit far outweighs the risk. Still, that decision does not prepare me for the surge of emotion I am experiencing today. The risk is now a reality.

The police are faced with the gravity of a situation far beyond their experience. A group of Christian foreigners is at their mercy. With black clouds hovering over the hearts of our team, we wait as the investigation begins.

Resting on a bench against the cement wall, I listen to the hushed whispers surrounding us. The villagers, gathered in circles on the grass, try not to stare. Like trying not to look at the monstrous goiter, it's impossible; all eyes are upon us.

The scenery in the courtyard has changed: two men with a small pile of wood are building a child-sized coffin. Each strike of their hammers drives the reality of death through my heart. The pain is piercing.

"The police want your passports. They are taking Ben and Helen for questioning."

"Don't be terrified," an official tells us.

Without passports, we sit, vulnerable and powerless, like criminals in a lineup. The medical examiner is summoned and more police arrive from LPB.

In Laos, a party responsible for the death of a person is expected to pay compensation and funeral expenses. Although no monetary value can take the place of life, we are ready to do whatever we can to recompense the family for their loss. The authorities aren't satisfied with closure; they have other plans.

Hours pass, the tension increasing every minute. Long after sunset, five of us are ordered to load into the van. Ben and Helen are gone. We aren't told where they have been taken. Dropping us off at our guest house in LPB, we spend hours praying for the two surgeons, committing the situation to the Lord.

Several days go by before we learn Ben and Helen are locked up in a small jail on the other side of town. Reports of their condition come to us through our translators, who periodically check on them.

Spending the next week under house arrest, the five of us are told several times by officials and authorities, "Don't be terrified." Fasting and prayer help me stay fixed on the Lord.

On my knees, I tell Him what He already knows: *Lord, I want to go home to my kids. I want to see my country again.*

Weeping bitter tears, I stop. Internally, a shift takes place. Peace descends on me. For the first time, I can say, *Whether I die, spend my life behind bars, or am released, I am Yours. Your will be done.*

We are told someone is offering to return our passports for a price. Knowing bribery is a corrupt action displeasing to God, we refuse. Interrogated separately at the police station, Helen's questioning lasts over three hours. Determined to answer truthfully, I state my faith in Jesus Christ. Although my flesh wants to squirm out of this mess and be free, my spirit remains strong. While working with those who have been arrested and persecuted in other countries, I have often wondered how I would hold up if I found myself in a similar situation. His grace is sufficient.

Reports reach us that two government authorities are working in our favor and two against us. They are deciding whether or not to take us to court and sentence us, implicating all seven of us. The message from one official is meant to be encouraging.

"Don't be terrified. We have decided not to ask for the death penalty."

Over the next week, the US Ambassador and Embassy Consul visit. No words can describe how much their support is appreciated. Congressmen in the States are advocating on our behalf. Knowing we haven't been overlooked is reassuring. Hopeful for our release, the ambassador explains, "We are here to support you, but, unfortunately, you are at the mercy of their decision. The US has no jurisdiction in Laos," adding, "I will be glad when I see the wheels lift."

After the interrogations, we are called to a meeting. Five of us are free to go. Ben and Helen will be released from jail but kept under house arrest. Wrapped in a white piece of paper is a stack of passports. As they are passed out and I take mine in my hand, I am overwhelmed by the sense of freedom it represents.

The others, having missed their original flights are eager to buy tickets and leave. Unclear until now, I understand my purpose in staying the extra week in Laos is to support Ben and Helen.

Once released to the guest house, they fill in the story, "The police told us we would be interrogated when they brought us to town on Friday night. There was no one here to question us. Then they said they had a place for us to rest. That's when they took us to the jail and locked us in separate cells."

Our reunion is sweet. Hearing their stories confirms the Lord's faithfulness to answer my prayers. Helen was placed in a cell with two women. Though she couldn't speak their language, the ladies had cheerful dispositions and filled the cell with joyful gestures and laughter.

"They helped me set up my mosquito net and tucked me in," she laughs.

I had been praying for God to send His angels to watch over Helen all week. These sweet ladies were those angels.

Having prayed specifically for the Lord to shine His light on her, put a song in her heart, and make her aware of His presence, I have to smile while she tells her story, "There was a light on all the time. It never went out. I put newspaper on my mosquito net to block it so I could sleep. One thing I always planned to do if I was in prison for my faith was to sing. I sang all the songs on our team song sheet twice a day. I realized I serve a God I don't have to fear or try to appease, but a God that meets me when I am in the pit and comes and sits with me."

Thank You, Lord, for sending Your angels, Your light, a song, and Your presence to Helen. Thank You for sitting in the pit with her.

* * *

Needlepoint clutches and silk pillows lay in neat stacks on the ground. As Ben, Helen, and I wait for the hourglass to run out, we fit in well with the tourists at the open market. It is strange to wear an impression of freedom while standing naked without passports. Though I have mine, I am aware of the fickleness of the authorities and pray for Ben and Helen's release. If charged, the authorities could implicate me as well; I gave the epinephrine injection.

Doubt and fear linger at the back door, waiting for a chance to sneak in. Refusing to focus on the negative, the three of us spend the next week together at the guest house. Having facilitated debriefing sessions in numerous crisis situations, my training proves helpful in framing our conversations. Sweet times of worship and prayer lift our spirits above the circumstances.

Meeting with the family brings a beautiful closure. The boy's parents are filled with gratitude for the generous compensation. They harbor no hostility. Helen talks to them about the sadness we feel and how one can never put a price on the life of their child. She asks for their forgiveness. Weeping and embracing, the healing begins.

Miraculously, Ben and Helen receive word: No charges will be made. After two weeks of suspense, their passports are returned. They are free to go. They book a flight leaving in the morning. I keep my original itinerary.

Hailing a tuk-tuk, the driver of the motorized rickshaw pulls up and smiles. A large bumper sticker on the passenger seat reads *Stay Another Day*. Sitting against it, I wave goodbye to my friends, eager to get to the airport.

Boarding the small plane, an unsettling tension persists within me. I am still in Laos. Buckling the seat belt and pulling my journal out of my backpack, I gaze out the window. Like a muscle manipulated by gentle massage, the initial vibration of the engine begins easing the tightness I didn't even realize was there. With pen in hand, I begin to relax and write.

I'm in the plane, taxiing down the runway, holding back the tears. Oh Father, thank You. The wheels have lifted. I'm so flooded with emotion. The river below is muddy. The air brown. The paths winding. The mountains huge. I see nothing now for the haze. It is all behind.

View of the Laotian sunset from my plane—as the wheels lift

Zimbabwean patients spend the night at the grain storage building

Chapter 20

Zimbabwe: Who They Are

> Consider it all joy, my brethren, when you encounter various trials, knowing that the testing of your faith produces endurance. And let endurance have *its* perfect result, so that you may be perfect and complete, lacking in nothing.
>
> James 1:2–4

Adjusting a plastic poncho over my daypack, I lock the door behind me and head for my tent. Normally I look forward to walking, but today I accept a ride with our Zimbabwean driver, who is also returning to camp. It's raining. Not a sprinkle, but the kind of rain that drives people inside their homes to escape the downpour. With each stroke of the windshield wiper, I capture still shots in my mind. Villagers with swaddled babies on their backs. Villagers standing under umbrellas in mud puddles. Villagers with plastic bags wrapped around them for warmth. Villagers lying on the ground under thin blankets. They are all preparing for the long, cold, wet hours ahead.

Miles away, on the horizon, where the sky is cloudless and blue, a shadow of the African sun settles into a mirage of waves drawing it down to the ground. Our medical clinic is closed for the day. The villagers I see from the windshield of the pickup will spend the wet night where they are, in the open field, hoping to save their place in line. Due to the overwhelming numbers, some, having already waited from sunrise to sunset, were turned away at this late hour. They will be here, waiting in line, when I return in the morning.

"This is what makes them who they are," my driver affirms in a dignified manner, catching me off-guard.

"What do you mean?" I ask.

As though reading my mind he says, "This is all they know—suffering. They live with it every day. They know what they must do to get something. They are persistent and patient. They will persevere to obtain what they need. Their suffering is what makes them who they are."

As I crawl into my warm, dry tent for the night, I can hear the voices of those strong, committed souls in the distance who are suffering: lined up in the driving rain, determined and hopeful to receive care tomorrow.

The staccato tapping of raindrops is replaced by a cool wind, exposing the starry brilliance of the galaxies and luring me from my sleeping bag. Crawling out, my senses are awakened by fresh air. This tent city, my temporary dwelling place in the African bush, is home to our team of fifty. We are here to treat thousands of patients in five days of clinic.

Serving the surrounding area, we are hosted by Jewish rabbis of the Lemba tribe. Tucked away in remote bush communities, groups of persecuted African Jews are hearing the gospel for the first time. Having observed their Old Testament laws and customs for centuries, they are now receiving the Good News: "Yeshua," Christ, also a Jew, is their Savior. As God opens their spiritual eyes, Messianic congregations are challenged to keep up with the growth.

In the pre-dawn darkness, I walk around the periphery of the camp and pray, preparing myself for the demanding day ahead. A simple cement structure, serving as a grain storage building, sits alone in the distance. Its character has changed since yesterday. Bundles now cover its dimly lit patio. My sleepy brain thinks of hotdogs. As I get closer, I tell myself they must be grain bags, until they move. Now even closer, I can see clearly. Rolled in blankets, side by side, are patients. The grain storage patio has become a hotel.

Further in the distance, I hear layers of conversations and laughter. It is the line at the clinic, the people who have been standing all night, waiting for the darkness to pass.

After breakfast I toss my daypack over my shoulder and walk to the clinic site, ten minutes from camp. Grabbing these few moments before work, I love to make a special connection with the people.

Though I know there will be a large crowd, I am never emotionally prepared to see what awaits me. On the hilltop, pressing together against one another is a rainbow of brilliant colors. Wrapping back and forth and around and back again, it fills a large field. The line management team is already at work, sorting patients according to their needs and cordoning them off for medical consults, glasses, ob/gyn, dental, minor surgeries, pediatric consults, and cataract surgeries.

Hundreds of joyful people stand patiently. In the next few hours, they will be joined by hundreds more. Each one greets me with a warm smile. With my cheat sheet in hand, I speak to them in Shona. "Good morning, how are you? Be patient and wait. God bless you."

Looking at a tiny baby swaddled on the back of her mother, I tell Mom, "You have a beautiful child!" And to the baby, "Yeshua loves you." They are humored by my knowledge of their language, not aware how long I have had to practice to reach this beginner level—visiting Zimbabwe eleven times in seven years.

Clapping my hands, I begin to sing a popular worship song in Shona. They all join in. Slowly walking the length of the line, I reach the entrance gate, wave, and bid them "Goodbye!" using a popular slang term. The crowd roars with laughter.

Not a single complaint about the harsh night or how exhausted they are, their warmth has beat the sun in a race to reach this place. With blankets in their arms, and babies on their backs, sleep-deprived and hungry, they are bubbling over with joy.

* * *

Remembering a recent office visit in the States, I can still see the apologetic nurse's anxiety on her face, "I am so sorry. The doctor is running behind today." She nervously fiddles with the clipboard in her hands. "It will be several more minutes before she can see you. I apologize."

Sitting on a couch, color-coordinated with every item in the waiting room, I look down at my watch. It is five minutes past my appointment time.

"Oh, it's OK. I am fine. I just returned from a place where people wait days in the rain to be given a few tabs of Tylenol for their pain. I'm grateful and blessed to have access to good medical care."

She is curious about my work and asks me more questions. Excusing herself to return to the back room, she adds, "Thank you for being so understanding. Not everyone has an attitude like yours."

Thinking about the Zimbabwean driver's comment, I wonder if abundance and *lack* of suffering for material need in my country don't produce impatience and a feeling of entitlement.

Lord, never let me forget these lessons You are teaching me.

* * *

Our team of physicians and specialists, including a large number of Zimbabwean practitioners, occupies the building for the week. Though this regional clinic serves a large population, there is no doctor on staff. The nurses do everything with what little supplies they have.

One year, arriving with a small advance group to set up, I am in my minor surgery room, stocking supplies. Chipo, the Zimbabwean nurse in charge, is excited to see me again. Giving me a report, she fills me in, "We've been busy. I've had six deliveries this week. Tinotenda gave birth this morning. She tore and needs to be sewn up. I was just getting her ready."

"Do you have lidocaine?" I ask.

"No, I don't."

"I have some. I'll get it for you." Thrilled to be able to accommodate her, she thanks me for the lidocaine.

"How about instruments? Do you have what you need?"

"No."

"Suture?"

"No."

Realizing she has next to nothing to work with, I tell Chipo I can get her the things she needs. Since my surgical stretcher is already set up, I arrange the supplies on a stand in my room.

I am surprised at how little she has with which to perform the surgery. *Would she have done it without lidocaine? Is there any suture in the entire clinic? Without instruments, would she have used her bare hands?*

My bush training has equipped me to serve people in developing nations. I have spent years excising tumors, removing foreign bodies, and suturing wounds. Never having repaired a perineal tear, I look forward to learning something from Chipo. With everything in place, I go to find her.

"I've got the room set up for you. Do you mind if I watch?"

"Oh, Dr. Kris," she pauses, "I was hoping you would do it."

I shouldn't be surprised.

"I have never done this surgery, Chipo. I was hoping *you* could teach *me*." I admit.

"You have more experience than I do."

The team, including the doctors, will not arrive for another week. There is no one more qualified around. I pray, *"Dear Lord, please give me wisdom and guide my hands. Bring healing to Tinotenda, who has her life before her. I am asking You to do what I can't."*

Hoping her tear is not complicated, I introduce myself to Tinotenda and prepare her for the surgery. Chipo assists me. As I work, I silently pray over every stitch of the long, jagged wound. In the end, I am satisfied with the results. The new mother thanks us, grateful for our work.

Chipo updates me when I return the next year.

"Tinotenda healed perfectly and is doing fine."

Reminded of Saiesha, the Sudanese nurse, and her comment,

"God's grace covers us," I am beginning to understand.

Thank You, Lord, for covering me. Never allow me to forget my dependence on You.

* * *

After the team arrives, the stream of patients is nonstop. Their needs are great.

Pushing Alick through the clinic door in a wheelbarrow, his wife, Julie, removes their one-year-old infant from her back and sits beside her husband. She has pushed him an hour through the bush to reach us. While chopping wood, the thirty-nine-year-old farmer also chopped his foot, the blow of his ax cutting deep into the tissue, resulting in a compound fracture: an open wound at the site of the break.

After medicating him for pain, I give him the best treatment available: a thorough cleansing, suturing, and antibiotics. We have no access to X-rays.

"Alick, you need to stay off this foot while it heals," I tell him.

Updating his tetanus vaccination, I send him home with medication. Making the hour-long trek each way, with baby in tow, Julie transports Alick back and forth every day in the wheelbarrow for a dressing change and wound check. He is healing well, and thankful for our care, which is far more than he would have received had we not come.

Nestled in Momma's arms, a healthy two-month-old baby boy and his twin brother, Nawe, are awake, but quiet. Unlike his brother, Nawe is failing to thrive. Weighing in at four pounds, he is HIV positive, like his mom, and is barely holding on to life. Placing an IV in his tiny arm, the size of my index finger, I make arrangements for an ambulance to transport him to the nearest hospital, three hours away, accompanied by a physician. Praying with Momma before they leave, I have done all I can. His short life comes to an end before the week is over.

Young and attractive, a woman with a fatty tumor protruding from her forehead sits with several family members in my triage area, having finally graduated from the long line in the sun to a group of plastic chairs, shaded by a tarp. Like a beauty pageant contestant, they are all hoping she will be chosen. Many cases are too complicated to be treated and, sadly, I must turn them away after evaluating them. Chloe jumps up excitedly when I call her name.

Under my mask and gown, I perform her surgery. Reflecting on my childhood dream to be a missionary doctor in French-speaking Africa, I think of the thousands of hours I have spent, not only in the Francophone nations of Africa but worldwide, performing minor surgeries.

God has made my heart's desire a reality in a way I could have never imagined. As a nurse, trained and mentored in the field by surgeons, I do this work in primitive areas, where my expertise is of great value and my credentials are sufficient.

For years, I tried to correct my patients when they called me "Doctora" or "Docteur".

"I am not a 'doctor'. I am a nurse with specialized training."

To which they reply, "¡Graçias, Doctora!" "Merci, Docteur!"

Getting nowhere, I stopped trying to explain. What I am doing for them is what a doctor does for them, which makes me a doctor in their eyes.

Chloe's lipoma, or walnut-sized fatty tumor, is easily removed. After suturing the wound closed, covering it with some gauze, and removing my sweaty gloves, I wrap a bright royal blue pressure dressing around her forehead and escort her outside to her family.

She takes my hand and starts dancing. All of her family members join in, clapping, singing, and jumping. It's time for all of us to celebrate. Today, Chloe's life has been changed while a vision given to me over sixty years ago continues to be fulfilled. The bush doctor is dancing too.

* * *

Patients line the corridor. I bring an elderly woman into the treatment room, her arm supported under mine. The limp in her step reveals her unspoken pain. As she sits down, I ask, "What brings you here today?"

Jessie lifts her dress to show me a baseball-sized lesion on her knee.

"How long have you suffered with this?"

"Twenty years," she answers.

Our surgeon takes a look, then prepares the site for surgery. Betadine. Anesthetic. Sterile gloves. Suture. We have brought all the supplies he needs. The procedure is simple. After the wound is bandaged, I provide crutches for her. She cannot contain the joy she feels. One of the Zimbabwean nurses comments, "Jessie will not forget this day."

No, she will not forget. After twenty years, her suffering is relieved in less than an hour.

Attending to a few less time-consuming cases, I dress a wound on a small child in our little African emergency room. Overwhelmed with gratitude, her mother repeatedly thanks me, "Please come back. Come back every year. We need you. Our children get sick and we can do nothing for them. Thank you so much! Thank you!"

Another little girl sheds big tears when I start an IV in her arm to infuse antibiotics. Without the slightest squirm, she braves the procedure better than most adults. Minutes later she is smiling.

"She is so happy!" her mom assures me, "She is so happy you are here to help her get well!"

Almost mechanically, without any emotion, Dominic's mother removes her baby's clothing. An invisible cloud hovering over her shoulder darkens the cheerful brightness of her yellow outfit.

Exposure to the heat of the afternoon sun while running a fever, Dominic's skin is hot to the touch. On his bottom is a large abscess.

As Mom sits and I care for Dominic, I wonder about this dark cloud I am discerning. Wanting to know what is behind her sadness, I start asking her questions.

"Where do you live?"

"I live in a village about three hours away."

"How did you get here?"

"I walked. I got here yesterday morning and waited in line all day, but I couldn't get in to have Dominic seen. There were too many people. We spent the night in the field. Then I got in line this morning."

"Were you able to get some food and water? I saw some women preparing and selling food in the field."

Entrepreneurial women set up little restaurant stations where the hungry people waiting in line can buy a hot meal.

"No, I was afraid I would lose my place if I left the line. I didn't want to leave. I haven't had anything to eat or drink since yesterday."

Long past lunchtime, this young mother is wilted. Parched and hungry, she silently sits, not seeking anything for herself but only thinking of her baby. As soon as I finish, I get some snacks and water for her. Like the plants in my garden, she perks up in minutes. Her whole countenance changes; she is radiating like a sunflower.

"When you bring Dominic back in a couple of days, you won't have to wait in line. I will give you a pass. You can come straight to me."

Water, snacks, and medicine in her arms, she turns and smiles, thanking me again before she and Dominic make the three-hour trip home in the African sun.

I forget how much this simple care means to these people. In their African world, a small wound becomes infected resulting in the loss of a limb—or life. In their African world, a simple fever leads to dehydration and becomes a life-threatening condition for an already compromised and malnourished baby. This is their African world.

* * *

Lying straddled on the barren bed, Jeanette prepares for her next contraction. Felistas, the midwife, Dr. Doug, and I are attending her delivery. Monitoring her closely, I look for physical signs to indicate she is having a contraction. From past experiences with births on this continent, I know most African women labor in silence.

"Do you have a name picked out?" I ask between contractions.

"If it is a boy, I will name him after Dr. Doug. If it is a girl, I will name her after you."

Without a sound, she bears the pain of her last contractions before giving birth to her fourth child, a beautiful baby girl. Honored and filled with joy, I get to hold precious little Kristine in my arms.

* * *

Feeble hands hold on to sticks fashioned into canes. Cloudy eyes, framed in weathered, wrinkled faces, glance up at me. What can they see? A blur? Something moving in front of them? They are all awaiting cataract surgery.

* * *

Taking a break from my station for a few minutes, I slip into the surgical theater where the ophthalmologist is operating. Making an incision, she slips the clouded lens out, opens a small box, and removes a clear artificial lens. Gently inserting it into the empty pocket, she carefully replaces the old one. After finishing the operation, she tapes a patch over the eye and gives the patient instructions to return in the morning.

Groping around their huts for years, did any one of these patients imagine a day like today would come—when a foreign specialist would arrive at their doctor-less clinic to perform eye surgery free of charge and restore their vision?

Early the next day, as the first rays of sunlight cut through the crisp air, there is an unspoken anticipation stirring at the clinic. Bundled up in bulky sweaters, a group of elderly patients, each with a patched eye, huddle together on a long bench—their canes resting beside them. One by one, as each dressing is carefully removed, a crystal-clear version of the world is revealed to another grateful soul.

Lord, through these rich experiences, You have given me a clearer perspective of what it means to consider it all joy while encountering various trials. Thank You for the Zimbabwean people, the joy they express through hardship, and the lessons they have taught me. Let me learn from their example so, like them, I can "sing in the rain" when suffering comes.

The endless line of Zimbabwean villagers hoping to be seen in our clinic

Bangladeshi nurses using the kris-rack at our satellite clinic in Kutupalong

Chapter 21

Bangladesh: Kutupalong Camp

He has filled them with skill to perform every work.

Exodus 35:35

A DIRT PATH continues where the road left off. The mountainous terrain looms before our van, a temporary home to the thousands of Rohingya people displaced from neighboring Myanmar. Years of ongoing conflict with the Buddhist majority and militia has erupted into a violent massacre leading to their mass exodus into Bangladesh. Forced from their villages, the ethnic and religious cleansing of this stateless people group has resulted in the displacement of approximately seven hundred thousand individuals. Kutupalong camp is now their home.

I am deployed to this disaster to work in satellite medical clinics within the camp, serving this Muslim-majority people group during the height of the crisis in 2018.

One of the biggest challenges is the language barrier. Having learned to navigate around this obstacle over the years, I still yearn to speak to the heart of the people I am serving, to know their stories and comfort them with words. Often, that is not possible. This lack of communication is painfully present in Kutupalong camp. Relying heavily on prayer, my faith is tested while trusting God to break down barriers.

Our team gathers next to a stack of bricks. A little boy is diligently moving one brick at a time to a different location, his spindly body bent over and strained by the load placed on his malnourished frame. His persistence reminds me of the persistence I see in the majority of the Rohingya in the camp. They don't stop. They are resilient. They work. They persevere.

Adjusting my daypack, I am joined by an American doctor, an American nurse, and two Bangladeshi nurses as we begin our hike into Kutupalong. After a brief stop at our primary health care center to pick up a trunk of medications and other supplies, we continue to one of the remote satellite clinics.

Entering the trailhead, I am amazed by the agility of the crippled elderly who navigate the rocky dirt paths and steep bamboo steps with calloused, bare feet. The constant traffic of human bodies on the trail allows them little time to pause and rest. They don't stop.

Bamboo bridges stretch across stagnant ponds of water which have become playgrounds for the children. Laughter cuts through the air. Looking up at the blue sky, I see several kites rippling in the breeze. The little ones have taken plastic bags from mounds of trash and crafted their flying toys with strips of bamboo. On an embankment nearby, three children giggle as they slide down a steep slope on their bare bottoms, with nothing to protect their tender skin. A couple of older boys toss a square of cardboard in a game of frisbee. Such simple pleasures bring the children hours of joy. They seem oblivious to the reality of their situation. They are resilient.

Men wearing traditional *longyi*, a piece of fabric resembling an ankle-length skirt, pass by carrying loads of brick and bags of sand. Twelve-foot stalks of bamboo, wrapped in bundles with rope and suspended by a long branch, are balanced on the shoulders of two young boys, one at both ends. Carefully, they negotiate the twists and turns of the trail as the bouncing bundles keep time with their steps. Moving in ant-like formation over the hills, the army of workers presses on to reach its destination. Taking measures to reinforce the structures already in place, they are hoping to beat the monsoons which will soon flood the water-logged deltas where they are camped. They work.

Crossing over the path behind them, I notice small sections of trail covered with bricks laid in a herringbone pattern. The beauty of creativity and design has not been abandoned, even in these difficult times.

Vicariously built on the shifting slopes are thousands of shacks. Perched on deforested soil, they are vulnerable to severe landslides during the rainy season. Bamboo frames provide structural support for blankets, tarps, and laminated tin. Stacked one next to the other, these dwellings form a labyrinth of overcrowded neighborhoods. Water runoff is everywhere. Lack of sanitation is a major problem. There is a scarcity of outhouses, most of which are full, while human waste litters the ground around them.

Boreholes within the camp are gathering points for women and children. Clothing is washed and buckets of water are gathered to take back to their homes. Naked toddlers splash in mud puddles forming around the water sources. In busier areas, a line of almost one hundred empty containers sits on the ground next to the pump, each waiting its turn at the spigot. Some will be waiting all day.

Spotting our primary health care center in the distance is not difficult. Under a shade covering are rows of benches with women clad in long flowing black outfits and head coverings holding limp babies in their arms. Though the day has just begun, the waiting area is already full. Others who cannot find room to sit are standing in the heat. They persevere.

Gathering medical supplies for our trunk, I double-check the inventory list before rounding up a couple of strong young men to carry it to the satellite clinic. Walking miles back and forth throughout the day, these runners serve to make connections between the satellites and the main clinic.

Our communication by walkie-talkie is often interrupted. It is difficult to arrange transport for the critically ill from the smaller satellites located in the more remote areas of the camp. Makeshift stretchers of plastic chairs supported by bamboo poles are the quickest means available to evacuate patients to the dirt road where transportation can be arranged to take them to a nearby hospital. After the patients are stabilized, porters carry them through the camp on their stretchers. Praying for a good outcome, I trust they will make it to their destination in time.

High on top of a hill on the outskirts of the camp is a fifteen by fifteen-foot open bamboo frame covered by a tarp. It is empty, except for several chairs. This is one of our satellite clinics. A line has formed before we arrive.

My first patient sits quietly under a layer of cascading black fabric. While she removes some of her covering, I am struck by the fact she is just like me. The mystery of her shrouded body is no longer a barrier. I feel a connection with her on a human level. Her heart is beating. She has a pulse. In her hopes, her dreams, and her suffering she shares emotions similar to mine.

Fatima complains of pain. Only as I lift her thin bared arm to get her blood pressure and gently place my stethoscope on her bony chest do I realize the extent of her severe malnourishment. Her body is skin and bones except for a large malignant tumor on her abdomen. There is little we can do for her advanced illness. She allows me to pray for her.

With each breath, a tiny baby's chest retracts as he struggles to draw desperately needed oxygen into his sick lungs, a sign of advanced illness. His eyes have a wide glassy stare that screams at me in silent desperation. He is dying.

While the doctor prescribes medications, the Bangladeshi nurses work from a trunk on the ground which serves as our pharmacy. Sorting through the dressings and medications, bottles of liquids are set aside to dig for others. Armfuls of supplies keep the nurses from being free to find what they need underneath everything sitting on top. Our system is totally inefficient. The nurses are taxed in their attempts to keep up with the demands. Frustration is written all over their faces.

As each patient graces my presence, I wonder what he or she has experienced. Unable to talk to them, I can only imagine the horrors they have encountered. I picture Rahenah, whom I visited one afternoon with a translator. Her terrifying narrative replays in my mind as I remember the frightened expressions on her and her children's faces.

* * *

Rahenah is standing in front of her shack clutching a swaddled baby with three small children pressing in tightly around her. Greeting her and the children, I wait quietly, praying they will feel safe with me.

Through an interpreter, she tells me her story. "I was in my village when it was raided. Marching through the village, the soldiers set fire to everything in sight. They were killing everyone: men, women, and children, and burning them alive in their houses. They raped me in front of my family. My husband tried to protect me and my children. They shot and killed him, then burned our house to the ground. I ran with all the rest of the villagers who were still alive. We were able to escape."

"I am afraid. I cannot sleep. I still have to hide. I hide my children. Men come from Cox Bazar. Strangers. They want to take Arefa. She is twelve. They say they can get her a good job that pays good money. I am so scared."

I know Rahenah's account is one of thousands like it. The reality of what the Rohingya have experienced is beyond comprehension. Their exploitation has not ended. It continues. Yet I see their God-given instinct of survival rising to the surface despite all they have been through and the struggles they face ahead. They don't stop. They are resilient. They work. They persevere.

How can I express compassion and love without words? I can pray. I know my prayers are heard. I am thankful for that truth.

* * *

There is an outbreak of diphtheria in the camp. A highly contagious disease, it is rarely seen in the US due to immunizations. Taking measures to mask and isolate a patient with diphtheria is important as it is spread by airborne transmission of respiratory droplets and saliva. In camp, this poses a problem. I see several patients with the telltale sign: a sticky grey pseudomembrane in the back of their throat. Assisted by an interpreter, I place them in an isolated area with a mask, explaining why this is necessary. In the meantime, doing my best to communicate via walkie-talkie to the primary care clinic, I attempt to facilitate the transportation of these patients to a nearby treatment center. This presents a logistical challenge. The patients remove their masks while they wait and wander away from the designated isolation site. One young boy is carried out on his father's shoulders to the road in the heat of the day. After a thirty-minute hike, we meet the transportation van at the roadside, and the child, still wearing his mask, is taken away.

It is an overwhelming situation. The physical needs are far greater than the resources we have available. Doing all that is humanly possible, I know I must trust God in recognizing our limitations. He loves the Rohingya more than I can fathom and I must remember: He is God. I am not.

* * *

As I think about the work I am doing in camp, I begin to ask Him to show me how I can contribute in a more effective, lasting way.

Lord, what can I do during my time here that will benefit the Rohingya in the long run after I leave?

One of the significant problems is the organization and mobilization of medications and dressing supplies to the satellite clinics. The trunks we are using are bulky and heavy. When monsoon season arrives, it will be next to impossible for porters to carry them over the muddy trails. They are also hard to organize. Finding medications, dressings and other supplies is an ongoing battle for the nurses. How I would love to come up with a solution.

An idea starts brewing. In many developing nations, I have implemented an organizational system for medical clinics with a great deal of success: a soft organizer with clear pockets hung with fasteners. They are often sold as over-the-door shoe organizers but can be used for other things. Having always bought them ready-made, I have never attempted to make one from scratch.

While living in Guatemala, our medical teams hiked into the mountains with mules carrying a portable pharmacy. The soft organizers were pre-packed with medications, rolled up, and stored in heavy-duty bins strapped to the mule team. Arriving in the village, we took them out of the containers, unrolled them, and hung them on the walls of the hut: a neatly organized instant pharmacy. Over the years, I started using them in other countries: for earthquake relief supplies in Haiti, for urgent care clinics and operating theaters in Zimbabwe, and for refugee clinics in Iraq. Surgical supplies, dressings, instruments, and medications. They work for just about anything.

Thinking about the organizers, I land on an ambitious idea. In Kutupalong camp, some of the refugees have set up shacks where they sell wares or run small businesses. I have hiked by one shack housing a tailor, complete with several treadle, or foot-driven sewing machines.

Sharing my idea to commission the tailor to make a custom organizer with our team of doctors and nurses, they are excited to see my project succeed. With permission to take a day off from the clinic to make the purchases, I ask my best interpreter, Syed, to escort me to the open market. Together we set out on a scavenger hunt.

Arriving at the maze of tiny specialty shops, Syed informs me he lives locally and is familiar with the vendors. He directs me through the tangled jungle of merchandise to find every item: heavy denim fabric, clear heavy plastic, zippers, rivets, thread, and binding. After a half day of bartering in the labyrinth of open shops, we have all the supplies we need.

During my shopping spree with Syed, I get to know him on a different level. Taking time for a short tea break, he asks me, "I am Muslim but I want to know about your faith. I don't know much about Christianity."

Explaining the gospel in detail, I draw simple illustrations on a piece of paper to show him the effect sin has on our relationship with a holy God. He probes me with deeper questions, showing a genuine interest. After our hour-long conversation, I am convinced our morning together was about much more than shopping for supplies.

With our bag of purchases and a simple sketch I have drawn, Syed and I hike back into camp to visit the tailor. Tobias is in his small shack with a couple of employees busy at work on their treadle machines. Sitting on the dirt of his open shop while curious onlookers crowd around us, we propose our project. Syed interprets my simple sketches while I lay them on the ground. Showing Tobias what I would like him to create, I explain, "Please put individual zippers on each of the sixteen pockets. This binding is for lining each pocket as well as the border of the organizer. These rivets need to be placed across the top for hanging.

I'd like the completed organizer to be square in shape. The measurements I have given you will fit perfectly in the bamboo huts serving as our satellite clinics."

Tobias shakes his head affirmatively as if to understand. Satisfied, we settle on a price and leave him with the materials.

While waiting to pick up the "kris-rack," as one doctor names it, I pray God will give Tobias wisdom while making it. Has he understood my simple drawings? Will his work be quality? I am both excited and nervous to see the end product.

While reading through the Bible in the Old Testament during this time of waiting, I come to the story where God has given certain select men the skills and abilities to complete the sewing of the curtains and coverings for the Tabernacle: "He (God) has filled them with skill to perform every work of an engraver and of a designer and of an embroiderer, in blue and in purple and in scarlet material, and in fine linen, and of a weaver, as performers of every work and makers of designs" (Exodus 35:35).

I can't help but draw a parallel. My design is nothing Tobias has seen before. The drawings are primitive at best. It will take a miracle for him to create the prototype I have in mind. But didn't I ask God to help me contribute something that would be of lasting value to Kutupalong and the Rohingya? Is God confirming through His word He has chosen Tobias for this very job?

When Syed and I arrive at the shop several days later, I am shocked. The rack is finished. It is beyond perfect. Tobias has taken the initiative to add tucks in the pockets to accommodate more supplies, something I had not asked him to do for fear of complicating my instructions.

In all my excitement, I fail to notice our commotion has attracted a huge crowd of curious onlookers now gathered in front of the little shop. Seizing the opportunity to speak to our audience, Syed interprets for me: "God chose talented men in the Bible to be skilled tailors who could accomplish the work of His temple for His people, Israel. God has blessed Tobias and his helpers with skills to meet the needs of the Rohingya, just as He did for the Israelites. Why? Because this personal God loves each one of you and is looking out for you. How can you know He loves you? He sent His son, Jesus, to die for your sins and give you eternal life."

During the month I am in Kutupalong, this experience beats all others in terms of communication. With my translator at my side, one who is interested in the Christian faith, the Lord gives me a chance to speak to a crowd of fifty people about His love for them.

We start using the prototype immediately. The Bangladeshi nurses are beside themselves with delight, proudly displaying their kris-rack in the satellite clinic, its pockets stuffed with neatly organized medication and supplies. Before leaving Bangladesh, I commission Tobias to make several more.

Monsoon season arrives just after I return to the US. I receive word that the racks are being successfully used to deliver medications and supplies. The porters simply roll them up, stuff them in a backpack, and deliver them over muddy trails and lagoons to the distant satellite clinics of Kutupalong camp. *Because of Your love for the Rohingya people, You have answered my prayers. Thank You, Lord.*

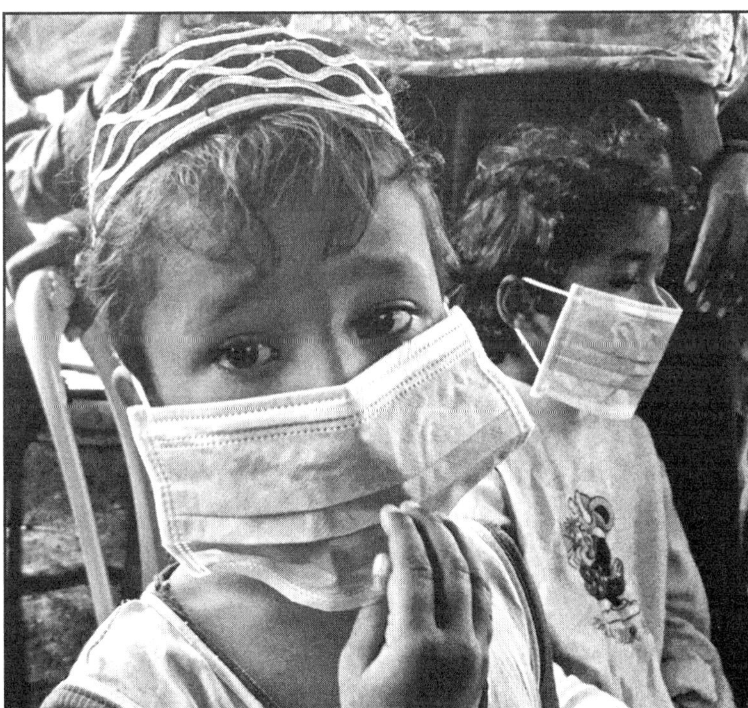

Rohingya boy with diphtheria in Kutupalong camp

Vintage car in Havana, Cuba

Chapter 22

Cuba: The Car Show

> God sees not as man sees, for man looks at the outward appearance, but the Lord looks at the heart.
>
> 1 Samuel 16:7

It all seems so quaint, so cool. Everywhere I turn, there is a relic of a car rolling down the street. I feel like I have traveled back in time. These cars were born when I popped out of the oven in 1952. Pink, turquoise blue, green, and purple—the colors match their striking personalities. A man sporting a muscle shirt adjusts his rear-view mirror; kids heading to the beach squirm on the front bench seat, their towels and floats thrown in the back; all passengers have their eyes on the road as each antiquated car heads toward its destination. Joining the parade, our taxi leaves the airport.

Relieved to get past customs with my suitcases full of Bibles, I can still picture the face of the young officer in charge. Standing motionless, his slender body, decorated by the military uniform bearing his rank, is leaning over the table. Having ordered other officials to go through my luggage and remove the contents, his eyes are fixed upon a Bible he has opened and placed in front of him. He is reading it. Deliberately. Intently. He does not move, nor is he distracted by the officers under his command who are busy rummaging through my suitcases, pulling out stacks of new Bibles, and placing them beside him.

For a moment, my interrogation has ceased. Like a statue, his position is fixed. It is as if this young officer has been taken captive by an invisible force, a force infinitely more powerful than that of the communist government for which he works. He continues to read, uninterrupted, for five minutes. Then, gently closing the Book, he places it on the stack with the others and resumes his duties.

Having been ordered to fill out a long form for my guitar, I declare its value, sign my name, and wait. When asked if it is for sale, I explain it's for personal use and I have no intention of selling it. After being told I must present the form upon leaving the country, I agree and am told, "If you do not return the form to us, you will be taxed for the value of the guitar."

Several more minutes of questioning in an attempt to flush out information regarding my Christian contact in Cuba get them nowhere. My refusal to divulge information does not make them happy.

Asking me to stand off to the side, I take in everything happening around me, keeping my eyes on the officer in command. Showing no emotion, he goes about his work mechanically, directing all the moving parts of his well-oiled machine. Decorated on the outside, he is empty on the inside. My heart is moved to pray: *Lord, I would love to give this officer a Bible. If You want me to do that, put him in a place, alone, where I can approach him discreetly. I am willing.*

While flights come and go, passengers arrive and exit under the green *nothing to declare* light. As ordered, I remain standing. Being detained is surely a tactic to make me uneasy. It works. With my Bibles on display like a Christian bookstore, I am ignored.

After a long thirty minutes, everything is thrown back into my suitcases and I am ordered to leave. My interrogation is over. Baffled by the whole ordeal, I am not about to ask any questions.

Though I am disappointed I don't have an opportunity to give the officer a Bible, I know I can trust God's sovereignty in the matter. Walking under the green light, I'm out the door and in a taxi.

* * *

"That's a '57 Chevy. There's a '55 Buick Special!" The taxi driver prides himself in knowing his cars, their models, and their years. Like a time warp, the scene around me is surreal.

My Cuban host tells me car sales in Cuba stopped in 1960. Only recently have prohibitively expensive vehicles been made available to the public for purchase. This antique car show is a picture of survival. Vintage cars have been pampered, restored, and refurbished, their engines replaced by Russian Lada and other foreign motors. While billows of black smoke pouring from their exhaust pipes belie the cosmetic beauty of some, I am impressed they can roll down the street and do their job. The alternative: a country without cars.

Seeing things from a purely external and cosmetic perspective is a distortion of reality. Looking at myself in the mirror, I am reminded of this truth daily. Beneath my skin is another person the world cannot see. My engine. My soul. White and American, I've been rebuilt on the inside.

Having spent a lifetime working among primitive and impoverished people in developing countries, I have changed, though I look the same. My perspective on life is different. My core values have been dramatically altered. In many ways, I relate more easily to the foreign cultures in which I work than my own. Living in the African bush for a month without seeing another white face doesn't phase me. After thirty years of a major overhaul, my soul resides in a vintage body with a foreign engine.

During a trip to Africa, I come face to face with my dilemma. Trying to stay on my feet in the middle of a crowd of cocoa-brown children pressing in on all sides, I feel a tiny hand grab hold of mine. The light eyes of a freckle-faced albino girl look up at me while dozens of dark ones are fixed on the two of us. These mischievous kids have brought this little outcast with pale skin and frizzy white hair to me. Like some strange specimen they've found in the bush, they're curious to see my reaction.

I wonder what her life has been like. Isolated. Lonely. Misunderstood. Embracing her with a smile, I pray my love is conveyed through the touch of my hand. White on the outside but African on the inside, I feel an immediate connection with her.

Lord, You are the One who takes our hand when no one understands. May this child come to know You, her Creator. Please forgive me when I judge based on appearance.

Cuba's surface is enchanting but it doesn't provide an accurate picture of the soul of the country. Oblivious to the plight of the people living in this communist nation, I have evaluated them from a distance, through the eyes of the world: a culture of colorfully animated and musically inclined people living ninety miles off the coast of Florida. Now I am close enough to hear their heartbeat.

As we pull up to a small, gated yard, the taxi driver lowers the volume of his radio and lets us know we have arrived. Pastor Estevan and his wife, Mariel, invite us inside.

Rolling our luggage down a narrow hallway, we rearrange things in the tiny room to make space for our bags. Medication, clothing, toiletries, and other supplies are temporarily stored here until they can be taken inland to the missionaries.

With little space to help out in the kitchen, Mariel's mother, Helena, insists I relax while lunch is being prepared. Striking up a conversation with her, I am grateful I took the time to listen to online newscasts and programs in Cuban Spanish before my trip. It is very different from the Guatemalan Spanish I know. Anticipating I might be asked to translate for our group, I prayed the Lord would help me understand the dialect while I did my homework.

Immediately, Helena opens up and bears her heart, "My son drowned recently. I learned of his death in February. He was trying to get to the States in an overloaded boat. There were thirty people in it." She wipes her tears with her apron and continues to share her heart-wrenching story, "He wanted to be free of this horrible life. Living here is like being in prison. We are prisoners in this country. He was willing to do anything to gain his freedom. The boat was full of people who shared the same hope. It cost all of them their lives."

Having walked a similar path in different shoes, my heart feels the weight of her burden. In January, my son, Cory, died of a brain tumor.

In her distress, Helena talks about knowing her need for a deeper relationship with God. "I have seen Estevan and Mariel live out their faith in their daily lives. I lack that and I know I need it."

Brought together in a tiny Cuban home, two mothers, strangers from distant countries, have a common bond. Waiting several minutes before speaking, I share, "I lost my son to cancer in January. In my deepest pain and sorrow, when I felt like I couldn't take anymore, Jesus carried me. He wants to carry you, Helena. He loves you and knows what you are going through. He is our only hope for real freedom; freedom from the prison of sin."

Ten minutes into our visit, I am communicating with Helena in her mother tongue, able to comfort her at a time when she is drowning in her sorrow and hopelessness. Broken and crushed on the outside, my words bring her inner strength. She reminds me of this throughout my stay. It is apparent the Lord's hand is working silently in our midst from the moment I arrive.

* * *

Cuba has been held in the clutches of communism for over sixty years. The government dictates and controls almost every facet of the lives of its people. Freedom as many of us know it is nonexistent. Estevan pulls out his *libreta*, a small pocket-sized ledger indicating the food rations allotted to his family.

"Here are the names of our family members, our gender, and our age. All of this information determines the quota we receive. This is a list of what we have bought and how much of it," he points to the columns filled with numbers.

"Everything is recorded and purchased at government-regulated grocery stores where commodities are controlled. Items are much cheaper than market price, but the quantity allocated is small. For example, one chicken and four eggs per month for a family of four. If I have extra money, I can buy more food from a private grocer. Many people don't have the luxury of supplementing their meager rations."

Taking me to one of these stores, I walk right past it before Estevan redirects me. The location has no identifying signs. Inside is a wooden counter with bare shelves behind it. A scant amount of rice, beans, and a few dozen eggs occupy very little shelf space, making the emptiness more obvious. A clerk, protecting the goods behind the counter, gives me a suspicious look. Several items are out of stock. We will have to come back.

With an extra day to spend downtown, we take a walk through the city. Havana's architecture is exquisite. The downtown buildings, like the cars, present a luxurious facade while hiding their crumbling structures.

In an open café, a band of musicians plays a lively song, creating a cheery atmosphere and adding a beat to my step as I walk by. We turn a corner onto a street where a crowd of people are sitting on the curb cradling laptops. Others are leaning against the buildings and standing on the sidewalk with their heads down and eyes fixed on cell phones. Estevan explains.

"This is where people come to get network. It is one of the few places in the city where you can do that unless you have a means on the black market."

Starting to make my connection between what is seen and what is not seen, I am kept from being swept away by the fascination of the culture. My perception is slowly beginning to change as the paint is chipped away.

* * *

Our team has come to support the Cuban pastors and missionaries living in the rural areas of the country. Traveling with Estevan, an American couple, and their two young sons, the six of us leave Havana for the interior. We spend the night in a village tucked away in a range of beautiful mountains surrounded by tropical forests.

Awakened by a colorful parrot contentedly perched in a wire cage on the patio, I take a walk through the countryside, admiring the quaint homes and rustic wooden horse carts parked in front of them. Brightly painted windowsills display potted plants, their foliage happily absorbing the rays of the early morning sun.

A thin man in black rubber boots sweeps trash and water off the road. His old cart, supported by metal wheels with thin spokes, is decorated with CDs suspended by string, reflecting the sunlight off their surface, like the beauty reflected in the simplicity of this rural lifestyle.

Returning to the church, Estevan is excited to get started. Drawing the curtains over the windows to cover our activity, we empty our suitcases and stage everything on wooden benches. We have eight heavy-duty garbage bags and begin to fill them with clothing, medication, and more. These will be distributed to eight missionary families. Seeing the stacks of over three hundred Bibles, I am blessed knowing how much encouragement they will bring to these faithful workers. I'm grateful they miraculously cleared customs.

Once everything is packed in trash bags, we carefully tie them off. They have been filled randomly, no two are alike in their contents. While we finish up, Estevan discreetly loads the bags, one by one, into the back of our van. Government officials are eager to stop any activity related to the church. In theory, religious expression is allowed, but hostility against the church runs high. It is best to keep a low profile.

Our first stop is a one-room dwelling where we are greeted by a family of five. Living on less than twenty dollars a month, they have been forced to move nine times within the past year. They have been targeted because they are Christians. We sit with them in their dirt-floored hut.

"The government can force us to move out at any time. They can make up whatever reason they want," José says, pulling his youngest son up on the bed with the rest of the family.

Despite hardship, they are full of joy. The mother sings a beautiful a cappella song for us while the three young children cuddle with their dad. Willing to serve Christ whatever the cost, they have chosen to endure persecution. We learn they have no refrigeration and arrange to buy a refrigerator for them. A small thing for us; I know it means more than I can imagine for them.

Traveling deeper into the mountainous jungle, we arrive at Julio's small ranch-style house. The Cuban cowboy trots up on his grey horse. Jumping down and removing a heavy grain sack from his saddle, he invites us to sit on the patio with him and his wife. Gentle and soft-spoken, they share their struggles with us. Woven through their story is an enthusiasm for reaching their neighbors for Christ.

Translating for our group, I find myself choking back my emotions as I interpret the testimony of these committed heroes of the faith. Five years ago, Julio experienced a radical conversion from witchcraft. He is on fire for the Lord. By appearance, I would never dream this kind man could have lived such a tormented life.

Sliding the van door closed, Estevan carries one of the trash bags to the patio. Opening it, the couple is ecstatic. Seeing their reaction to our delivery of Bibles, I realize these sacred Books are as rare and priceless to them as the purchase of a new car.

"We need to go if we want to complete our deliveries," Estevan reminds us.

After praying together, we leave the couple to visit Lydia in another village.

Lydia has moved her congregation to the outskirts of town due to persecution in her neighborhood. The new location is prone to flooding during monsoons. Those wanting to come may not be able to find transportation.

Another church in disrepair collapsed, killing a member, before the congregation could obtain permission to rebuild. Believers there are continually harassed. Restrictions placed on buildings and meetings make it difficult to gather.

Everyone we visit has a story. Despite the hardships, persecutions, and prohibitions they have faced in serving God, they have been built up internally. Possessing a supernatural strength that keeps them going, the oppression and opposition under which they live has fortified their internal makeup.

It's quite a hike from the road to reach our final destination before returning to Havana. Trekking through the mud, we wind our way over the narrow trail, lit only by our headlamps. Heavy tropical rains have left puddles for us to navigate. Carrying the last black plastic bag to be delivered, we arrive at the home of Diego and Julia. Young and small in stature, Julia's large bump of a tummy carries their hope for a family after having lost their first baby. Their struggles have been intense. Trying to develop relationships with their neighbors, they have been met with intense hostility. Diego explains while we listen.

"Because of misconduct, the last pastor was forced to leave the church. We came hoping to bring healing to the congregation. There has been no end to our suffering. The church is still broken. False accusations fuel the hatred the community continues to express toward us. They have even stoned us. By God's grace, we want to persevere. We are praying His love will win them over. It has been hard. We are tired. Sometimes we want to give up. We know God is with us. At times it can be very lonely. What an encouragement to know believers are praying for us. Thank you for coming."

His transparency brings his emotions to the surface. Taking Julia's hand, he can barely hold back the tears. Their concern for the eternal destiny of this hostile neighborhood is a powerful testimony of God's persevering love.

After enjoying a cup of coffee, we encourage them to open the plastic bag. Pulling clothing and other items out, they are like kids in a toy store. Reaching down to the bottom, Diego pulls out a bottle of folic acid, an important nutrient needed in pregnancy to prevent serious birth defects. His face lights up.

"I went to the pharmacy to try to buy folic acid for Julia and was told I could not buy it without a prescription. I tried, but I was not able to get a prescription."

With a huge stack of Bibles on their lap, surrounded by the contents of our gift bag, we pray together. Before we leave, I remember I have one umbrella left in the van. It is the last of three I bought to give away. Diego and Julia trudge through the mud with us, enjoying our company until the last moment. I grab the umbrella out of the back and hand it to Julia. Her expression is one of surprise.

"I need one of these. I don't have one!" Bag number eight and an umbrella have reached their God-ordained destination.

These ordinary-looking common people are made of gold. Their interior has been overhauled by the Master mechanic. In mint condition, they are running on God's strength. His internal force is moving them forward like the antiquated cars rolling down the road.

In a country governed by a philosophy whose manifesto declares God does not exist, these humble workers are determined to bring Christ to their nation.

Cuban street sweeper with his cd-decked cart

Life vest graveyard on Lesvos Island, Greece

Chapter 23

Greece: Moria

This is how we know what love is: Jesus Christ laid down His life for us. And we ought to lay down our lives for our brothers and sisters.

1 John 3:16 NIV

Driving the van through the cobblestoned Greek village, I stop and pick up a couple of volunteers standing in front of the coffee shop. The van's manual transmission poses a problem for young European workers who have never learned to drive one. Happily, I accept the duty of chauffeur, which gets me on the road early in the morning. In the evening, driving the team home from camp, I get to hear stories about everyone's day.

Turkey's coastline is barely visible in the distance. With my window rolled down, the cool air arouses my senses while the picturesque countryside bathes my soul in tranquility .

"Your faithfulness is new every morning. Your hand is in this beauty. I can feel You. I can see You. Into the crucible of human suffering, I go. Fill me anew with Your love, patience, and strength."

Two years have passed since I last worked here on Lesvos Island. At that time, in 2017, the camp was at capacity with three thousand asylum seekers—respectfully called persons of concern (POCs). Today the number hovers at fifteen thousand.

Bursting at the seams and overflowing into nearby olive groves, Moria is situated on a mountainous incline. Cleared out by the Greek government to accommodate POCs on the island, the former prison facility greets new arrivals with a grim first-time impression: razor wire, barred gates, endless chain link fences, wall-to-wall people, tents, and mountains of trash.

Fleeing from war, political upheaval, and persecution, the POCs have left all that is familiar to travel for months to reach Turkey. After hours at sea, they successfully make the perilous seven-mile crossing to Greece. Others are not as fortunate. Tragic accounts abound.

"My baby's twin washed overboard and drowned."

"A family of five fell out of the raft and we couldn't pull them back in."

Cold, wet, and hungry, with all their belongings and loved ones in their arms, they are placed on a bus. Traveling an hour south, they reach Moria, the "hot spot." Sadly, their new home does not hold the promise of peace that lured them here.

I work with a frontline organization. Warming them up while providing food and water is our first step in reception. Introduced to waiting, they experience what will become a daily ingredient for all activities. Tent? You must wait. Food? You must wait. Doctor? You must wait. The answer? You must wait. While passing out bottles of water, a memory from my last experience revisits me.

* * *

Volunteers, new at the food distribution area, are being mobbed by new arrivals. Frantic, desperate men, deprived of sleep and shelter, are shouting in their mother tongues. It is beyond chaotic. Leaving my station to help, I become a human gatekeeper, extending my arms to keep the crowd back far enough for food to be distributed rather than trampled.

Wearing despair on his face like a transparent mask, one father demands meals for his family of eight. More aggressive than the rest, he pushes and shoves to get to the front. Panic is in his eyes. Trying to calm him I say, "Sir, there is food for everyone."

He speaks enough broken English to paint a vivid picture of his plight. "You must understand. I am *very* hungry. I have not eaten for two days. I came over in the boat last night and have no other clothes, no food, no water. *I am hungry*. My family is hungry!"

Suddenly I feel his desperation. He does not know that food and water are distributed every morning. He does not know there will be a hot meal at lunch and another at dinner time.

What untold stories are shared by this agitated crowd of men desperate to feed their families? He is right, I *must* understand. Looking at him, I think of my son, Jacob. This could be him. Deeply touched by his words, I reassure him.

"Don't worry. You will be fed. There is more food. Your family will eat."

In two years, the stories have not changed. The number of POCs has. There is no end to the hundreds of desperate individuals arriving in small lifeboats from Turkey. Once they are registered, we start working on housing and non-food item distribution.

* * *

Info Point is a long wooden counter under a tin roof. Here, we answer questions regarding almost every aspect of camp life. Behind the counter is a container housing our headquarters where a few dedicated personnel process records and scramble to keep things together.

Hiking up the steep hill to our location, I brush shoulders with Moria's residents. Lines have already formed: people with medical problems waiting for the clinic to open, people with empty stomachs waiting for breakfast rations, and people clutching legal paperwork waiting to discuss paths toward asylum.

New arrivals, trying to catch a few minutes of sleep, take cover in the dirt under their blankets. They wait at Info Point in hopes of receiving tents and tarps when we open. Children dart in and out through the obstacle course of restless bodies. A color palette of nations is represented in this mass of humanity who has arrived with their shattered dreams.

Under the corrugated roof, the noise level is noticeably higher. A crowd of people is already pressing against the information counter with stacks of paper in hand. I push through, taking care not to step on the families still under covers on the ground, and enter our container for the morning briefing.

Inside there is standing room only. I see many new faces and miss others. There is a constant turnover of worldwide volunteers. The little box is shaken from outside as the deafening roar of voices escalates.

Our group takes a few minutes for devotion and prayer before receiving our work assignments.

Lord, I want to see with Your eyes. Please give me compassion and respect for each person with whom I speak today. Give me wisdom to answer their questions and solutions to offer them. Let them sense Your love through me even when I have to say No.

After grabbing a walkie-talkie and donning my red vest, I go to my station outside the door at Info Point with two other volunteers. This is where I am called to love. This is where my love is tested. A position most of the volunteers try to avoid, I ask for it. I like the challenge. Sometimes.

Immediately we are met with a barrage of desperate individuals firing requests at us in Farsi, French, Arabic, and a handful of other languages. Grabbing the correct translator is a challenge.

"I need a tent. My family has been sleeping on the ground for days."

"I want to change my container. It is too small. I am stepping on my children. None of us can sleep."

"We haven't received tarps or pallets. It is raining and we are wet."

"I need a doctor's appointment."

"I have a sick father. My baby is bitten." Laying the baby on the counter, pushing extended arms and papers aside, the mother points to a series of welts on his swollen legs and continues, "We have to move. *Now*!"

Fists pound the gate blocking the entrance to our little box. One lady throws a handful of pebbles, hitting a volunteer in the face. Papers are thrust forward. A frantic wave of human energy against the wooden counter threatens like a tsunami.

Falling to the ground, a large Somali man has a seizure in the arms of his sister.

"This is his fifth seizure today," she tells me with resignation. "We are new arrivals and he hasn't taken his medicine. I need to live in the same tent with him to care for him."

She holds his head in her lap. Another POC tears a cardboard box apart to cushion his body from rocks on the ground. Kneeling in the dirt with her, I sense her despair.

"He needs a wheelchair. You need to take him to the hospital before we house you. I am *so* sorry. I know how frightening it can be. My son had seizures."

Let my words comfort her, Lord.

She looks at me tenderly and nods her head. Peering into her eyes, I add, "Your brother is fortunate to have you to care for him."

The dedicated translators are my intermediaries, interpreting every communication. They, too, are POCs who live in the camp, volunteering their time to help. At the end of the day, I leave. They return to their tents.

Filtering the meaning of all of the words behind the angry outbursts, the translators bear the brunt of defending my inability to satisfy requests. Absorbing the blows like a punching bag, they offer me a gentler version of what is actually said. I can't imagine what they are hearing.

With sparkling eyes and a confident smile, a five-year-old is brought to me. Another child, holding her hand, tells me the little one is lost. Taking her inside our container, I find someone to accompany her to the police post across camp. Looking up at us, she laughs. Not a nervous laugh, but a happy laugh.

We must be funny.

She bursts into a series of high-pitched giggles. She can't contain herself. For a moment we forget the clouds of sorrow looming outside. Everyone is laughing. Standing in our midst, like a toy doll that has had its chain pulled, this precious little one has brought us joy.

"Lord, like this beautiful child, give me joy amid the suffering, and help her to be reunited with her family."

I am constantly trying to understand: what is the *real* need? What horrors has this man experienced, causing this trigger? What does it feel like to live in her skin? How can I express genuine concern and love, while constantly saying, "No"?

"Lord, You know the answers. You know their heart. Help me."

A single mother with two wiggly children spilling out of her arms, breaks down in tears as I tell her, "No, I am *so* sorry. I cannot move you into a larger tent and I have no extra blankets to give you." Taking her hand in mine, I tell her, "I know you are suffering. I can't imagine how hard this is for you. Unfortunately, I can't change your housing situation today, but I *can* give you some suggestions. Keep your tent as clean as possible. See that your children drink plenty of water. Bundle them up in extra clothing at night. Cover their heads and feet. These things will help keep them warm and can improve their health. You *can* do these things for them!"

Our eyes meet. She smiles sweetly. For a moment, we make a deeper connection. Two mothers who love their children.

"Thashakor." Thanking me in Farsi, she turns to leave, struggling to hold onto the children as she pushes through the crowd.

Leaving camp at the end of my shift, I am stopped several times on the way to the van.

"Just one minute, please."

"Please, just one question."

Driving the team home, I ponder the unrelenting demands of the day. Never have I experienced such intense needs on such a large scale. "BIG PROBLEM!" is the mantra of the camp that shouts at me from black spray paint on a brick wall in the village.

"Lord, the crowds constantly pressed in on You. When You tried to get away, the people followed. It never ended. Was it like Moria? You tell me to trust You. Your Word teaches You are a loving, just, and sovereign God. I believe that. Don't let me grow weary. Remind me of Your truth. Be my refuge and strength, a very present help in trouble. You are in the midst of this overwhelming crisis, drawing many to Your love. Your ways are not my ways. Help me remember that."

More than six hundred unaccompanied minors roam the camp. Seventeen-year-old Amir arrives from war-torn Somalia with Fatima, his fifteen-year-old sister. Al Qaida killed their father and mother, then gave Amir money to make wedding arrangements, intending to force Fatima into marriage. Instead, Amir used the money for their escape to Turkey where he worked until he could pay a smuggler and flee to Lesvos.

Having experienced hatred all his life, he is shocked when Becca, a volunteer, smiles at him and says, "Good morning!"

"Why are you kind to me?" he asks her.

"God has placed the love of Christ in my heart for all people. His love is what brought me here," she answers.

Housed with the minor boys, Amir befriends one of his roommates who has an *Injil*, the *Gospel of Jesus* in Arabic. Curious, he secretly reads it. Believing what he has read, he takes a step of faith and receives Jesus as his personal Savior. God's love is birthed in him, replacing the fear, bitterness, and hatred residing in his heart.

The noonday sun is not the only thing ablaze. A crackling noise from inside a nearby container tips me off before a flame bursts from its window. Triggered by memories of 2017, I have a sense of déjà vu.

* * *

I see clothes, neatly hanging on racks, and sized. A curtain serves as a makeshift dressing room. Our camp boutique is full of customers. Appointments are scheduled every six weeks for each POC to come and pick out a new set of clothes. Rather than handing them a bag of random garments, being able to choose an outfit helps restore a sense of control and dignity to their lives. Most of that has been stripped away.

While working at the boutique, I enjoy chatting with some French-speaking Africans and listening to their stories. Some have been here months, some for years. The prospect of asylum is uncertain. Some are facing deportation. Mounting tension coupled with overcrowding is taking its toll.

Moria's neighborhood is blended: Syrians, Iraqis, Iranians, Afghans, Congolese, Algerians, Eritreans, and Somalians, to name a few—the people of warring nations, ethnicities, and religious groups brushing shoulders and their teeth at the same sink. Separated by a curtain in an overcrowded tent, their families are forced to coexist. The environment is thick with rising tensions and hostility.

Angry shouts escalate among a large group of men, pushing and shoving their way past us on the other side of the chain-link fence. Several gunshots are fired. Rioters begin throwing rocks and storming the area where deportees are held in detention, just above my boutique. Evacuation procedures are activated.

Running past the riot police, a spray of tear gas sends a burning jolt to my eyes and lungs. Looking back, I watch as a huge cloud of black smoke billows into the sky, rising from where I have come.

Our team returns to work the next day.

* * *

"I'm sorry. We have no clothes to give you, they were all burned."

"You will have to wait. I'm *so* sorry. Our office was burned down and we have no supplies. We will help you as soon as we can. Everything was destroyed."

Moving our headquarters into a cramped space, we start from ground zero, continuing to help victims as well as those responsible for the trouble.

"*It's so easy to be angry at the perpetrators but I have come to love in Your name. Please help me, Lord.*"

Aware of the horrific circumstances from which many of these people have come, I understand why they rely on violence to resolve conflict. It is all they have ever known. It gives a voice to their unheard pleas. My choice is to allow love to govern my reaction to their behavior. In His power, I can do what is humanly impossible.

A week passes. Another violent riot breaks out. Buildings in camp and vehicles on the street are vandalized. Riot police are summoned. Dumpsters are overturned. Fires ignited. Rocks hurled. Windows shattered. An angry mob chants threats. Once again, our team evacuates safely through the tear gas, leaving the police behind to arrest numerous POCs responsible for the violence.

* * *

There is nothing new under the sun. Two years later it's happening again. This time, a young man, driven by the power of love, is moved to act. Amir, sensing a compelling force, heads toward the raging fire consuming a housing container below Info Point. Some Somali women and their babies are trapped inside. Hundreds of bystanders watch but do nothing, their cell phones poised in the smoky air to capture the story.

Overcome by a deep compassion for these women and their children, Amir remembers something he has seen in a movie. Drenching a blanket with water, he covers himself and runs toward the fire while the crowd shouts, "No! No! Don't go in! You're crazy! Don't go! You will die!" Ignoring their protests, he enters the blazing container and rescues one woman, carrying her to an ambulance, unaided, a half mile away.

What ignited this heroic act of selflessness? A simple smile? A kind "Good morning?" On so many levels, Amir's life speaks to me of the power of God's love. Transformed by the life-saving sacrifice of Christ, he receives eternal life, reducing his fear of death to ashes. Now healed from the scars of tragedy, hatred, and sin, this burning passion in Amir's heart compels him to risk his life to save another.

"Lord, thank You for Your love which surpasses understanding. Help me remember the power of a smile, a touch, a word. Through them, You work miracles."

* * *

On my day off, I hop on a public bus and grab a front seat. The scenery on the island has changed. On the roadside, competing for space with the bus, large groups of POCs are walking into town. Pristine beaches, no longer visited by families, are filled with asylum-seekers congregating on the shore and in the water. Stopping frequently through the village, empty seats become occupied by island residents returning home with shopping bags in hand. The full bus winds through the countryside as it heads towards Moria, one of the last stops.

Approaching the camp, at least fifty POCs are waiting to board. As the driver pulls up, they storm the bus, rocking it and pounding on the door. It is terrifying. The woman next to me shakes her head in disbelief.

No longer welcoming these guests with open arms, this is now a BIG PROBLEM for the residents as well. Life on Lesvos Island has changed.

* * *

Several volunteers tell me about a "life vest graveyard" on the north coast of the island, a two-hour trip. My first attempt at finding it is a failure. People living in a nearby village flatly deny its existence.

"I don't know what you are talking about," they insist, "There is no such thing." They would rather forget this whole ordeal ever happened.

Disappointed to have spent most of my free day riding a bus to nowhere and back, I gather more specific details on the graveyard's location from volunteers who have been there and make another trip the next week, determined to find it. Trekking through the hills, the Turkish coastline is visible in the distance separated by the expansive blue waters of the Aegean Sea.

What amount of desperation would it take to make that journey?

After a long trek, I start to wonder if I'm facing a second round of defeat, when, far off in the distance, I notice a vast sea of red, orange, yellow, and blue. Hiking toward the color, I arrive at mountains of abandoned vests, dinghies, rafts, and children's floaties sprawled over the hills, alive and breathing in the wind. Walking through them, I am overwhelmed, knowing there is a heartbreaking story behind each item. Lying silent on the ground, the hopes of thousands are represented in this solemn memorial.

"Lord, for those who have come seeking a new life, help them find peace in You. Thank You for the opportunity to share in their pain and suffering. Even when it hurts. Even when I don't have answers. And, like Becca and Amir, help me love well."

POC mantra graffitied on wall in Mytilene, Lesvos Island

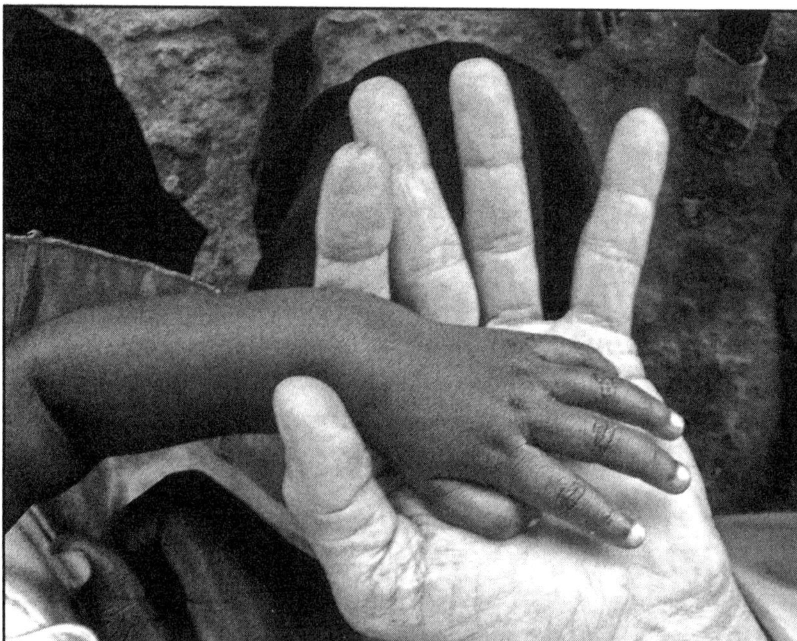

Reaching out in love in Uganda

Chapter 24

Vision

Your eyes have seen my unformed substance
And in your book were all written
The days that were ordained for me
When as yet there was not one of them.

Psalm 139:16

Some of my deepest revelations have occurred in the most unlikely places, catching me off guard and reminding me how far I've traveled from where I started. One of those memories stirs in my heart today.

* * *

It is 2013. My tour of the Holocaust Museum in Jerusalem has left me emotionally and physically exhausted. Surrounded by chatter in as many languages as choices on the menu, I've come to the cafeteria to get lunch. Grabbing the last available seat, I slide my tray onto the table and sit down. Mouth-watering hummus, Kalamata olives, and other Mediterranean delights begin to tickle my taste buds as I settle into people-watching. Suddenly, from the opposite end of the noisy room, a large imposing man begins to push his way through the throng with a sense of urgency. He is heading straight for my table.

"Those hands! Let me see those hands," he commands, staring at my hands, which are now lifted in the air.

Could I be under arrest?

"What do you *do* with those hands? I have *never* seen hands like that on a woman."

Though alarmed, I realize I can relax. The man is simply curious.

Slowly bringing my hands down, I look into his eyes.

"Well, sir, I do a lot with these hands. I am a nurse and use them to treat sick people. My hands perform medical and dental surgeries. They relieve suffering. I am an artist and a musician. These hands enjoy creating things and playing music.

"Sir, I worship God with these hands. *He* gave them to me."

He looks at my hands one last time. Then, as quickly as he arrived, he turns and disappears into the crowd.

* * *

I often think back on my conversation with this man and the impact it had on me. My Creator's "eyes have seen my unformed substance"—including my hands. Embracing this truth, I am no longer living to please people, or overly concerned with their opinions of me. I am free to live a life pleasing to God. My confidence comes from knowing I am His. What *is* important is that I am using what He has given me for His glory. If I were to run into Mr. Curious today, I would love to tell him, "Sir, these hands write. Yes, they've written about the one true God who is reaching out to you with *His* hands of eternal love."

* * *

Connecting the dots of every experience in my life, God knows my every day, my every thought, my every move. Only He sees within my soul. Detours, pitfalls, joys, suffering, pain, successes and failures—all add to the total picture. Realizing each one plays a vital role in my life, I choose to take *His* hand, knowing He will complete His artistic work within me in His time.

Created in the image of God, my existence has a divine purpose behind it. Every decision I make sends ripples into eternity. To choose wisely, I need His wisdom. To endure hardship and overcome weaknesses, I must rely on His strength. Daily I surrender, confessing my sins, seeking His Word for guidance, and trusting Him for the outcome. Sometimes it *feels* as though He has abandoned me but I *know* I am not forgotten. He is faithful and can be trusted.

The reality is—life isn't always what I had hoped for. Whether I end up on a beautiful tropical island basking in the sun or lying on a hospital bed in intense pain, there is nothing sweeter than holding *His* hand through it all.

In 1974, at the age of twenty-two, before I became a nurse, went on a mission, or served the poor, with years of addiction still ahead of me, my hand penned the lyrics to *Vision*. It is the story of my life today, written in *His* book long before *Vision* was written on a page in mine. Inspired by the One who would reach beyond my own brokenness to heal me, His infinite love has taken me to the ends of the earth to reach beyond broken to others—this Love is reaching for you as well.

VISION

There's a land far away I can see
I feel somehow that's where I should be
People there don't have the things I thought livin' naturally brings
Oh, Lord, would You lead me
I'll let Your spirit feed me
Fill my heart with love, my soul with faith,
My words with truth, and my life with peace
Show them, Lord, how You've freed me

Always had all I needed to eat, clothes on my back, shoes on my feet
Only way to show that I care
Take what I have and begin to share

Oh, Lord, would You lead me
I'll let Your spirit feed me
Fill my heart with love, my soul with faith,
My words with truth, and my life with peace
Show them, Lord, how You've freed me

Time's getting short, I know it's true—we can be saved because of You
To man You've given the gospel to bring
Touch my lips that they might hear me sing

Oh, Lord, would You lead me
I'll let Your spirit feed me
Fill my heart with love, my soul with faith,
My words with truth, and my life with peace
Show them, Lord, how You've freed me

Honeymooning with Jesus—Kris

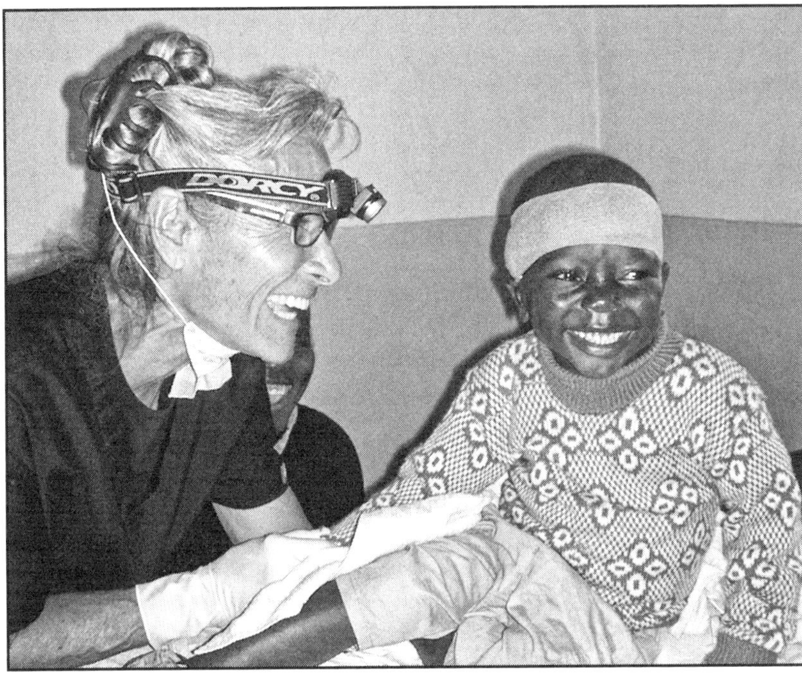

A happy little patient in Zimbabwean village clinic

If the Lord is drawing you to Himself, you can enter into a relationship with Him today by praying a simple prayer of faith like the one below.

Dear Lord Jesus—
I know I am a sinner and need Your forgiveness
I believe You shed Your blood and died for my sins
I believe You conquered death and rose from the grave
I turn from my sin and turn to You as my Savior
Help me, Lord, to follow You
I give You my life today
In Jesus' name, amen

* * *

To grow in your new relationship–

- Pray by simply talking to God. His Spirit now resides in you.
- Read your Bible, asking God to help you understand what He wants to teach you.
- Share your faith.
- Cultivate Christian friendships.
- Find a healthy Bible-teaching church where you can grow and encourage others.